Countries the Wycliffe Bible Translators are serving in the Western Hemisphere

TWO THOUSAND TONGUES TO GO

The Story of the Wycliffe Bible Translators

TWO THOUSAND

THE STORY OF

ETHEL EMILY WALLIS

and

MARY ANGELA BENNETT

drawings by Katherine Voigtlander

TONGUES TO GO

THE WYCLIFFE BIBLE TRANSLATORS

Harper & Brothers, Publishers, New York

Contents

v

3196

FOREWORD *by Clarence W. Hall*

SENIOR EDITOR, *The Reader's Digest*

To anyone whose profession requires him, as the Book of Job puts it, to travel "to and fro throughout the earth and walk up and down in it," there comes a constant surprise, both startling and satisfying. That is his discovery of the ubiquitous Christian missionary.

That surprise—and that satisfaction—is heightened as he visits particularly those remote areas far off the beaten track of the tourist. Where "civilization" as we know it is just beginning to come. Where peoples only recently savage are getting their first glimmerings of a way of life totally beyond their dreams. Where, until the missionary came, vicious tribesmen clothed only in superstition were unblissfully unaware of any better kind of life than killing and witchcraft, disease and oppression.

When the full story of the lifting of such forgotten peoples to a place of dignity and responsibility is finally told, I venture that none will be more honored for his contribution than the Christian missionary who, now largely unrecognized and unsung, has helped them achieve that place.

During constant rovings about the world, in search of stories of human courage and devotion to high duty, I have met hundreds of such missionaries, observed them at work, noted the results of their long labors, seen at first hand the revolutions they have wrought.

But in all the far-ranging and infinitely varied missionary enterprises there is none, to my mind, that is more imaginative, more intelligently conceived and more heroically pursued than the Wycliffe Bible Translators, whose story is so dramatically told in this book.

I have met representatives of this group—as well as graduates

vii

of its Summer School of Linguistics who work under other mission bodies—in the stone-age villages of New Guinea's interior; in the still wild provinces of the Philippines; in Brazil's incredibly primitive Mato Grosso; in the tangled jungles of Peru and Ecuador. There and elsewhere I have seen them braving almost unbelievable hazards to wage their war against world illiteracy. Spending their lives analyzing unwritten languages. Creating primers and dictionaries, setting up schools, training native teachers. And creating churches and congregations whose brand of Christianity often shames our own.

Best of all, I have come to know Wycliffe's statesmanlike founder, William Cameron Townsend, surely one of the most remarkable men of our time. In developing his world-girdling group for Wycliffe's audacious onslaught against ignorance and supersitition, Townsend has cut out for himself a niche in missionary service that is utterly unique and unduplicated.

Since the day when, while trying to interest a Guatemalan Indian in a Spanish edition of the Bible, he heard the plaintive plea, "Why hasn't God learned *our* language?" Townsend has been busy recruiting and training a young army of linguists to give God other tongues. Thus far his army has entered 175 different language groups in 11 countries—and is almost daily entering others. His institutes of linguistics, begun only 25 years ago in a renovated chickencoop in the Arkansas Ozarks, now train some 500 students annually. Graduates number more than 4000. And Wycliffe is only in its adolescence!

"We have," Townsend says, "two thousand tongues to go." Nobody who knows him and his zealous army of translators has the slightest doubt that his goal will be achieved.

A careful reading of this thrilling account of Wycliffe's achievements thus far will warm the heart, inspire the soul, stretch the vision. I know of no more daring acceptance of the Divine challenge, "Go ye into all the world . . . to every creature."

Acknowledgments

Credit for the title of this book goes to Clarence W. Hall, author of the popular article of the same title published in *The Reader's Digest* for August, 1958. We are indebted to Mr. Hall for granting the Wycliffe Bible Translators, Inc., permission to write the book growing out of his article.

The Central American Mission generously shared with us information of Cameron Townsend's early missionary years in Guatemala. His sister, Lula Townsend Griset, supplied facts and photos of her brother before and after he went to Guatemala as a young recruit. Mary Vandever of the Pioneer Mission Agency painstakingly gathered data concerning the early history and sessions of the Summer Institute of Linguistics, and of the beginning years of translation work in Mexico. We are also grateful to Otis Leal, Wycliffe's historian without portfolio, for fruitful suggestions concerning the early history of the organization in Mexico, particularly with reference to policies of operation.

In a characteristic spirit of helpful co-operation the members of the Wycliffe family furnished pictures, historical details, and background material which made possible the telling of their story. Some of them—particularly Kenneth Pike, George Cowan, and Philip Grossman—gave valuable help on the manuscript.

Without the early guidance and continual encouragement of Melvin Arnold of Harper & Brothers the project could not have been consummated. And to Eleanor Jordan, also of Harper, we are indebted for skilled editorial assistance. To them and their associates we are deeply grateful.

E. E. W.
M. A. B.

1. Undergraduate Adventure

William Cameron Townsend had not really expected the National Guard recruiting officer to release him to go to Guatemala. Perhaps it was his physical appearance that had prompted the officer to say, "Sure, go ahead, Townsend. You'll probably do more good selling Bibles in Guatemala than shooting in France." Boyishly blond and of average height, Townsend was slightly built, tipping the scales at one hundred and thirty-one pounds. He apparently did not impress the officer as a sure-fire military risk. At any rate, he had been cleared to go to Guatemala under the auspices of the Bible House of Los Angeles at a salary of twenty-five dollars a month as a salesman of Spanish Bibles.

It was 1917, the United States had just entered World War I, and Townsend had recently completed his junior year at Occidental College in Los Angeles. Many of his classmates had enlisted and were on their way to the fighting in France. But Townsend had been arrested by the blunt remark of an artless old-maid missionary: "You big cowards, going away to war and leaving the mission field to us women!" This scornful challenge triggered his decision in favor of Bibles over bullets.

The two-week trip down the Pacific coast to Guatemala had been a novel and exhilarating experience for Townsend, tired though he was from the summer's work preceding it. He had earned his passage by loading crates of fruit at the dock, a job that taxed his strength to the limit since some of the loads weighed almost as much as he did. His college chum, Elbert

Robinson, with whom he undertook his work, was big and husky and had not tired so easily.

But the struggle was forgotten in the joy of departure as the steamer *Peru* glided through the Golden Gate of San Francisco on that magic evening of September 15, 1917.

Inside the dining salon the merrymakers had already begun their initial round, for it was a big occasion. The room was festooned in green, white, and red, the patriotic colors of Mexico, in celebration of the eve of her Independence Day, September 16. Coincidentally this day of departure also marked the commemoration of Central America's liberation.

The two boys observing the mounting merriment inside relaxed in the quiet shadows of the deck as they enjoyed the effortless beauty of twilight on the Pacific. They watched the lights on the shore dim and darken as the *Peru* began to roll in the unsheltered waters of the open sea. While most of the passengers drank patriotic toasts to Latin America Townsend wrote in his journal:

"What a great day for the outgoing colporteurs carrying the message of the Great Liberator who said, 'If the Son therefore shall make you free, ye shall be free indeed.' "

"Robinson will do all right, but Townsend won't last two months," was the pessimistic prophecy of one veteran missionary who appraised the new recruits. But at the end of two weeks in Guatemala City, the "City of Eternal Spring," the unimpressive pale blond had more color in his cheeks.

Two weeks after their arrival they were invited to attend a Bible conference in Antigua, the old capital of the country, twenty-five miles from Guatemala City. The boys were delighted as they set out in a carriage drawn by four mules. They clicked and clattered over stone streets, constantly twisting and turning their heads to catch glimpses of the passing drama. Dogs and donkeys, Indians and soldiers, hooded nuns and braided generals—it was like flipping quickly through the pages of a *National Geographic*.

On a steep rise outside the city the carriage driver announced that the passengers would kindly alight to relieve the load. For this invitation the boys were grateful. By walking they could enjoy more leisurely the pine forest and trails through which they were now traveling. They also began to observe in detail the

2

variety of Indian dress dotting the roads leading to the city. The inhabitants of each village were marked by a characteristic color or weave of blouse. Men's hats of many shapes and brightly embroidered trousers of varying lengths threaded in and out among the pine trails. But all the Indians, men, women, and children, were heavy laden with firewood, corn, live chickens, bananas, and other produce to be sold or bartered in the big market. How far had they trudged with their bulky freight? To Townsend's horror he found that some had already walked thirty miles with the towering loads which bowed their backs.

After reaching the climax of the grade near the town of Mixco, the party soon began to descend into the valley of Antigua. It was a hair-raising experience. Townsend wrote:

"The descent into Antigua is very steep, and the coachman, eager to arrive ahead of all the rest, lashed his mules into a gallop on the downgrade. The seemingly springless old diligence creaked, bounced, and rolled over the bumps, around the bends, and downward so fast that the collars were often pushed up on the heads of the galloping mules. Even then the coachman was not satisfied, but leaned out over them so far it seemed he would fall, and from this dangerous point of vantage screeched out threats upon them and lashed them most unmercifully."

Finally, the harried pair arrived at the Antigua mission. After supper they were thankful to drop onto their army cots in the small room assigned them above the stable.

The sightseers were up early the next morning investigating the town. They found that contemporary life was moving over and around the mountainous stone ruin of a former city shaken and shattered, it seemed, by some giant hand. They saw the walls of a great cathedral and other mammoth buildings in heaps all through the town. Roofless sanctuaries gaped at them through stone arches still partially standing. What a place it must have been, this former capital of the republic! The great earthquake of 1773 had done a most spectacular job of destruction.

Until that time Antigua had been one of the meccas of the New World, vying with the capitals of Mexico and Peru in wealth and power. Her society was composed of the highest Spanish nobility, and monasteries representing great religious power had been built alongside her brilliant courts.

3

As Townsend and Robinson attended mission meetings during the following days, they also sought to piece together the sad history of the country which was becoming home to them. They learned that Antigua was actually the third capital of the republic. In 1524 Cortez' captain, Pedro de Alvarado, had established the first capital near the present town of Tecpan about fifty miles northwest of Guatemala City. He had arrived on the scene at a propitious time for the Spanish conquistadores.

Tecpan had been originally known as Iximche, a Mayan name meaning "Corn Plant." It was the seat of power of the Cakchiquel nation, an important branch of the prehistoric Mayan stock. At the time of the Spanish conquest the ruling house of the Cakchiquels was Xahila, or Clan of the Bats. The Cakchiquels were one of three powerful peoples descended from the ancient Mayans who once occupied the northern area of Guatemala. When they migrated southward they fell into three nations, the Maya-Quiche, the Cakchiquel, and the Tzutuhil. The powerful Cakchiquel ruler Sinecan Belejebcat was on the point of subjugating the Quiche branch of the old Mayan empire when Alvarado arrived on the scene.

The warring Mayan nations had been warned by Montezuma, king of the Aztecs in Mexico, that white men had arrived in their land to the north. The Guatemalan tribes disregarded the warning, however. Thus when Alvarado marched in, he conquered the warring Quiche and Cakchiquel nations with comparatively little fighting. He established his base at the Cakchiquel capital of Iximche.

The Tzutuhils were harder to subdue. They had built a fortress on a promontory jutting out into beautiful Lake Atitlán lying seventy miles west of Guatemala City. They also had a large fleet of dugout canoes for protection. The Tzutuhils were a rich, powerful people, unconquered by the grasping Cakchiquels. Alvarado found strong resistance in the Tzutuhils, but finally aided by the Cakchiquels with three hundred canoes the Spanish overcame them. Thus the last of the three ancient powerful Mayan nations was made the servant of the Spanish gold-seekers.

Alvarado had named the first capital built on the Cakchiquel site Santiago de los Caballeros. In 1527, weary of the constant uprisings of the rebellious Cakchiquels, he destroyed the Indian

4

seat of power and moved his court to the valley of Almolonga. Now known as Ciudad Vieja, it was demolished by flood in 1541. Finally, the capital was established in Antigua where the Spanish continued to rule until 1773. In that memorable year the wealthy metropolis of Central America was shattered by the devastating earthquake which left it in the ruins visible today.

Townsend now began to understand the reason for the endless processions of dialect-speaking Indians who were ruled by Spanish-speaking "Ladinos," New World Latins. Although actually constituting three-fifths of Guatemala's people, the present-day Mayan descendants were separated from their fellow countrymen by high walls of speech, race, dress, and custom. Two worlds of men had been thrown by the caprice of history into one small geographic area. Now they lived peaceably side by side, the once proud Mayan outwardly subservient to his Spanish-speaking superior.

Although Spanish was spoken in the mission services and in the shops of Antigua, Townsend observed that trade in the market was carried on principally in the dialects of the Indians who brought the heavy loads of food and firewood for the Spanish speakers who were dependent upon the human beasts of burden for the basic needs of living. The Indian, however, was to the young colporteur a mysteriously closed chapter of human history, sealed and set apart by his unintelligible, unwritten language. Yet Townsend began to get the vision of reaching these people with the gospel in the only tongue they really understood.

5

2. "Why Haven't You Come Sooner?"

Reticent and unaggressive, Townsend dreaded the new experience of talking to strangers about so intimate a subject as their faith—and in a foreign language! But he felt obliged to try. One day the struggle reached its climax on the stony streets of Antigua where he made his first attempt at "witnessing." He planned to walk up to a person and say, "Do you know the Lord Jesus?" He memorized the question in Spanish, *"Conoce Ud. al Señor Jesús?"* But he did not know that in Spanish *señor* may mean "Lord" or "Mr." and that "Jesús" is a common first name for a man.

After practicing the question many times, he finally gathered courage enough to accost an unsuspecting pedestrian with the query. When the gentleman replied politely, "Sorry—don't know him—I'm a stranger here myself," Cameron Townsend had all that he needed for complete discouragement. Back in his room above the stable, he dropped to his knees beside his cot and prayed in despair, "Lord, I've come more than two thousand miles to tell these people about You and I can't do it. I'm a complete failure."

Without realizing Townsend's difficulties with Spanish, and ignorant of his deeper turmoil of heart, mission leaders suggested that he begin his work with a group of believers in the town of Santa Catarina, about four hours' walk from Antigua. Robinson had decided to go to Tecpan. He was drawn to the humble tribesmen and had expressed a desire to help them. On October 23 the college chums parted company, each going to his own field of labor.

The road leading out of Antigua was bordered with beautiful shiny green coffee trees and luxuriant corn. Townsend enjoyed the company of his Guatemalan brothers who regaled him with stories of how the gospel had entered the little towns around Antigua through much trial and persecution. During the lapses in conversation Townsend thought of California and how, if he were there now, he would be in his senior year in Occidental College. But he was learning many things here that he never would have learned in college and was glad he had come.

Late in the afternoon the party arrived in the Indian settlement of San Antonio where the newcomer was welcomed by other believers who offered him the choicest hospitality of their dark hut. This involved being seated alone in the place of honor on a low wooden stool at a table about eighteen inches high, and eating red hot chili pepper stew.

Cameron Townsend was trying desperately in his spotty Spanish to convince an old Indian that he really liked her peppery potion. But the steady trickle of tears coursing down his cheeks was eloquent token of a struggle.

"Look, Grandmother, the American brother is crying! He isn't accustomed to eating our food. See how many tears are flowing down his cheeks. Poor thing!" But the granddaughter only giggled in amused pity as the obvious novice continued to lap up the fiery stew with a tortilla, an Indian corn cake that served as both spoon and sopper. By blotting up the liquid fire with the tasteless tortillas torn in bite-sized pieces he was managing to satisfy his youthful appetite.

It was not just the Indian fare of rural Guatemala which occasioned the conflict, however. As the old Cakchiquel Indian stirred her savory stew in the big black pot on the smoky fire she was engaged simultaneously in another operation. Her little granddaughter was sitting with her back to the old lady who between stirs was inspecting the child's head. Occasionally she would pop something into her mouth, something taken from the child's head. After another stir of the pot she would make another furrow in the girl's long black hair and continue searching with gnarled and knotty fingers.

7

As Townsend continued his hassle with the stew the significance of the scene began to break in full force upon him. The old Indian was perfunctorily delousing her granddaughter. The big juicy ones went into her mouth, and the scrawny ones into the fire. For a boy who had been finicky in his eating back home in California this break-in was rather brusque. His stomach churned as a ripple of nausea interrupted the struggle with the stew. He made a tactful half-turn on the low wooden stool so that the delousing ceremony was not so squarely in front of him. Then he continued eating, for he was hungry.

That night as the believers gathered in the hut dimly lighted by a candle to hear the Word of God expounded, Townsend's heart was moved by what he saw. He remembered what the brothers had told him as they traveled on the trail to Santa Catarina. The gospel had entered this region with much tribulation through the work of faithful colporteurs who had prepared the way for subsequent mission work.

Although few in the area could read and only a limited number could understand Spanish, the Word of God had taken root. Now healthy congregations gathering in humble huts such as this one dotted the hillside. Huddled around the candlelight the earnest brothers whose faith had cost them dearly were eager to learn more from God's Word.

Townsend had also learned that about forty Protestant missionaries were at work in Guatemala as a direct result of action taken in 1871 by President Justo Rufino Barrios. This liberal president who brought among other reforms religious liberty to Guatemala, visited the United States requesting that Protestant missionaries be sent to his country. Until that time the Roman Catholic faith had been accepted as the official religion. The Presbyterian Board of Foreign Missions complied with the request and a Protestant school and chapel were established on the main square of the capital. President Barrios sent his own children to the school.

With Barrios' encouragement missionaries of the Central American Mission also entered Guatemala, as well as colporteurs of the American Bible Society and of the British and Foreign Bible Society. They began evangelizing the rural areas of Guatemala on foot. Thus it was that towns such as Santa Catarina had

8

heard the gospel. But this new teaching had caused great up-heavals in the quiet communities which had known nothing but the incense-burning of ancient Mayan worship, or the veneration of Catholic saints. Reaction to the message of salvation by simple faith in Christ had resulted in eruptions as violent as those staged by the volcanoes which at intervals had laid waste various areas of Guatemala.

Townsend joined his Guatemalan brothers in inviting neighbors to the meetings in the humble hut. One day while passing a beer garden, he offered a tract to an Indian who was drinking. The man refused the paper, saying that he could not read. Townsend cordially invited him to attend the meeting the following night. As he walked away, he was surprised to find the man running after him and calling to him. He was saying that he would take the paper after all, because his neighbor could read. Townsend prayed earnestly that the man would come to the service, and he did. However, he was under the influence of liquor. Townsend preached "in almost unintelligible Spanish," but the drunkard Tiburcio responded to the invitation to accept Christ. The be-lievers then explained the gospel to him more fully in "good old Cakchiquel," and prayed with him.

Tiburcio was thoroughly converted. He remained faithful in spite of the rage of his cronies who in derision threw liquor all over him. Later he was all but hacked up by a long sharp machete wielded by one who disliked the new teaching. In spite of such severe treatment Tiburcio became a witness to his own people and never tired of telling how Christ had changed him.

Tiburcio's conversion was a great encouragement to Town-send whose effort at evangelism had failed so miserably in An-tigua. "It showed me that God could use even a poor instrument like myself when willing to be led into the place of need," he chronicled in recounting the experience which was a turning point in his early missionary life.

Within a month's time after leaving the conference at Antigua, Townsend had tramped the trail to thirty villages telling humble peasants the gospel story in his very simple Spanish. And in spite of many meals when his "stomach almost turned" he was gaining in weight and strength. "These discomforts counted for little in the joy of the work," he wrote. He was not without homesickness, for there were times when he was "greatly reminded of home."

Near Santa Catarina Townsend met Francisco Díaz, a faithful Cakchiquel believer who agreed to accompany him on a tour through the sugar and coffee plantations near the Salvadorian border. At the end of November they set out, Townsend taking from time to time the thirty-pound pack of books which Francisco carried. The sickening heat of the tropical sun at times nearly overcame Townsend, and slogging through trails deep with mud was fatiguing. But he was becoming more accustomed to the tiring trails. He could now enjoy almost any food placed before him, even tortillas once so tasteless.

Labor on the coffee and sugar plantations in southern Guatemala was done chiefly by Cakchiquel Indians from the highlands who migrated to the hot plains to work. These Indians served for very low wages, and were constantly in debt to their Ladino overlords. Townsend was moved as he saw the abuses and cruel treatment meted out to defenseless Indians.

As they traveled from plantation to plantation Townsend observed the immediate acceptance of Francisco among the workers because of his ability to speak Cakchiquel. Few of them had mastered Spanish, but Francisco was able to explain the way of salvation fully and freely in a language which the majority of the laborers understood. And on the trails and over their tortillas Francisco never missed an opportunity to impress upon Townsend the need of his own Cakchiquel tribe.

Townsend found that there were two hundred thousand Cakchiquel Indians in the highlands of Guatemala, most of whom spoke no Spanish. And he had plainly seen that Spanish was as foreign a language to them as it was to him. Most of them were not eligible customers for the books he carried, for they could not read, nor could they understand the language in which the books were written. He was also learning much by observing the success which Francisco had in evangelizing the unlettered tribesmen. The need for a translation of the Scriptures in their language began to weigh upon him.

At Christmas time Townsend went to Guatemala City where Robinson and he had a happy reunion with their missionary friends. However, they found that several recent earthquakes had made the city dwellers nervous as they remembered other times when quakes had in a few moments leveled towns and taken many lives.

On Christmas Eve there was a tremendous jolt which catapulted some from their beds. Robinson was awakened and alarmed by the shake, but Townsend slept on. "At the risk of my life," said Robinson, "I went back to rouse him." The city was literally falling around them. As they ran out into the street "the earth began to roll like the sea." Through a series of upheavals following in rather quick succession, the city was soon reduced to a heap of rubble and a shaken, suffering mass of humanity.

Townsend and Robinson went everywhere helping the injured and relieving the suffering where possible. During a stretch of forty-two hours when help was needed on every hand, Townsend was able to snatch only two hours of sleep. In the confusion the minister of war took up his post in the city square in an effort to restore order. Townsend went to him and offered his services. He was commissioned to several errands, one of them being a trip to Antigua to buy corn, beans, and firewood for the destitute sufferers in the city.

When the days of emergency had passed Townsend was eager to resume the trek with Francisco, and accordingly made preparations by gathering together his few possessions that had survived the destruction. Soon the two were on the trail again, going southward toward Salvador. It was the beginning of a tour that would take them through four of the Central American countries, Guatemala, Salvador, Honduras, and Nicaragua, tramping the treacherous trails foot by foot and evangelizing all the while.

Again Townsend passed through the sweltering plantations where Indians sweated in the cruel sun. One day as he and Francisco were eating their humble fare under the shed on a large coffee plantation the owner rode up.

"Who is your foreign companion?" he asked Francisco. "And what is he doing here?" Upon discovering that the pair were engaged in evangelistic work the owner warned them against spreading their propaganda among his workers. However, he later found that his best workers were those who had been converted to the gospel. He watched their behavior. Indeed they were among his best producers, and he concluded that the effects of the foreign religion were not so bad.

Afterward when this wealthy land owner became the president of Guatemala, he showed no little kindness to the foreigner whom he at first would have expelled from his domain.

Townsend's practice was to obtain permission from the mayor or the first officer of every town where he intended to sell Scripture portions. In one such town on the Salvador frontier, he had received permission from a military officer, but the mayor later challenged the liberty and summoned Townsend to his office. This gave Townsend a further opportunity to explain to all assembled the purpose of his visit, "making quite clear the way of salvation." He stressed "the necessity of having a portion of God's Word in one's possession." He told of its wonders, adding that "President Wilson and King George were constant readers of the Bible and that it would be very appropriate for His Honor the Mayor together with his underofficials to do likewise. The result was better than expected, insomuch that the last Testament was sold. God had turned defeat into victory."

Indeed the timid faltering witness was becoming an adept salesman. Not only did Townsend and Francisco leave a trail of satisfied customers, but they instructed them in the Word of God. In some places they were encouraged by groups of listeners who professed faith in Christ.

Perhaps without his realizing it this practice of speaking to all in his path about their responsibility to consider eternal values was establishing very early a pattern which later was to become the heart of Townsend's ministry. Although drawn to the humbler Indians, he also felt an obligation to recommend God's Word to literate authorities who had ignored its treasures. Some were grateful and responded cordially to the spiritual invitation, while others decorously refused it, but Townsend made it his business to dispatch his duty to them.

At the Salvador border a rather gruff officer scowled at Townsend and asked for his passport. He scrutinized it, and finally gave permission to the foreigner to pass. Before leaving, however, Townsend spoke to the officer about the need for trusting

Christ for salvation. Whereupon the officer glowered again, touched his sword, and said, "This is my creed."

In other cases an interest in the welfare of civil and military authorities brought a warm response, and the Bible venders were given royal hospitality.

At the same time Townsend was acquiring a firsthand knowledge of the conditions under which the oppressed poor were existing. His love and sympathy for the socially and spiritually needy increased day by day. Through living with Francisco, he saw the latent possibilities of a race which was considered inferior. Francisco was intelligent, and possessed a grand capacity for learning. Townsend taught him more about the Bible, for his knowledge of it beyond the bare rudiments was limited.

As they journeyed into Honduras the trails became worse, for it was the rainy season. In places the jungle was so thick that they had to keep close together to be visible to each other. Monkeys howled in the trees, and jaguars made traveling at night hazardous. In one forest the guide was so convincing in his stories about jaguars that Townsend followed his advice and put his hat on a stick so that the animals would leap at it instead of at him.

Crossing rivers and streams was always a complicated adventure. The current was sometimes swift, and frequently the pack animals would refuse to swim. On one occasion Townsend swam a river pulling the lead rope of a mule after him. When he reached the other side a horrified native asked him if he didn't know that the river was infested with large and hungry crocodiles.

Evidence of a once-mighty Mayan empire spreading from Mexico to Honduras often arrested Townsend's attention as he traveled. It seemed incredible that a race equally as cultured and skilled as the ancient Egyptians and Romans could have been reduced to the servile condition of the Cakchiquels now toiling like serfs on the coffee and sugar plantations. He saw stone pillars bearing carefully carved hieroglyphics in mute testimony of a near-literate society. He learned also of mathematical notations indicating an intricate computation of time still a wonder to modern scientists, as well as of the architectural and engineering skill of a race who so efficiently erected edifices unsurpassed by modern methods.

13

And Francisco continued to remind Townsend of the need of his own Mayan tribe. But how could the need be met? No portion of the Scriptures in Cakchiquel was in existence, for no missionary had learned the language, and no native speaker had had the training necessary for making a translation. The learning of an unwritten language would be extremely difficult, thought Townsend, to say nothing of the complications of a translation.

However, toward the end of their journey which lasted far into 1918 Townsend had made an important decision. Regardless of the difficulties, he would set himself to the task of learning the language and making a translation of the New Testament.

Francisco was lighthearted on the return trip to Guatemala. He was overjoyed at the prospect of a missionary to his own tribe, and in the anticipation of the Word of God in his own language. In Guatemala Townsend found that Elbert Robinson had already taken up work among the Cakchiquels surrounding beautiful Lake Atitlán where there was much interest in the Word among the Indians. Town after town was opening to the Good News. One old chief had challenged the first bearers of the gospel to his village in these words:

"Why haven't you come sooner? We have heard that you have told this wonderful story in other nearby towns and we have been wondering what sin we have committed against God which kept Him from sending you to us."

Townsend, upon hearing the news, wrote in his journal:

"The fault is not theirs. God has sent, but we have refused to go. The children of Mammon are more faithful to their Lord. In these very Indian villages, for instance, as in towns the world over, Singer Sewing Machines are a common sight. In little more than a generation one commercial organization has sold its wares throughout the entire world whereas the church of God after nineteen centuries has not made the gospel as commonly known. We have been negligent and inefficient. These villages around Lake Atitlán shall all soon hear the call, 'Come unto me, all ye that labour and are heavy laden, and I will give you rest,' for Elbert has settled there and will give his life to ministering to them. But there are thousands of other Indian villages from Mexico south to Tierra del Fuego whose chiefs might cry, 'What sin have we committed that you do not come?' "

14

3. Wrestling with the Language

Townsend had fallen in love with the Cakchiquel Indians. He had pledged his life to them, to give them the Word of God in the language that would reach their understanding and move their hearts. Tramping the trails with Francisco had been pure joy, and now he looked forward to settling down with his tribe, learning his language and translating the Scriptures for him and his people.

As Townsend's thoughts turned to rugged research on the Mayan dialect, he found his heart turning also toward a charming Swedish girl from Chicago whom he had met in Guatemala City. Elvira Malmstrom drew Cameron Townsend like a magnet. And he could not resist the dream of a home, after some of the scant meals and skimpy lodgings that had been his portion in traveling through Central America.

Elvira spoke Spanish well—and she could probably learn Cakchiquel, thought Townsend. She was musical, and also an efficient secretary. She had lived in rural Guatemala and knew the hardships and privations of Indian work. When Townsend shared his dream with her, she too felt that her place with him had been planned.

Upon their marriage on July 9, 1919, the Townsends joined the Central American Mission under whose auspices they were to work in the Cakchiquel Indian field. Townsend was the first missionary in Guatemala to devote his efforts to the translation of the Scriptures into an Indian dialect. Heretofore workers had evangelized the Indians in Spanish though most of the dialect-speaking Guatemalans could not understand it. With the commencement of the Cakchiquel work, a new pattern was being formed in missionary effort in the country.

The Townsends made their first home in Antigua where the young missionary had so unpropitiously begun his work almost two years before. Antigua served as the center from which they could minister to the many groups of Cakchiquels where Townsend was already known and accepted.

Elvira Townsend was thrilled to spend her honeymoon on muleback visiting groups of Indian believers scattered far and wide throughout Cakchiquel country. She rejoiced with her husband in the progress evident in the young work. In addition to their work with groups of believers they also supervised a school for Indian children in San Antonio, the town near Santa Catarina where Townsend had had his first encounter with hot Guatemalan food. Of the busy honeymoon Mrs. Townsend wrote:

"No doubt you would be interested in knowing how we spent our honeymoon. The first week we were busy arranging our home, and also holding meetings here in Antigua. The second week we went off on an evangelizing trip covering eighty-five miles on muleback. . . . Each week on Sunday we mount our mules and go to San Antonio and Santa Catarina where we hold services. We remain over until Monday, giving Monday morning to the children in the school. . . . We have been so happy to see the brethren take new interest, and especially because some of them have come and asked Mr. Townsend for further instruction in the Bible in order that they might lead a meeting among their people. . . .

"You will be interested to know of the school at San Antonio. At times we are almost inclined to give it up. But then it seems it is the Lord's will for us to keep it going, especially as you know so few Indians are given the privilege of even learning to read. You would be surprised at their intelligence. Last March when the school was opened none of the children could even read, and now we find that three of them are able to read difficult passages in the Bible, and they are taught a Bible verse each day, so we feel it is a great blessing to these children."

Although living in Antigua, the Townsends had made plans to move to San Antonio where there were many more Cakchiquel speakers. Antigua was made up of Ladinos and Indians, and they found that working with these two strata of society, straddling a wide racial and cultural cleavage, was difficult. They knew that they would have to concentrate their efforts if the New Testament was to be translated. In the first place they needed to live where they would hear and speak the Indian dialect, and San Antonio was a better environment for this goal than Antigua. Accordingly they were joyfully anticipating life in the cornstalk hut, soon to be built. It was the predominant type of structure in the Cakchiquel village. The Townsends were desirous of adapting their life as much as practicable to Cakchiquel ways, without sacrificing efficiency in the work.

With no tools for attacking the difficult Cakchiquel language except their own ingenuity and persistence, it was a challenging task, to say the least. In speaking of the difficulties of learning the language Mrs. Townsend reveals something of her trials of soul:

"How we wish you could step into our Indian parlor with Indian curtains, centerpieces and other little trinkets that they make. Our little home is cozy and nice and we count it a privilege to be here amongst our Indians. Do pray that we may quickly learn this awful language. With no grammar or books of any kind from which to study, it is indeed hard. We have a little book of our own in which we mark down different words and phrases which the Indians tell us when we visit them. However, some of these words have such awful sounds that it is almost impossible to write them down. But surely the language of the Cakchiquels is the Lord's just as much as English, Spanish, or Swedish, and we know that He will give us this Indian language that we may soon be able to explain the gospel to them in their own tongue.

"We are sad at this time because of the death of our beloved Indian brother, Francisco Díaz, the Lord having called him Home. During Mr. Townsend's travels through these republics, when Francisco accompanied him for a whole year, he was always so faithful, and at all times he has stood ready to help in the work of the Lord. It is only a short time since he was placed as pastor for the congregation at Patzum and surrounding towns. 'His ways are not our ways.' It is hard for us to understand why, but the Lord must have had some purpose in taking Home our beloved Francisco."

During Townsend and Francisco's travels through Guatemala

17

and other Central American countries, the political weather had been calm. It was controlled in Guatemala by Manuel Estrada Cabrera who had ruled from 1898 until 1920. But finally wearied by his despotic rule, other forces gained momentum and eventually exerted themselves. In 1920 the country was torn by volcanic political eruptions that shook the land with gunfire and cannon roar. Travel became quite unsafe. Letters from the Townsends written during the outbursts give a glimpse of some of the political fury:

"April 26, 1920: How we praise God that we got out of Guatemala City safely, and yet at the last hour before the awful conditions arose there. Mr. Townsend had intended going on that day and I was going to remain until the next day, but finally decided to go along with him. . . . When we came from Guatemala City two Indian believers came with us, carrying some of our things. We got ahead of them in the road, but they were to arrive in Antigua that same day. As yet we have heard nothing from them or about them. . . ."

"May 3, 1920: The box of clothing, books, etc. which we thought had been lost has been found. The *mozos* had left it at the home of another believer on the road from the capital and had fled to their homes on hearing cannonading."

By May the storm had subsided, and the hut in San Antonio was finally completed and ready for its occupants. The Townsends moved to their new center of operations to work in earnest on the Cakchiquel language. But there was much to do in addition to desk work, as was clearly evident from their correspondence. On May 3, 1920, Townsend wrote one of his typical letters full of Indians, education, and related activities:

"We are all settled now in our home. It is an Indian home in an Indian town, and though its inmates are white yet their hearts are chock full of Indian-ward love. We are so happy to be here, and we are sure it is the joy of being in the center of the Lord's will. Here we have a congregation of some eighty believers. One of the beauties of it is that there is a strong representation of young people, as well as adults and children. It's a great joy to open up the Word of God to them and to pastor them the best we can in view of the many other duties we have.

"Some of the brethren who don't know how to read are today

putting the finishing touches to a room for the schoolteacher so that he can live here and thus start a night school to teach them to read. He has been living in Antigua and going back and forth on foot. Their one interest now seems to be to learn to read God's Word. If it were not for this, they would very contentedly go through life without knowing a single letter. What they have heard of God's message to men gives them a burning desire to be able to read it for themselves. The desire is so strong that after carrying heavy burdens all day long, at night they light a piece of fat pine for a torch, take out their Spanish Bibles; and after asking the Lord to open their understanding, they begin to spell out the letters. Over two dozen in the various congregations have learned to read with no other teacher than a brother who can read a little already and with no other textbook than the Bible. God grant that some day we may be able to put large parts of the Bible into their own tongue. For even when they learn to read the Spanish, they do not understand a large part of it. . . .

"Though neither of us has had any experience in medical work, we find the need so great that we have laid in a supply of simple remedies and already have considerable practice. One day we doctored four patients. Our specialty is chenopodium which we give for the hookworm. According to Rockefeller Foundation reports, eighty per cent of the people here in San Antonio have this disease. There is considerable malaria, too, and sores resulting from insect bites abound."

Always with the goal of the Cakchiquel New Testament clearly in view, the Townsends later made another move in the interest of learning even more Cakchiquel. They found that the town of Patzum where they had been shepherding a group of believers was more monolingual Indian than San Antonio.

Medical work continued to open doors for gospel witness. It soon became apparent that a doctor, or at least a nurse, could be kept busy by the droves of medical cases that came to them. And Townsend, who saw other possibilities in the local situation, wrote in the month of November, 1920:

"This has been a week of great blessing. Through the sickness on all sides many homes continue to be opened to us. Only last night a youth from one of the homes where Elvira has been doctoring made public confession of faith. This is a special work of grace, as in the same home a witch doctor from a neighboring town had been called in to work in competition with Elvira. The witch doctor in Santa Catarina is doctoring many by her magic arts, but when she herself or some of her family gets sick she comes for Elvira. We are now being called upon to doctor many cases other than malaria. They come with sore eyes, bruises, colds, dysentery, baby colic, etc. Surely our limited knowledge is sorely put to the test, and we need a good doctor book. However, at least six who were at the point of death are now well. Many now come to the services who before persecuted us, and on all sides we are greeted in friendly terms by those who formerly feared and hated us."

In November of that same year a government conference was held in Antigua to consider the union of the Central American countries. This meeting, coinciding with Townsend's visit to the believers in the town, afforded him the opportunity of making the occasion one of witnessing to the government officials. He wrote of the event on November 15, 1920:

"Perhaps you have already read of the Congress that has just been held in Antigua for the purpose of negotiating or arranging for the union of these republics. Delegations were sent from each of the other republics and it was an epoch-making event. Toward the end of the sessions a mass was held in one of the cathedrals in honor of the delegates. . . . At the suggestion of one of them, we decided to hold a special gospel service to give a strong testimony for Christ before all these representative men. Accordingly we sent them written invitations to a service to be held in their honor in the chapel at Antigua, making as a special drawing card the promise that the Indian believers would have a part in the program.

"The response was far greater than we had expected. Most of the delegates attended and the big chapel was filled, even though it was Friday afternoon. We took over from here a large group of the Indian believers. They sang two special hymns as a group, then there was a splendid quartette composed of two Indian young men, an Indian girl and Elvira. One of the delegates had come in a mood to make fun, but when the children sang a special hymn in Spanish and another in English, he changed as though by magic into one of the most respectful listeners present.

20

The message was short and to the point. It was a clear testimony to the power of the gospel to save everyone who believeth, be he Indian, or foreigner.

"As we were closing the meeting one of the delegates asked for the floor. His address was the most sincere I have ever heard from a Guatemalan. It seemed that the Lord had touched his heart to the quick, and though he had a wonderful command of Spanish, words seemed not to satisfy him in his appreciation. He marveled to see what the gospel had done for the Indians, a race which their conquerors had always considered as beasts. The service, he said, had been a real banquet to his soul. The brother of the President of Honduras was the next on his feet and expressed himself in the same glowing terms. The Secretary of the Congress was just as hearty in his appreciation. It was a wonderful meeting in every sense of the word."

Characteristically, in addition to his spiritual emphasis Townsend also discussed with the government representatives the need for physical and social betterment of the area where malaria was an endemic deterrent to progress. In response "one of the delegates promised to try to interest the government in the drainage of the lake and swamps which make these towns so unhealthy in this season of the year."

By the end of 1920 it was clear that the Townsends would require help with some of their activities. The pressure of school supervision, medical work, church meetings, evangelistic trips, as well as the routine of pioneer living left no time for the analysis of the language and Bible translation.

The Lord had already begun to answer their prayer for reinforcements. Elbert Robinson, who had started to work with the Cakchiquels even before Townsend, had gone to California to be married and was returning with his bride. Thus the Townsends were delighted to know that soon there would be four laborers in the promising Cakchiquel field. The prospects could not have been rosier.

4. Cakchiquel Conquest

Christmas, 1920, marked an important milestone in Cakchiquel history. Two visitors from the United States had arrived for the first general Cakchiquel Bible conference Townsend had planned for the holiday season. Howard Dinwiddie of the Victorious Life Testimony in Philadelphia had come to visit the Indian congregations and to speak through interpreters. The other speaker was Leonard L. Legters whom Dinwiddie had recommended to Townsend.

Legters' earlier efforts to communicate with the Comanche Indians of Oklahoma had been frustrating. The mission under which he had worked did not favor the use of the Indian language and forbade him to learn it. But so eager was he to give them the gospel that he learned their sign language and thus taught them the truths of the Bible as best he could.

After twenty years with the Comanche Indians Legters next became pastor of the Southern Presbyterian Church of Bishopville, South Carolina. But as missionary and minister he had been plagued by a habit he could not shake: he was bound to tobacco.

Through an address given by Dr. Robert McQuilkin at a Bible conference at Stony Brook, New York, Legters found deliverance from the tobacco and other practices that were a detriment to him and his work. McQuilkin had stressed the need for dependence upon God alone through the power of the cross for victory in the Christian life. Legters soon began to preach the message that had gripped him. Through his testimony another was also delivered from the use of tobacco. That man calculated that he would save five hundred dollars during the remainder of his life because of freedom from smoking, and gave that amount to Legters as a memorial of the occasion. At the moment Legters had no need for the money. On the way home from the conference, he gave it to a fellow passenger who had been with him as a speaker during the meetings.

"Here, take this," he said. "I don't need it."

The man at first took the money—then reconsidered.

"No," he said. "This was given to you," and he returned the five hundred dollars.

Upon arriving home, Legters found the cablegram from Townsend inviting him to come and minister to the Cakchiquel Indians at the Christmas conference in Guatemala. The five hundred dollars was obviously earmarked.

Later Townsend wrote:

"In 1920 Legters accepted my invitation to be guest speaker at the first general Bible conference for the Cakchiquel Indians, and on this, his first trip to Latin America, he became greatly burdened for the evangelization of the Indian tribes. Thereafter he was a man possessed by a vision. From then until the last year of his life, he made yearly trips to Latin America in the interest of pioneer work among the Indians."

No wonder Legters was sold on Indian work after what he witnessed in that 1920 Cakchiquel conference! He saw that the gospel of the cross which had liberated him was working in the same power among the Indians of Guatemala. In recounting some of the blessings of the conference Townsend wrote on January 3, 1921:

"Saturday the conference began in earnest with four meetings a day. From the very start the Lord was present in a marvelous way. Sunday was the culmination of all. Over sixty surrendered their lives entirely to the Lord, sixteen volunteered to go out and preach the gospel in eight different groups over the greater part of the territory in which we are working. Don Catarino, a rich old Indian chief who at Mr. Dinwiddie's first meeting said he was the hardest of all, surrendered himself and all that he has to the Lord, as did also his son. The chief with tears in his eyes said: 'At last the Lord has touched my heart, and I surrender

23

myself to Him. If I am able to go out myself and preach the Glad Tidings, I am ready. Perhaps I can at least go along with a worker, or my beast may be of use in the Lord's service. At all events I will help in all the ways I can for I and my property from this day forward are entirely consecrated to His service.'

"Another of the well-to-do believers had recently refused to give permission for his son to go out into the work. Today both he and his son are far from here preaching the gospel in different sections. As soon as his other son recovers from chills and fever he plans to go out into another section. Marvelous are His works!"

But Robinson reported the results of the conference from a different point of view, noting particularly the way in which God was using Townsend as His instrument of blessing to the Indian tribe. He wrote:

"The conference among the Indians of San Antonio was deeply inspiring and greatly blessed of the Lord. Mr. Leonard Legters and Mr. Howard Dinwiddie brought the messages, with Cameron Townsend interpreting with clearness and in the power of the Holy Spirit. Our blessed Lord worked in a mighty way in the hearts of the humble, bronze-skinned folks, some sixty giving themselves in a full surrender to the Lord. With the Indian such a step comes from the depths of the heart and seems to be thoroughly genuine and lasting.

"Mr. Townsend is having splendid success with them and seems to be greatly loved by each and all. In everything he is humble and leans entirely upon the strength of the Lord, and the Master is using him in a very blessed way."

After the conference Robinson and his bride set off for San Lucas Tolimán, the town near Lake Atitlán which Robinson had selected some time before. However, the presence of so many Ladinos rendered the area unsatisfactory for Indian work. In searching for a more strategic center that would also include a training school for workers, Robinson decided upon picturesque Panajachel. It was an idyllic Indian village gracefully curved along the edge of Lake Atitlán. Of his plans for building a home there and of the need for concentration on the Cakchiquel language he wrote on February 21, 1921:

"On February 1 the Lord opened up to us part of a home here in Panajachel. We believe this is a far better location for the work of the whole department than in San Lucas, and we are praying that our Lord may soon make it possible for us to build our own permanent home, which is not the very expensive proposition that such an undertaking is in the States.

"We are endeavoring to devote as much time as possible to the study of the language of the Cakchiquel Indians, that we may as speedily as possible bring the glorious gospel to them in their own tongue. We have already had many blessed opportunities to give them the gospel both individually and in groups. But owing to the limited number among them that understand Spanish, and the obscurity with which the minds of these seem to be clouded when thinking in the Spanish language, we are discouraged at times when giving them the precious Word, and are made to realize that until it is given in their own tongue but a very small proportion of the Holy Seed will fall upon fertile ground."

Meanwhile Legters was busy visiting the whole Cakchiquel field. He was captivated by the interest of the Indians in the gospel, and by their responsiveness to it. The need for the translation of the New Testament gripped him.

He was a great stimulus and blessing to the young missionaries. Robinson wrote of him on April 8, 1921:

"We have been greatly privileged in having in our home for a few days Mr. Leonard Legters. The hours spent with him have been indeed inspiring and helpful to us, and we have also taken two very interesting trips of evangelization among the Indian villages of this lake region. . . . We did some real sod-breaking in an absolutely virgin field. . . . In the evening some thirty crowded into that little black-smudged cornstalk hut, standing and squatting, while perhaps as many more were grouped about the door without. I doubt if any of them had ever before heard the true Word.

"It was a most picturesque scene, and never have I been in a more inspiring religious service. Mr. Legters brought the message, preaching in English, I interpreting into Spanish, and our Indian worker into the heart language of the listeners, the Cakchiquel. Every moment or two our audience would break out in exclamations of 'Isn't it wonderful!' 'That's the truth!' and many times we heard the ejaculation in their language, 'Thanks be to God! Thanks be to God!' "

25

Back in San Antonio, Townsend kept as steadily as possible at the job of translation, in spite of interruptions and a constant round of other duties. On April 30, 1921, he wrote:

"We are getting the Gospel of Mark into the Cakchiquel now. It seems to be the easiest to translate. . . . For several reasons we believe that it should be a diglot edition, Spanish and Cakchiquel, though of course it will cost more."

And two weeks later:

"Margarito (my informant) and I are working hard on the translation of St. Mark. I think it's the most delicate work I ever did. To be used as a transmitter of God's own precious Word, which He has so marvelously preserved through all these years since He gave it to the inspired writers! How careful we must be to get the exact thought into the Cakchiquel! We have to look to Him for every word, and He does not disappoint us. You would be interested to watch us as we work day after day, out in my little room off the corridor. We occupy half the table, while the other half is covered with books. There are three Spanish translations before us, as well as two in English, one in Greek and one in Latin. . . . The work progresses very slowly as every difficult passage has to be explained to Margarito, and at times just one word will baffle us for quite a while."

Townsend also made frequent trips to many other Cakchiquel villages, including new places where the gospel had not been introduced. Of one such trip he wrote on May 26, 1921:

"We came to a hamlet of Indians where we sought something to eat, only to find that they would give us nothing, due to fear. The fact that I spoke a little of their language, however, quieted them sufficiently so that they sold us a few tortillas. When we tried to give them the Word they listened very poorly which I was sure was because of lack of confidence. I determined to do a daring thing to win them over. One of the women was toasting a large quantity of flying ants, caught just before their wings were sprouted. I knew that it was a purely Indian dish, and that if I would eat them I would be in their eyes more like one of them. Accordingly I purchased some, and much to their surprise ate them with relish. Their confidence was won. I had found the point of contact. . . ."

26

The work at Panajachel was moving ahead with encouraging speed. Under Robinson's skillful supervision temporary buildings were up and permanent structures under way. Toward the end of 1921 prospects for a "splendid center" of Cakchiquel work were nearing realization.

Robinson and Townsend were soon deeply entrenched in their respective corners of the Cakchiquel field. Toward the end of June, 1922, the Townsends, needing a break from their strenuous routine, visited the Robinsons at their lakeshore home. In the afternoon of June 24, Townsend and Robinson went for a dip in the beautiful lake. The sun shone brightly, and Cakchiquel fishermen splashed quietly nearby in their canoes. Suddenly and with no warning Robinson, a strong swimmer, slipped from sight to disappear under the peaceful waters of Lake Atitlán. In a moment Townsend's college chum, his brother in the Cakchiquel work, was gone.

The stunned leaders of the mission wrote in the *Central American Bulletin:*

"With heavy hearts we chronicle the death by drowning, while bathing in Lake Atitlán on June 24th, 1922, at 3 P.M., of our beloved Brother W. E. Robinson. . . . Another name has been added to the Roll of Honor of the Central American Mission."

Witch doctors in and around San Antonio continually lost business while Elvira Townsend's flourished. In 1922 the need for an evangelical hospital and at least a nurse to help carry the medical load became urgent. The Townsends were praying—and writing letters too about the opportunity for service. Cameron had briefed his brother Paul and his wife in California about the great future of the Cakchiquel work, especially the medical ministry. By October, 1922, they were both in San Antonio happily constructing the hospital that Townsend had planned.

About the same time the much-prayed-for nurse came in the person of Signe Norrlin. She was immediately initiated into her strenuous duties. Elvira Townsend served as go-between until Miss Norrlin could manage in the language for herself. In addition to caring for the steady flow of patients in San Antonio, she also went with the Townsends to Patzum where another large

27

circle of friends awaited treatment. She happily conducted a full-scale clinic, thus releasing the Townsends to hold a year-end Bible conference for the Cakchiquel believers of Patzum.

Townsend would have been more than busy with the activities in San Antonio and Patzum along with his ever-present translation task, but with the death of Robinson Panajachel fell to his hand also. With Robinson he had planned and prayed, dreamed and designed buildings in Panajachel. They had sketched school buildings, chapels, and rest homes to be built on the shores of Lake Atitlán. Some of the structures were almost completed. A curriculum for a Cakchiquel training school had been outlined. In fact, some classes had already been held but because of the pressures of other duties they had had to be dropped. And many of the planned activities had slowed down considerably. Townsend and Robinson had prayed together often for more helpers, especially for someone to undertake the training program for Cakchiquel leaders. After Robinson's death the Townsends began to spend more time at Panajachel, for the Cakchiquel Christians missed the feeding from the Word which they had received from Robinson.

Ever working toward the prize of the finished New Testament, Townsend looked for translation helpers in Panajachel and found them. Trinidad Bac, one of the first students in the Bible school, proved to be a steady, intelligent informant. Thus Townsend was able to push ahead on the translation even while overseeing the other work at Lake Atitlán.

In January, 1923, God's man for the job in Panajachel appeared on the busy scene. He was Archer Anderson from the State of New Jersey who had had the Cakchiquel work before him for some time, but without Townsend's knowledge of it. In recapitulating the events leading to his appointment he later said:

"Robinson is the man whom God used to get the property which is now our school home. He, with Mr. W. Cameron Townsend, is the real founder of the school. They are the ones who at one time tried to open a training school, having classes for two months, and after seeing that their hands were more than full, were forced to let the matter drop, visibly, although they continued to pray that God would raise up someone for just that work. Mr. Robinson is the one who chose Panajachel as the site for the training school and therefore I call him the ground-breaker. For these reasons, coupled with the desire to prove to this country that 'precious in the sight of the Lord is the death of his saints,' as well as to show that even though Moses be taken away God still has His Joshua, we chose to name this school the W. E. Robinson Bible Institute.

"The history of this school to me . . . is one of the marvels of God's working in answer to prayer. While I was a student in the Philadelphia School of the Bible the folks here in Guatemala were praying that God would call someone to establish a Bible school for the Indians to train them in the 'ministry of reconciliation.'

"With the death of Mr. Robinson, Mr. W. C. Townsend, his intimate friend and now mine as well, continued in prayer that God would send His man here. Mr. Townsend was looking to California for the man, but it pleased God to get him from New Jersey on the other side of the continent. In my first year in the Bible school in Philadelphia I felt the call of God to Guatemala and for the first time got in touch with the Central American Mission. Then in my second year I read a statement in the *Bulletin* from a letter by Mr. Townsend asking people to pray that God would send someone to establish a training school here. All I can say is that God spoke to me then and I gave myself to Him for this work.

"Upon being accepted by the Mission I was assigned to the work in San Antonio, then under Mr. Townsend's supervision. I came to Guatemala, reaching the capital on the 28th day of January, 1923. In about two days I met Mr. Townsend and immediately asked him what had been done about the training school for the Indians. I wish that you could have seen the surprise on his face. It was really good fun. His reply was the question, 'What do you know about the proposed school?' I said that I only knew that I had been praying for some time that God would establish it; whereupon he told me that they had been waiting for me for two years. What an example of the way in which God works!"

So Anderson carried the school load while Townsend plodded ahead on the ponderous job of translation. Much of the work was done now in Panajachel where he could help in the supervision of the school and in evangelism, and where he had informants

29

from the Robinson Bible Institute. Trinidad's maturity as an older believer continued to be a mainstay in the phrasing of the Cakchiquel Scriptures. José Chicol, a promising lad, also helped Townsend while attending the Institute.

Although Townsend's strength, nourished as it was on a tortilla-and-bean diet and toughened by periodic treks on the trail, was a constant marvel to those whose predictions had been pessimistic, yet the strain of heavy work began to tell. Occasionally, sickness interrupted the translation. He was often forced to rest. Many times, half sick, he would sit at the desk and, by sheer determination, push out another chapter, or at least a few more verses. In the process he was training Cakchiquel helpers who assumed more and more of the responsibility of the tedious, exacting work. He taught them to write in their own language, and to make drafts of portions of Scripture in Cakchiquel which he could check later. Thus translation slowly and steadily moved along, in spite of threats to the completion of the task.

Archer Anderson, who had an amazing aptitude for learning languages, was soon speaking Spanish well, and was learning Cakchiquel. The Institute was growing in numbers and in spiritual strength, for the students who could not understand the Spanish Bible were helped by the Word in their own language as it was being translated. That Word, once veiled in mysterious Spanish phrases, was coming alive to them in vigorous homespun Cakchiquel. Students were preaching it in their own tongue, and tribesmen in villages far and wide were turning to Christ and abandoning their witchcraft. Just what one would expect the Word in their own tongue to do, thought Townsend. It brings forth fruit, reproduces, just as God said it would.

An increasing number of students came to Robinson Bible Institute annually and went out teaching the Word to the Cakchiquel Indians. The Robinson-Townsend dream was coming true. When in 1953 the Institute celebrated its thirtieth anniversary, long after Townsend had left Guatemala, he was providentially able to be on hand for the occasion. Of the celebration the *Central American Bulletin* reported:

"Believers came on foot and horseback, and in chartered buses, jammed with people and belongings. By actual count 1112 persons registered, but the numberless children and the unregistered pushed the total to nearer 1500. Who were all these Indians? To the praise of the Lord, they were believers who had been raised up, for the most part, through the direct work or influence of the Institute. . . . Thus Robinson Bible Institute became the first organization in Guatemala to train nationals in Christian work.

"These thirty years have shown the fruit of that project. . . . Two of the graduates now serve on the Institute faculty, and an estimate puts some 50 others as very active in their local churches. An exact census of the numbers evangelized and led to Christ by former students is impossible to compile. The Judgment Seat of Christ alone will give the full story. . . .

"On the afternoon of the 20th this great company of believers marched by fours to the tomb of Mr. Robinson. . . . Some of the older believers told of incidents in their contacts with Mr. Robinson, and praised God for the work of the Institute. . . . A wonderful message of encouragement and hope was given by Mr. Townsend in Cakchiquel." (This after his absence of more than twenty years from the Cakchiquel field.)

In 1924 while Archer Anderson was busy with the embryonic school in Panajachel and Townsend was battling with the completion of the Cakchiquel New Testament, another Indian enthusiast was at work in the Amazon basin, surveying aboriginal tribes. L. L. Legters had caught a vision of the evangelization of unreached tribes during his visit to the Cakchiquel field in 1920, and he was restless. He had to see for himself other Indian areas where wild Indians had been reported.

By this time Legters had helped found the Pioneer Mission Agency, with headquarters in Philadelphia, for the reaching of un-Bibled tribes. Each year he made a trip to see the field firsthand. At home he was a dynamo on church and school platforms, and now he had one message: reach the unreached tribes with the Word *in this generation.* Comfortable conservative Christians, singing properly in their pews, began to sit up and rub their eyes. What was all the excitement about? "A thousand tribes without the Bible!" roared Legters. "It's time we got excited about it!" His unecclesiastical behavior barred him from some pulpits but made him welcome in others. He was an uninhibited flame for God, burning from coast to coast with one message which consumed him.

Fire answered fire in correspondence, too. Legters wrote Townsend of what he had seen along the Amazon and Xingu Rivers in South America, and sent him pictures of "fine, stalwart, naked Indians" who had never heard the gospel and with whom no communication was possible. These other tribes began to crowd into Townsend's already full mind, buzzing as it was with Cakchiquel verbs and Pauline phrases which he was trying to recast into the Mayan mold of expression. As he pressed toward the completion of the New Testament for one tribe, the claims of a thousand more began to weigh upon him. A thousand tribes without the Word—and who will go to them? Who will dare to struggle with their weird unwritten words?

Finally in 1929, the long struggle in Guatemala was over when the manuscript of the Cakchiquel New Testament was sent to the American Bible Society for printing. Plans were already under way for extensive literacy campaigns to teach people to read the New Testament. But Townsend was looking into the future when he could leave the Cakchiquel work in the hands of tribal leaders and be free to pioneer again. Legters' pictures of the Indians were fastened in the album of his mind. He would translate the Word for at least one of the tribes of Amazonia. Of his plans at that time he wrote later:

"The decision to pioneer again had been made even before the Cakchiquel New Testament was in circulation. I met with a group of missionary-minded men at Moody Memorial Church in Chicago in May of 1930, and presented to them my project in behalf of the unreached tribes of South America. One of the men had worked for twenty-five years in South America and had heard of the atrocities committed by one of the tribes when geologists and their aides went into the jungle in quest of oil. This man urged me to stay with the Cakchiquels. 'It is impossible to reach these Indians,' he said. 'There is no hope for them.'

"After an hour's conference I became convinced that he was right and decided to return to the Cakchiquels whose language I could speak, who lived in a beautiful and healthful area and whose needs were very much upon my heart. We left the room and went to the Sankey auditorium where a prayer meeting was being conducted as a part of the Annual Missionary Rally. A feeling of contentment had come over me at the thought of returning to the beautiful section of Guatemala where the Cakchiquels live and of settling down for good among them. As I took my seat in the prayer meeting, however, I felt a chill come over my soul. The old fervor and burden for the unreached tribes had gone. I shuddered and cried to the Lord, 'Return to me, dear Father, the warmth of soul that has accompanied the vision of pioneering, and I shall be glad to go wherever you say, even though the task seems impossible.' Immediately the old zeal returned, and I knew that God had called and that He would do the impossible.

"I had realized that it would be impossible to reach many of the tribes by the old methods, and for two or three years I had been corresponding with an aviator whom I had met in Guatemala in 1926, Herbert Dargue. He had been in command of the good will flight that our country had sent to Latin America, a flight that had taken him and his crew of five airplanes to visit all of our Latin American neighbors. He had assured me in numerous letters that the best way to reach the Indians of Amazonia was by the use of airplanes. In 1930 I had drawn up a plan and presented it to a number of Christian leaders."

Back in Guatemala early in 1931, on the eve of receiving the finished New Testament from the printer, Townsend was already actively working toward the South American project. One of his colleagues in the Cakchiquel work, Frank Bundy, whom he had recruited from the Moody Memorial Church of Chicago, told of Townsend's sharing of some of his dreams with him. For one thing, he saw aviation as a necessary adjunct for pioneer work in isolated areas. A large lake in the Petén jungles in the north of Guatemala would probably make a good site for experimental techniques. This would be similar to conditions along the Amazon River where Indians lived scattered in almost impenetrable jungle.

Finally in May, 1931, the long-looked-for New Testament arrived. Even before it came Townsend had planned to present a copy to the president of the republic and had arranged a ceremony for the occasion. This would be a superb setting for witnessing to government officials. Townsend and his Cakchiquel Indian helper Trinidad were received by President Jorge Ubico on that day when a new page in Guatemalan history was written. The *Central American Bulletin* reported the event in these words:

"Early in May, 1931, Mr. and Mrs. W. C. Townsend of San Antonio, Guatemala, received from the American Bible Society the first shipment of the Cakchiquel New Testament. It is not difficult to imagine what an indescribable joy must have been theirs, after twelve years of faithful and tedious persistence, to hold in their hands the finished product of the years of patient prayer and labor.

"It was indeed a fitting thing that the first Guatemalan to receive a copy of this epoch-making Book was the republic's President Jorge Ubico himself. R. R. Gregory, the Caribbean secretary of the American Bible Society, came up from Panama to be in Guatemala on the occasion of the presentation. Mr. Townsend, Mr. Gregory and Trinidad Bac were graciously received into the President's quarters, and after the fitting exchange of greeting Mr. Gregory put into the hands of Trinidad Bac, the Townsends' faithful and loyal Indian helper in the translation work, a beautiful, leather-bound copy of the Book, having an inscription in gold letters on the cover. This then, in turn, Trinidad officially handed over to President Ubico. The President most graciously received the New Testament, expressing his gratitude and stating that this work was a real step of progress for his country."

Concerning the translation of the Cakchiquel New Testament Gregory said:

"The Indians of Guatemala are coming into their own. For the first time in the history of these folks has the entire New Testament been translated and published in one of their dialects. A few years ago the evangelical work among these people was a negligible factor. Today the situation has changed. Present-day missionary effort in Guatemala must reckon with the ever-expanding work among the aborigines of the country. . . ."

(On May 19 and 20, 1931, the Cakchiquel New Testament was presented to a representative group of Cakchiquel believers in Patzum.)

"I shall never forget the eleven days' trip on muleback, accompanying Mr. Townsend in visiting a section of the Cakchiquel field some six years ago. . . . God has wrought a mighty work through His humble servant. The story of giving the New Testament to the Cakchiquel Indians is but a part of his services. There are scores who through his personal ministry have been brought to a miraculous change of a new life. He is still dreaming dreams. The last few days I have listened to him as he has hinted at some of the big problems yet to be met, the great needs of the backward Indian tribes of Guatemala and of all the untouched millions of Indians of South America."

Scarcely pausing to receive felicitations from many who rejoiced with him in the translation triumph, Townsend began a series of literacy campaigns in Patzum. Many believers there were waiting for the Book for which they had long prayed. Soon Townsend was in academic action, making Cakchiquel primers and training teachers to help in the gigantic task of educating thousands of illiterates.

The venture was successful. Many were learning to read, and were sharing their skill with others. Some, like one old man of the town, were saved through the reading of the new Book in their own Cakchiquel tongue. After learning to read in his language he found there was no literature except the Cakchiquel New Testament. Reluctantly he read it. Then he called the believers to a meeting in his hut. Standing before them in the shadows of many wooden images that filled his home, he said, "I want to believe in Christ." Later when one of the older believers visited him he noticed that the images were gone. The old man explained, "I served them all my life and I thought it was about time they served me. So I made kindling wood out of them and cooked my beans."

5. Tuberculosis and a Thousand Tribes

Townsend's continued battle with fatigue soon became serious. Not only was he tired, but he was ill. After consultation with doctors a sad diagnosis was made: tuberculosis. He would have to leave immediately for California. The only hope was a long undefined period of rest.

Near Townsend's boyhood home in rural Los Angeles his sister Lula, now married to Eugene Griset, had settled down on a small farm. Through the years the Grisets had prayed for the Cakchiquel work and had sent financial support as income from the farm allowed. The Griset children, Evelyn, Lorin, and Florence, had learned to love the Cakchiquel children through the pictures from Uncle Cam and from his colorful letters telling of the work. They had saved their money to send to him for the building of the cornstalk hut in the Indian village of San Antonio. The cost of construction—seventy American dollars—was borne mainly by the Grisets and their children. Now the family gladly opened their home in Santa Ana to him and Elvira.

There he was the object of loving care and constant prayer. With plenty of fresh milk, fruit, and vegetables from the farm, administered with large doses of California sunshine, Townsend began to regain strength.

But God was restoring his health beyond medical expectation. He had promised the Lord that given health he would pioneer again. Legters' pictures of the need of the Indians of Amazonia haunted him. He had seen the power of the gospel in an Indian language of Guatemala. He knew that the Bible in the tongues of South American Indians was their only hope. It would be a long, hard and costly job, but it was the only way.

As Townsend's health returned, the strain of the years in Guatemala also began to tell on his wife, and she was stricken with a serious heart ailment. This occasioned a further delay not without its compensation, however, for of it Townsend wrote:

"This time of waiting permitted further investigation. I found that there were at least a thousand tribes in the world, all speaking different languages, who had never received a single portion of God's Word.

"Early in 1933 Mr. and Mrs. Legters came out to California to try to persuade me that we should begin in Mexico rather than South America. Legters told me of the greater accessibility of the tribes there. He urged me to go to the big Maya tribe of Yucatán and Campeche. I pointed out to him that something needed to be done which would speed up the giving of the Word to all the thousand tribes who had never had it, and that it was not enough just for Elvira and me to go to one of the thousand.

"Inasmuch as one of the greatest barriers in reaching these tribes was the difficulty of learning their languages, I suggested that we found a summer institute where pioneer missionaries could be taught how to reduce a language to writing and to translate the Scriptures. I had found that there were only two universities at that time in the United States that offered much in the way of descriptive linguistics. These courses were spread out over a period of four years, making it difficult for the average missionary to take them. I told him how hard it had been for me to learn to pronounce unusual sounds in the Cakchiquel language and to master the extremely different grammatical system which called for the conjugation of a single verb in over a hundred thousand forms.

"The result of our consultation was a decision to go to Mexico the following fall or winter and ask permission of the Mexican government to send in Bible translators to learn the fifty or more Indian languages spoken in Mexico, and to translate portions of God's Word for them. But this was only part of the decision, for

37

we also agreed to start a training camp for pioneer linguistic missionaries to be conducted each summer."

Thus was born the idea of formally training Bible translators in the discipline of descriptive linguistics. Townsend's intuitive drive toward scholarly standards for missionary linguists led subsequently to the formation of both the Summer Institute of Linguistics and the Wycliffe Bible Translators, Inc., when academic and missionary activities grew beyond the proportions of efficient handling through one organization.

Providentially, it was a time of an awakening interest in the study of linguistics and of North American Indian languages. Franz Boas, who has been called the father of North American anthropology, and his brilliant contemporaries, Leonard Bloomfield and Edward Sapir, pioneers in North American linguistics, were at work in the scientific field pursuing new paths of investigation that differed radically from the classic disciplines of Hebrew, Greek, and Latin. In 1933 the first edition of Bloomfield's book *Language* was published, which for many years was to be the basic text for descriptive linguistic students.

Independent of linguistic scholarship in the United States, Townsend had discovered exotic linguistic structures in his study of the Cakchiquel language. He had pioneered in linguistic analysis and Bible translation with few tools. There was not much printed material about the science of descriptive linguistics, so he was forced to improvise the curriculum of his school for pioneers. He could teach Cakchiquel grammar and phonetics, but he realized the need of more technical help. He had devised an alphabet for the Cakchiquel, but what of other unanalyzed languages? A broader base of experience and scholarship was necessary. Townsend continued to think, and pray, and investigate.

Assuming that God would restore his health, Townsend made definite plans with Legters for the proposed trip to Mexico in the fall of 1933. Legters had left California with a vision burning in his soul and a message on his lips. Wherever he went he boomed out the need for Bible translators, for Christians who would wake up to the claims of Christless tribes—one thousand of them at least—around the world.

While considering the general requirements of tribes in all the world, one specific situation faced them. Townsend wrote:

"The biggest and most immediate problem that confronted us was the attitude of the Mexican government toward the immigration of foreigners in general and spiritual workers in particular. It had become impossible for mission boards to get new missionaries into Mexico and restrictions had become so numerous upon the activities of the older missionaries that many of them had withdrawn from the field.

"In the summer of 1933 Mr. Legters presented this problem very forcefully at the Keswick Bible Conference at Keswick Grove, New Jersey. Such a great burden of prayer fell upon the listeners that they forgot all about mealtime, and spent hours presenting the cause of Mexico's Indians to the Lord. A burden of prayer had also fallen upon a group of missionaries and national evangelical leaders in Mexico, and meetings were held early each morning in Mexico City where leaders would gather to pour out their hearts before God asking for a spiritual awakening throughout the land."

Lulu Reber, who in the summer of 1933 served as a waitress at the Keswick Conference and who later became a member of the Wycliffe Bible Translators, reported the events of that unusual day of prayer:

"The leaders announced that meals would be served in the dining room as usual for anyone who cared to partake of them, but that they would fast. When the meeting was dismissed we went to the dining room and set the food on the tables, rang the bell and waited. Not one person came to the dining room. We who always ate before we served were not hungry, and none of us cared for food. So we put the food away, and all of us got together in little groups to pray. All had the same burden. All claimed an open door to Mexico. . . . One woman at the conference donated her car to the cause so that the trip into Mexico could be made as soon as possible. Without anyone ever dreaming of such a fantastic work as Wycliffe has grown to be, I believe that that day in 1933 the Wycliffe Bible Translators was born."

In Santa Ana, California, the Grisets and the Townsends were praying too. As strength allowed, Townsend was talking to his friends and groups of Christians about the need, urging them to pray for an open door into Mexico.

Townsend and Legters started for Mexico in November, 1933.

39

They were filled with hope and optimism. Their faith, however, was soon to receive a severe test. Of that dark hour, Townsend wrote:

"Mr. and Mrs. Legters and I crossed the border at Laredo, Texas, and asked permission of the Mexican immigration officials to pay a visit to their country. Somehow word had preceded us that we were on our way to try to start work among the Indians. The officials had already made up their minds to refuse our request. For hours we sat in the immigration room on the southern side of the Rio Grande, wondering how God would undertake to get us in."

As Legters looked out of the Mexican office of immigration at the muddy Rio Grande, he hummed the tune of a chorus that had become his theme song:

> Faith, mighty faith the promise sees,
> And looks to God alone.
> Laughs at impossibilities
> And shouts, "It shall be done!"

By faith he saw the promise fulfilled for Mexico. Had not that unusual prayer meeting at Keswick last summer been an unmistable token of what God was about to do for the land to the south?

Townsend pondered and prayed too as he sat waiting for the officials' minds to change. But they didn't change. No, these preachers would not be given entrance to their land. Religion was not what their country needed.

The two men sat for hours in the office wondering what to do. Surely God would work some miracle to let them in. From time to time Townsend spoke politely to the man in charge, only to receive a repeated and curt refusal.

Townsend suddenly remembered a letter among his papers from a Professor Moisés Sáenz, an outstanding Mexican educator and official who had visited Guatemala. While Townsend was working with the Cakchiquel Indians in Panajachel he had noticed Moisés Sáenz walking one day through the streets of the village. Recognizing that he was a visitor to the region, Townsend welcomed him. He learned that Sáenz was a Mexican educator concerned with the Indian problem in his own country. He was therefore making mental notes of these Mayan descendants in

Guatemala who were racially and linguistically related to some of the tribes in his land nearby to the north.

Townsend conducted Professor Sáenz on a tour of Cakchiquel country. At the Robinson Bible Institute he introduced him to transformed Indians studying the Word in order to give it to their own people in their own tongue. Leaders, thought Sáenz, literate leaders for their own people. The program pleased him. He had seen nothing like this before. Then they visited San Antonio where Townsend had the Indian children recite and sing in their language and in Spanish. Sáenz examined the books Townsend had devised for the schools, and learned of the complete curriculum for Indian education which he had inaugurated. Sáenz was thrilled. Here was a kindred spirit, a man who was doing for Guatemala what he was trying to do for the peasants of Mexico barred as they were from the advantages of education by the language hurdle.

Then they went to Patzum and other towns to visit the clinics. This simple system of medical work was changing the lives of Indians blighted by witches' curses and everyday dirt. Indeed, the more he saw the more delighted Moisés Sáenz became. "This is just exactly what Mexico needs," he exclaimed. "Why don't you come to my country and do this for our Indians?"

Later he repeated his invitation in a letter on official stationery which Townsend now extracted from his papers and showed to the skeptical officials.

For a long time they studied the letter, discussing it among themselves. They had heard of Sáenz. They recognized the official government seal. But what should they do? They had had orders not to allow these religious racketeers across the border. Well, they would phone Mexico City and see what should be done.

"The official reply from the capital," wrote Townsend, "was that in view of Professor Sáenz' invitation, we should be permitted to continue our journey, but that Mr. Legters would not be permitted to preach, nor would I be permitted to study any Indian languages."

The officials reluctantly obeyed the orders from their superiors and gave the men the proper papers signed and sealed for their entry into Mexico for a limited time. But they were under bond not to carry forward the purposes for which they had come.

41

Puzzled, they traveled several hours down the Pan American Highway then under construction. It was night when they arrived at Monterrey, so with weary bodies and wondering minds they decided to stay over until the next day. Of that memorable first night in Mexico, Townsend reminisced:

"When we reached Monterrey, we gathered somewhat crest-fallen in the Legters' hotel room and opened the devotional book called *Daily Light* to read the portion for that day, November 11. As the verses were read it seemed as though God Himself was speaking to us from heaven.

"We felt like shouting after each verse, especially when we read, 'To bring thee into the place which I have prepared,' and 'They got not the land in possession by their own sword.' A few weeks later when we were again told that we would not be permitted to bring in Bible translators, we remembered those verses and they drove away every inclination to doubt. We were absolutely sure that God was going to do the work we had asked Him to do."

As they resumed their trip to Mexico City they saw evidence of a young nation in the throes of a complex domestic struggle. At many points soldiers were warily guarding the road, and often detained them until the proper papers were produced. Some small town officials were friendly, others hostile. Indians in tattered clothes trudged along the highway with heavy loads of firewood and pottery on their way to market where they would receive a paltry pittance for many days of hard labor. It all looked very familiar to Townsend. He longed to begin working with these Indians on the spot—but he remembered the bond hanging over his head.

With hearts more burdened than ever Townsend and Legters reached Mexico City. Later Townsend reviewed the events of those portentous days.

"In Mexico City we conversed with different missionary leaders, all of whom painted a very dark picture concerning bringing in workers. Some also told us that the government would not welcome our doing anything in the Indian languages. We found, in fact, that the head of the Department of Rural Education was bitterly opposed to teaching the Indians in any language but Spanish. God, however, brought me into favor with this man through a long chain of circumstances including a card of introduction from an Episcopal rector, a luncheon held in my honor at a downtown restaurant by an English writer into whose hands the card of introduction fell, and a radical socialist professor from Columbia University who was highly esteemed by the officials of Mexico. As a result, the director of the Department of Rural Education extended me an invitation to study the rural school system of the areas where most of the Indian tribes lived.

"During the following month and a half, I visited tribes in the states of Veracruz, Morelos, Mexico, Oaxaca, Chiapas, Tabasco, Campeche, and Yucatán, making word lists in the different Indian languages and gathering considerable data about the wonderful program that the Mexican government was developing in rural education."

This study resulted in several articles by Townsend, setting forth his educational and spiritual projects. One of these articles was published in the Dallas (Texas) *News* and others appeared in educational magazines. Townsend later learned that Mexican officials had somehow seen the articles and were thus better informed of his program. In writing of these publications, Townsend said:

"These enabled the Mexican government to understand that our type of work would be different from the ecclesiastical program to which they objected. The attitude of the officials concerning ecclesiastical work was revealed to me by a statement that the director of rural education made in which he said that the Indians ever since the days of the conquest had had too much religion. He referred to the religion that had been imposed upon them as a superficial veneer and which had not brought spiritual light into their souls or transformed their living conditions.

" 'Our government does not want the Indians to have more religion,' he said.

" 'The Indians have never yet received the Bible in their own languages,' I replied."

But one official had understood from the beginning. Moisés Sáenz was to be an enthusiastic exponent of the Instituto Lingüístico de Verano, as the Summer Institute of Linguistics is known in Spanish, from its inception in Mexico. Later as ambassador to Peru he was also to prepare the way in that republic for the work of the Instituto among Amazonian tribes.

6. College on Nail Kegs

Early in 1934, while traveling and talking with government leaders in Mexico, Townsend suddenly received sad news that interrupted his plans. Elvira, who had gone from California to her home in Chicago for further recuperation from her heart ailment, had taken a turn for the worse. She was gravely ill, not expected to live.

Lacking funds to fly to Chicago, Townsend set out immediately by second-class railway coach on a very slow journey toward the northern border of Mexico.

Townsend reached Sulphur Springs, Arkansas, in the northwest corner of the state where his brother Paul was teaching in the John Brown schools. Borrowing a car, Townsend drove day and night to Chicago. There he found his wife alive, but very ill.

As soon as Elvira was able to travel her husband made a bed for her in the car and drove her to the Ozarks. There, under the care of Dr. George Bast, she improved considerably. The doctor and his wife tirelessly attended the ailing missionaries, for Townsend too was still in delicate health. Springtime in the Ozarks and the prayers of the old guard of faithful friends and family, combined with competent medical treatment, resulted in a marked recovery.

Townsend was constantly drafting projects for the future. Each day as he hiked through the restful beauty of the Ozark hills, he planned and prayed for the opening of a linguistic institute. There were some who tried to discourage him against a new undertaking during those depression days, but Townsend was quite sure the time had come. As he wrote and prayed, the project became a reality in his own thinking.

He was carefully planning the curriculum for the first session of the linguistic institute, and exchanged many letters with Legters regarding it. Legters, who had also returned from Mexico, was traveling throughout the United States alerting young college and seminary students to prepare for work with Indian tribes which he believed were to be reached with the gospel in this generation. Townsend was also exchanging letters with William G. Nyman, a Swedish friend from Chicago who had retired in California with heart trouble. Nyman was a missionary enthusiast and had followed Townsend's work in Guatemala with interest. He was on the missionary committee of the Church of the Open Door of Los Angeles which for years had contributed to Townsend's support.

In a letter written on April 8, 1934, Townsend told him:

"Elvira is so much better here than in Chicago that I've about decided to start the Training Camp for Linguists here. Mr. and Mrs. Loren Jones . . . have a pretty farm about one and a half miles from town with a creek, wooded hills, wild berries, etc., where we can have the camp site at no expense. . . .

"Mr. Legters thinks that we should only take in about half a dozen picked fellows. I wish that I could get a young man who is learning Aztec in Mexico to come and live with them. He enjoys hiking with the Indians, sleeping on boards, etc., and would be a good one to set the example for the fellows. . . . I also want Joe Chicol to live with the fellows and teach them Spanish and to help with other subjects. He can spend his spare time working on the Cakchiquel dictionary.

"I'm wondering if it would be possible for us to get Dr. Mc-Creery to spend a couple of weeks here giving the men some intensive training in phonetics?"

Dr. Elbert L. McCreery, an instructor at the Bible Institute of Los Angeles, had been a missionary in Africa and had translated a part of the New Testament into a tribal dialect.

By the middle of April, Townsend had written out a tentative prospectus of courses for the linguistic school. In addition to the academic subjects to be covered, the prospectus emphasized the importance of training in pioneer living which, it warned, was to be "uncomfortably simple." The purpose was not only to train but "to eliminate all who cannot stand up to hard living conditions before they go to the expense and risk of a long trip to a pioneer mission field." The prospectus began as follows:

SUMMER TRAINING CAMP FOR PROSPECTIVE BIBLE TRANSLATORS
June 7–September 7, 1934

PLACE: Happy Valley Farm, Sulphur Springs, Arkansas.
TEACHERS AND SUBJECTS TO BE COVERED AS TIME PERMITS:

L. L. Legters: Indian Distribution and Tribal History
Indian Customs and Psychology
Indian Evangelization and Spiritual
    Development
How to Get Guidance
How to Work with Others

J. M. Chicol: Spanish
Indian Orthography and Pronunciation
Indian Superstitions, Vices and Religions

W. C. Townsend: Economic and Cultural Status of the Indians
Governmental Programs Regarding the
    Indians
Indian Translation—Field Problems
Indian Philology
Why and How of Reading Campaigns

Paul Townsend: The Indian Workers' Practical Living
    Problems

Some notions will also be given regarding the geography and history of Latin America and it is hoped that we can secure Frank C. Pinkerton, M.D., for courses on *Keeping Well in the Tropics, First Aid,* and *Indian Archeology,* and Dr. E. L. McCreery for a short course in *Phonetics.* Where the word INDIAN is used it refers to the Indians of Latin America.

46

Townsend personally delivered carbon copies of the approved prospectus to potential applicants at Dallas Theological Seminary and at Columbia Bible College in South Carolina. He also sent them to other schools. But the two regular students who applied for work the first year came from the two schools visited by Townsend, Richmond McKinney from Dallas and Edward Sywulka from Columbia. Sywulka had already heard Legters at the Keswick Bible Conferences pouring out his heart for workers to go to neglected Indian tribes. He recalls Townsend's visit:

"Just a few weeks before school ended Mr. Townsend came through Columbia. I don't recall that he even spoke in chapel but I saw him and he handed me a little typewritten sheet telling about his project for the linguistic school. It appealed to me very much and I decided to go. I think I was the first student to apply."

On June 27, 1934, Sywulka, secretary for the camp, wrote to friends who had followed the events leading up to the founding of the linguistic school:

"Greetings from Camp Wycliffe. We have chosen this name in honor of the great English Bible translator because each of us hopes to follow his example among the Indians of Latin America.

"We ask your prayer: 1. For the complete restoration of Mrs. W. C. Townsend's health, if it be our Lord's will. 2. For God's guidance in the plans and His provision of funds for two projects: a) A time of visiting several Indian tribes of the U.S.A. this summer; b) A period for the study of phonetics with Dr. E. L. McCreery."

When it developed that Dr. McCreery could not make the trip to Arkansas to teach the courses in phonetics, Townsend arranged for the students to go to Los Angeles. On July 16, 1934, Townsend wrote Nyman:

"Funds are in sight for the proposed trip to Los Angeles to get the lessons in phonetics from Dr. McCreery. . . . A missionary from Brazil who wants to go to the Indians will also give twenty-five dollars toward the trip as he wants to get the phonetics classes and visit the Indian stations en route. . . . Would you assume responsibility for them while they are in California and see that their classes are arranged, etc.?"

With a cordial invitation from Nyman the party set out for California. They visited Indian reservations along the way for

Townsend was eager that they should see the Indian field at home. When they reached California, they went to the Nyman home in Glendale. They did their own cooking as they had in Arkansas, living on a very simple fare to keep within the limited budget. Recalling the experience Sywulka says:

"We stayed with the Nymans in a little apartment above their garage. The Nyman children were very much interested in supporting missionaries. They had saved up about fifty-five cents and decided to give their offering to us. White grapes were cheap then, about three pounds for five cents. We practically lived on them. After a while one of the children said to Mr. Nyman, 'Let's don't give those fellows any more money. All they do with it is buy white grapes.' "

The grape eaters studied every day with Dr. McCreery, learning much about language sounds and how to reproduce them. This supplemented what they had already learned from Townsend. Thus the first session of "Camp Wycliffe," later academically known as the Summer Institute of Linguistics, was successfully concluded.

But the academic work was only a part of the vision Townsend had for the training school. He also taught his first students to look to God for open doors into lands then closed to Bible translators. Of those days of prayer Townsend says:

"We recall how hard the floor was to our knees and the nail kegs to our elbows as we spent considerable time in prayer asking God to undertake in behalf of the hundreds of tribes of Indians of Latin America as well as unevangelized tribes elsewhere in the world. The memory though is sweet."

7. Arkansas Travelers

A new president, Lázaro Cárdenas, had come into power in
Mexico, but the strict laws regarding missionaries were not relaxed. In fact, the religious situation was more tense. Cárdenas
had signed a law prohibiting the use of the mails for religious
literature of any kind. This had resulted in the impounding of
many boxes of Spanish Bibles at the port of Vera Cruz. However, Townsend was firm in his conviction that a change would
come.

"In the fall of 1934 after the students had scattered," Townsend wrote, "Elvira and I decided to go to Mexico to follow up
contacts already made there. We were able to drive as far as
Monterrey, but were held there by landslides along the new Pan
American Highway. We spent two months in Monterrey waiting,
writing, and interviewing officials and people of various categories
whose opinions I needed to know for my writing."

But once again the hope deferred that makes the heart sick was
Townsend's lot. His wife became desperately ill, "so ill," wrote
Townsend, "that the doctor instructed me to prepare for a funeral.
I went to the pastor of the Monterrey Baptist Church who told
me that the restrictions on religious services were so exacting that
it would be impossible for us to have a funeral service in his
church."

When it was clear that no service of any kind would be permitted an improvised bed was made in the car and the party set out for Dallas, Texas. There the patient was placed in the care of Dr. Robert Giles—who brought her through the crisis.

Returning to the Ozarks, Townsend continued to write about the training school and send out announcements about the second session to be held in the summer of 1935. Legters was energetically advertising it in his lectures and travels throughout the States. He was overjoyed when his own son Brainerd, a seminary student in Philadelphia, decided to attend. Legters had named his son for the early American missionary to the Indians, David Brainerd, with the hope that his son would follow in his steps. Brainerd had also recruited a classmate, Maxwell Lathrop. They both wrote to Townsend asking about the possibility of going to Mexico following the summer school to work with Indian tribes.

"In my reply to them," Townsend wrote later, "it was necessary to state that we had no human assurance whatever of their being able to enter the land to which we felt called. In fact the restrictions that faced us were insurmountable except for God. I told them, however, of how God had led us thus far and of my conviction that He would go before us and open the door. They felt that this assurance was sufficient and both showed up for the summer's work."

Richmond McKinney returned from Dallas for a second summer; William Sedat, a German-born student interested in Indian translation, had heard of the school and reported for the session. Another recruit was Kenneth L. Pike, a young man from Connecticut, who had been studying at Gordon College of Theology and Missions in Boston. He had applied to go out under the China Inland Mission but had been rejected for health reasons. He had heard of the linguistic project and thought he would try this approach to the mission field. Lacking funds, he had hitchhiked his way to Arkansas.

Dr. McCreery was able to make the trip from Los Angeles and join the others for the summer session, and soon a happy handful of young recruits and experienced instructors was at work in the rustic classroom.

One of the recruits failed to impress Legters as a good potential pioneer. Ken Pike was thin and delicate-looking. He obviously was not accustomed to rugged outdoor life, as Legters observed on the hikes and field trips made in the Ozark hills. One time when the boys were gathering firewood for the preparation of an outdoor meal, Legters spotted Pike climbing a high tree. It is reported that Legters shook his head in disappointment and murmured, "Lord, couldn't you have sent us something better than this?"

But Townsend appreciated Pike from the start. His physical frailty was no problem, for Townsend himself had been given only two months when he landed in Guatemala years before. Besides Ken Pike could imitate the Cakchiquel sounds remarkably well. Townsend thought he showed a real aptitude for phonetics and for language work in general. What if he lacked experience in building fires? He could learn that.

Townsend wrote to a group of friends who were following his work:

"This session of Camp Wycliffe has been signally blessed. God-picked men exceptionally well prepared have come from different spheres in answer to your prayers. God's presence has been preciously manifest all summer. Dr. McCreery believes that a movement is being born that should go forward until every tribe on the face of the earth has received God's Word in its own language."

Then Townsend told of the immediate plans for advance. In addition to the five single recruits who were expecting to go to Indian tribes, he and Mrs. Townsend were making similar preparations. Thus "six tribes of Indians are to feel the impact of this summer's encampment," he wrote. "Mrs. Townsend and I plan to join the students in this advance. We cannot tell you how happy we are over the prospect of breaking the Bread of Life once more to a people who have never had it. On the 17th of July Mrs. Townsend celebrated the eighteenth anniversary of her arrival on the mission field by spending four hours studying phonetics under Dr. McCreery. Just a few months ago at the edge of the grave and now four hours a day in the classroom preparing for a new task! Truly a miracle!

"You have been praying for our health and God has heard. You have also prayed that the door might open in Mexico, and a month ago the hinges began to creak."

The day in 1935 when "the hinges began to creak" was an unforgettable one at Camp Wycliffe. It had been designated as a

51

special day of intercession for the discouraging situation in Mexico. One who knelt by the nail kegs wrote later:

"The doors for the entrance of new missionaries in Mexico were still tightly closed last summer. At Camp Wycliffe a special day of prayer for the situation was set aside. It required more than usual faith to kneel down and ask the Lord to mold the policy of a government which had been radical in its attitude toward Christianity. Yet there were promises which God gave us grace to claim.

"As we rose from our knees, someone who had been listening to a radio in town came and announced a news report that President Cárdenas of Mexico had dismissed his cabinet including the fanatical atheists."

This confirmation of Townsend's faith was a great inspiration to the young recruits who were feeling their way into a new type of missionary venture. They had actually helped in prayer to "move the hand that moves the world."

The following days continued to bring good news from south of the border. Gradually the extreme position taken by the government leaders began to shift. There was continual encouragement to the pioneering party. One of the 1935 Wycliffe chroniclers wrote:

"The ban upon the mailing of evangelical literature was lifted on June 25; the immigration laws permitting a foreigner to remain in the country longer have been announced; the officials who formerly opposed the coming of translators for the Indian languages are at present recommending that very proposal to the government! Surely the Lord might well rebuke us by saying, 'O ye of little faith.'"

By August 15, a party of ten were making preparations to leave for Mexico. Some of the students who had not completed their studies at schools in the States planned to make the trip down and return in September. Others including the Townsends expected to remain for work in the tribes. Of the problems attending the beginning of the expedition, Townsend wrote:

"Elvira's health was so poor that we realized it would be necessary for us to take along a girl to help her, and that it would be necessary for us to have some conveniences in the Indian village where God might lead us. The first problem was marvelously solved through the willingness of our niece, Evelyn Griset, to take a year off from her studies at the University of California at Los Angeles to accompany us. The second problem was taken care of through the generosity of Mr. and Mrs. Tom Haywood who ran a hardware store in the nearby town of Gravette and who had given us the nail kegs for the school. Tom located a big old house trailer that was no longer being used, and without telling me what he was doing traded a washing machine for it.

"The house trailer weighed two tons and the rickety old car we were driving was not strong enough to pull it, but we had no other car and no money to buy one. Nevertheless something had to be done immediately, so I took the old car to the blacksmith shop to have a trailer hitch installed. The pastor of the Gravette Tabernacle, Rev. V. Canady, heard about it, and he knew that it wouldn't work. He came over with his wife and told us that they would give us their car at a sacrifice to be used in trading for a big car that would pull our house trailer. A huge old Buick was located in Siloam Springs and though its motor was in such bad condition that it burned a quart of oil every twenty or twenty-five miles, it was big enough to handle the trailer."

Some members of the party left Sulphur Springs in another car of comparable vintage, and the historic caravan was on its way. Bravely pulling the awkward trailer, the old Buick crawled cautiously over the bumps and around the curves of the narrow Arkansas roads toward the Texas border.

Upon leaving Arkansas the members of the party had been required to have in hand thirty-five dollars each for the trip to Mexico. Later Townsend wrote:

"Everyone possessed the required thirty-five dollars except Elvira, my niece and me. We had a little over five dollars among us, and no one knew of our shortage. In Dallas we were entertained in the home of the Central American Mission. On Monday morning at about ten o'clock, after the rest of our party had already started for the border, Miss Mildred Spain, one of the secretaries of the Mission, asked me when we expected to be on our way. I replied that we hoped to get away that afternoon. She said, 'What do you mean "hope"? Don't you have any money?' But she entered into the fun of waiting with her customary enthusiasm.

"An hour or so later the postman brought a letter from the Moody Memorial Church of Chicago with a check for ninety dollars. The immigration officials at the Mexican border were supposed to require us to show cash in our possession to the amount of sixty dollars per month per person for the time we expected to stay in their country. But we continued on our way to the border knowing that God would undertake."

To those unaccustomed to viewing such monstrosities the Buick-trailer was awe-inspiring. Clearly the Mexican officials at Laredo were unaccustomed—and impressed. Amazement betrayed their faces when one day, looking up from their humdrum duties at the drab customs house, they saw the monster moving ominously toward them.

"Look!"—one was ejaculating—"*señores ricos* coming! What a grand *coche* they have—with a house attached!" Instantly the whole shift of officers was in attendance upon this novel foreign invasion. They were looking from end to end of the mobile mass and commenting in rapid underbreath Spanish.

The chief of the crew walked respectfully up to Townsend and greeted him politely. After a lengthy conversation and the inspection of many documents he seemed satisfied. With the repeated exchange of cordial greetings, and variations of *gracias* for the kind treatment, the unusual immigrants in the curious contraption finally lumbered away from the customs house.

"What did they say, Uncle Cam—tell us all about it—" Evelyn Griset could hardly contain herself.

"Well, praise the Lord, they were very nice. They were quite impressed when I explained all about the trailer in which we will live and work in an Indian village. They wanted to know how we were going to cook our food and so forth. They were *very* interested in our work."

"And the money?" queried Elvira Townsend.

"They were evidently embarrassed to ask exactly how much we had on hand, and said to go right ahead and enjoy their land."

The caravan picked its way through ruts and rocks along stretches of the Pan American Highway still under construction. It was slow and precarious traveling through the mountains, especially for the Buick and its burden. At times heavy rains

W. Cameron Townsend as
a college student before
he went to Guatemala as
a colporteur in 1917.

Townsend reading the Scriptures
to village officials
in San Pedro de la Laguna,
Guatemala, shortly after he
had translated the New Testament
into the Cakchiquel language
in the 1920's. (p. 26)

An early photograph of Indian girls making tortillas at one of several schools Townsend established in Guatemala; one graduate became the first woman doctor in her country.

Members of the second session of The Summer Institute of Linguistics held in Sulphur Springs, Arkansas, 1935. (Seated, left to right) Richmond McKinney, L. L. Legters, W. Cameron Townsend, William Sedat. (Standing, left to right) Kenneth Pike, Brainerd Legters, Maxwell Lathrop. (Townsend and L. L. Legters were instructors; the rest, students.) (p. 50)

Cakchiquel women at the communal water well in Patzum, Guatemala,
the scene of Townsend's arduous literacy labors. (p. 35)

Townsend with Lázaro Cárdenas, president of Mexico, 1934–40,
who invited linguists to work with the Indian tribes
of his country in 1936. (p. 76)

Kenneth L. Pike, director of The Summer Institute of Lingui
at the University of Oklahoma, demonstrates the techniqu
eliciting and writing words from Comanche informants. (p. 1

Tarascan Indians living on Lake Pátzcuaro, Mexico, welcomed Maxwell and Elizabeth Lathrop in 1936. (p. 79)

Townsend with William G. Nyman (left), retired businessman responsible for managing a budget which maintains 875 missionaries in 11 countries.

Amuzgo women of western Mexico welcome returning translator Ruth Stewart who, with her husband Cloyd, has lived among them since 1943.

In a Mexican village where Paul and Dorothy Smith are translating the New Testament, termites force Chinantec Indians to rebuild annually their balsa wood and grass thatch houses.

Lacandón child wives of
southern Mexico display
their chief delicacy,
a roasted monkey.
(pp. 104, 143)

Benjamin Elson,
director of Wycliffe's work
in Mexico and translator
to the Popoluca tribe,
teaches a neighbor to read
his own language.

Marianna Slocum
receiving assistance from
curious Indians
as she translates the
Tzeltal New Testament,
which she completed in
1956. (pp. 116–24)

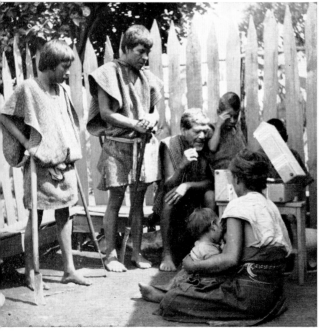

A Tzeltal family listens
to one of the gospel
records which aroused
interest during the early
years of translation
and helped to convert
some of the 5000
Christians in the tribe.

forced the party to stop until the storms had passed. The slippery mud was an additional hazard on dangerous mountain curves.

All along the road Townsend and his party had been impeded by construction gangs, but at Tamazunchale they were stopped completely by the blasting for the new highway. Townsend, writing of the experience, said in his journal:

"The blasting held us for nearly a week at the home of Dr. and Mrs. James G. Dale of the Mexican Indian Mission in Tamazunchale, and we were able to see a bit of their fine work among the Aztec Indians. Finally, we received word that we might proceed inasmuch as the road had been opened up for one day to let travelers pass. The grade was steep and the rains had been heavy so that our caravan made slow progress. We did not reach the place where the blasting was being done until twilight.

"There our car found it impossible to make the grade and the right rear wheel skidded until it was out over the precipice and the car was held on the road only by the weight of the big trailer. Below gaped a chasm whose depth was awesome. Breathlessly watching all our possessions precariously balanced on the edge of destruction, we besought the steam shovel operator to come to our rescue. He calmly hooked a one-inch cable to our front axle and prepared to pull. Fearing that something would go wrong in the dark and the drizzling rain I suggested to the man that he wait until morning. He smiled and replied, 'By morning your car will be buried under tons of rocks.'

"At that very moment a boulder fell just a few feet in front of the radiator. With my heart in my throat, I told him to go ahead. I rejoiced to see cable, trailer-hitch, and everything hold firm so that within a few minutes we were safely on the other side of the bad spot enjoying the hospitality of the Mexican road camp."

Finally, the caravan reached Villa de Guadalupe, a settlement at the northern edge of Mexico City which even then sprawled possessively over a large expanse of the central plateau seven thousand feet up in the rarefied air. To the south they saw the two famous snow-covered volcanoes Popo and Ixti, wrapped proudly in their icy ermine capes, towering aloof from the sooty world below.

Realizing that a ride through the traffic-mad city was fraught with dangers, Townsend stopped to check his tandem transport.

63

Coyoacan, his destination, lay on the opposite side of the city. Of this stop and its consequences Townsend wrote:

"I stopped along the side of the road to try to fix the tail light of our trailer. Two motorcycle cops rode up and asked if they could be of assistance. They discovered the purpose of our mission and saw Elvira's poor state of health. Realizing that we were going to have difficulty in crossing the large city to reach the home of friends in Coyoacan, one of them said in very good English, 'It was my privilege to visit your home state of California last year as a member of the Mexican shooting team, and I shall never forget the wonderful hospitality shown us by the chief of police of Los Angeles and others of your fellow citizens. My companion and I are going to help you across town.'

"Accordingly with a police siren blowing in front of us and the traffic officers holding back traffic on either side of us, we entered in regal state the city that had been the capital of Montezuma's old empire. Elvira and Evelyn completely forgot the weariness of the journey as they nearly convulsed with laughter to see buses, trucks, and automobiles brought to a stop to let us pass."

This triumphant traffic entry into Mexico City seemed to symbolize the welcome awaiting Townsend in official circles. His arrival coincided with the Seventh Inter-American Scientific Congress that was to make Mexican history and mark the birth of the Instituto Lingüístico de Verano. Because of his previous official contacts in Guatemala and Mexico, he was immediately recognized and given representation in the Congress. Writing of that important participation Townsend said:

"At the Congress we met some of the leading friends of the Indians of Mexico, among them the Secretary of Labor, Licenciado General Vásquez; the founder and director of the Mexican Institute of Linguistic Investigations, Dr. Mariano Silva y Aceves; the man who had formerly been director of rural education, Prof. Rafael Ramírez. Licenciado Vásquez prided himself on his own Indian blood and his knowledge of one of the main languages, Zapotec. All were great friends of the Indians. The secretary of the Indian section was another expert in Indian affairs who became a very helpful friend of ours, Prof. Javier Uranga. When these men learned that in addition to carrying out a thorough study of

64

the languages of the tribes and giving them some portions of the Bible, we also wanted to assist the government in its efforts to improve the living conditions of the Indian tribes and to promote literacy among them, they assured us of their help."

During the Congress, Townsend heard of an Aztec-speaking village sixty miles from Mexico City in the state of Morelos. It was conveniently located a mile off the highway, but was considered to be the most backward town in the state.

Townsend thought it the very place for them. As he wrote later:

"God wonderfully led Elvira, Evelyn and me to an Indian village southwest of the capital but at an elevation of three thousand feet lower than Mexico City, which was better for Elvira's heart condition."

8. Tetelcingo

"Eyes this way!" barked the teacher to a roomful of brown faces straining toward the door to catch a further glimpse of the drama in progress in the town square just outside.

Visitors were rare in the squalid village of Tetelcingo, but now some pale, mysterious foreigners had arrived the night before in a marvelous big vehicle!

At recess an excited melee of ragged Indian children burst through the small door of the school and raced across the barren dusty plaza to the town hall. There the tired-looking old Buick weighed down by the hulk of the outmoded house trailer rested in the thin shade of a small tree. The children squealed and giggled and skidded to a halt in a cloud of dust and pigs.

Townsend was talking with the mayor of the village, a short stocky Indian with a square firm face. Over his baggy white muslin suit he wore a black serape bearing as a shield on his chest a gaudy red and orange Aztec design. It was the only splash of color in the otherwise drab and dusty scene. He wore huaraches, the peasant sandals usually distinguishing the humble Indians of Mexico from the Spanish-speaking Mexicans in closed-in shoes.

"Look! He's talking to the mayor! . . . How pale he is! . . . He must be *rich*—just look at that automobile!" flowed the childish comments in rapid Aztec.

"Excuse me a moment, Señor Mayor," Townsend was saying, "but how do you say *buenos días* in your Aztec language?"

66

"Shimopanotli," replied the squatty Indian official.

"Shimopanotli," repeated Townsend, turning with a smile to the circle of eager faces. An outburst of surprised giggles went up from the children as they crowded closer.

"I must write that word down," said Townsend, fishing for a notebook in his shirt pocket. "Your language is so beautiful. How I would love to speak it! Please, Señor, would you say that word for me just once more?"

"Shimopanotli," said the Indian slowly, grinning from ear to ear.

"Look, he's writing it on paper!" gasped a wide-eyed little boy in a breathy Aztec stage whisper.

The foreigner, looking at his paper, repeated the word again, and then asked:

"Is that right, Señor Mayor?"

"That is *exactly* correct, Professor," said the mayor. "You will soon be speaking our language better than we do!"

Then Townsend practiced his Aztec word on several of the children, and each time the response was a delighted chuckle.

"Run along now and play," said the mayor in Aztec to the children. "The foreign man and I have things to talk about."

But the ragged pupils did not run along. They backed up a few paces and continued to point and whisper. Some moved over to look at the big Buick and appended trailer that was a second center of attraction. No such spectacle of transportation had ever spent the night in this poor village!

"As I was saying, Professor, you are welcome to our humble little village. We are poor Indians as you can see. Many do not consider us to be people of reason because we speak our Indian tongue."

"But I love your language, Señor Mayor," said Townsend. "It is very beautiful. I would like to learn it, and write it down!"

"That is very curious, Professor," said the muscular Aztec in pleased embarrassment. "No person of reason has ever been interested in us or our poor language before!"

But Cameron Townsend was very much interested in Martín Méndez, and in his village, and in his language. He knew that these Aztec Indians like other Indians of Latin America were considered to be less than "people of reason," as Spanish speakers

67

were called. They were all classed with animals, they were of lower intelligence and of general cultural inferiority to those who wore shoes and spoke Spanish. But that is precisely why Townsend had come, and for him this royal welcome into the dirty Indian village was made to order.

It's just like the Lord to do this . . . This is the place that He promised to bring us into . . . a place prepared, a perfect place, he mused, picking his way through grunting pigs toward the house trailer. I must tell Elvira. She is waiting to hear the verdict, and Townsend quickened his pace.

"You mean he gave us permission to stay, just like that?" asked Elvira Townsend.

"He's delighted to have us. I told him what we had in mind, and even mentioned planting a garden here in the town square."

"A garden? In this pigpen? Well, maybe . . ."

The foreigner had seemed innocent and sincere, reflected Martín, but it was better to be on one's guard . . . Perhaps it is a trick—or maybe he does mean well . . . We shall see . . . Anyway, if he starts any trouble I can handle him . . . I'm used to fighting!

Martín had thrived on fighting. When he was young he had joined the revolution under Zapata, and for eleven years had weathered the pain and privation of Mexican army life. Then he had returned to Tetelcingo. Barren, dusty, hot, it was a sordid collection of cornstalk huts and smelly pigs. But it was home.

He had heard of the way things used to be before the first white-faced foreigners came. His ancestors used to own the land . . . In fact, they were the rulers of it . . . How different it was now, Martín thought, eking a bare living from land that was not really his! How fortunate were his ancestors! How happy in those days before the foreigners!

More than four centuries had passed since the conquerors came from beyond the sea. It was a glorious land where food and gold were plentiful. If it had not been for the gold, perhaps Martín's ancestors would have been safe from the foreigners, but the fame of Mexican gold had reached the ears of the restless adventurers far away in Spain. Their fingers began to itch for the precious metal to be had in abundance in the New World.

Cortez had set his face toward the land of the ancient Mexicans long before he arrived on the Yucatán peninsula. He had found a ship sailing as far as Haiti, but there he was delayed. He chafed and cursed, but in 1504 ships bound for the glittering New World were scarce. Governor Don Ovando who had known him in Spain offered him a large grant of fertile land equipped with slaves.

"Land?" roared Cortez. "What do I want with land? I came to get *gold,* not to till the soil like a peasant!"

But he finally accepted the land, for there was nothing better in sight. In short order Cortez whipped his slaves into profitable action, with his prosperous farm soon producing a widening stream of gold in the form of sugar cane and fine cotton.

His appetite, however, remained unappeased as he hungered for solid gold. Relentless searching finally led to the discovery on his property of a puny gold mine. Under the blazing Haiti sun he now drove his slaves further to ferret out the thinning veins of precious metal, their backs beaded with blood drawn by the scourge of their greedy owner.

"Heaven only knows how many poor Indians died of neglect or were lashed to death in Cortez' mine, in order to line his purse with gold," sighed the pious friar Las Casas who had devoted his life to the cause of the oppressed Indians of the New World.

But Cortez, unmoved by their wounds, was sharpening his sword for conquests of land where gold was within easy reach and one did not have the bother of beating the slaves.

Finally in 1519, the great day came. Draped in velvet and studded with jewels the gold-hungry conqueror stepped from his winged water-house, as the Indians called his ship, onto Mexican soil. Brandishing his sword he claimed the land for his Spanish sovereign. From that moment he was conqueror of the ancient Mayas and Aztecs.

For two sad years the brave people of Montezuma fought to defend their land from the sword of the white-faced foreigner. Blood flowed, and the artfully penned scrolls depicting in intricate hieroglyphics centuries of Aztec history and learning were reduced to ashes. As Cortez watched mound after mound of parchments and paintings wither and die in the flames of his kindling, he smiled contentedly. He was deaf to the cries of a race whose spirit was dying, too.

"Silly scribblings of unlearned barbarians!" he scoffed as the

69

last precious volumes of ancient Mexican wisdom faded and sank on the pyre of a glorious civilization now doomed to bookless drudgery and the unremitting toil of slaves. The once virile spirit of the Aztec people lay buried in the gray ashes covering the valley of Mexico.

From the time in 1519 when the white gods were sighted off the coast of Mexico an air of defeat like a subtle rising fog began to spread and thicken on the high plains of the empire. For some time preceding the arrival of the Spaniards, the Aztec priests had been predicting a great catastrophe.

The astonishing precision of the solar calculations by which their civil calendar was ordered had resulted in the loss of only one day in five centuries. This was more accurate than any European calendar of a comparable era. In addition to the solar reckoning the Aztec priests kept their own lunar records by which they prophesied of things to come. Counting from the year 1091 of the Christian Era the Aztecs recapitulated their history in four great cycles made up of fifty-two-year periods. The time of the appearance of the foreigners in the Gulf of Mexico coincided with the termination of a great cycle predicted to end in disaster. Doom was in the air. Priests were bewailing the fast-approaching fall of the great Aztec nation.

In addition to the remarkably accurate calculations of the calendars cut in stone and the sacred recordings of the priests who were steeped in astrology, the mythology of the Aztecs also supported the premonition of impending tragedy. Quetzalcoatl, the ancient deity known to the Aztecs as the feathered serpent, had incurred the wrath of one of the greater gods and was compelled to abandon the country. Upon reaching the shores of the Gulf of Mexico he took leave of his many devoted followers but promised to return. Then he sailed away in a "wizard skiff made of serpents' skins." He was tall, with white skin, dark hair, and a flowing beard. This Quetzalcoatl myth had been dramatically preserved among the Aztecs who always looked forward to the reappearance of their vanished deity.

Cortez fit the description of Quetzalcoatl perfectly. The stage was set for the conqueror from Spain. When Montezuma heard of the coming of one from beyond the sea, he sent his personal representatives laden with gold and silver gifts to make peace with him and to assure him of his good will. Two circular plates of silver and gold which the embassy took as gifts were "as large as carriage wheels." These tokens surpassed Cortez' fondest dreams. He hastened his plans to take possession of the land.

When Cortez pressed his advance to the very gates of the Aztec palace, Montezuma offered little resistance, for tradition had already decreed him the last of the Aztec rulers. He did weakly resist the final assault but quickly capitulated with the fatalistic whine, "Of what avail is resistance when the gods have declared themselves against us?" His followers fought to save their land from the grasp of the conquerors, but the bloodshed was in vain.

Subsequent centuries saw the dispossessed Aztecs plodding their way up hill and down valley seeking patches of fertile land for their *milpas,* or cornfields. Their conquerors enjoyed the spoils of gold and of the choicest land, turning the glory of their heritage to the darkness of servitude to learned masters who spoke in another tongue and wrote much on paper. Their own language, once accurately symbolized on parchment and stone, became the unintelligible gibberish of animals. People of reason spoke Spanish!

Driven in small herds and scattered over the central plateau of Mexico, the Aztec groups eventually developed dialects peculiar to themselves, separated as they were by jagged mountains and deep arroyos. Other aboriginal groups—the Totonacs, the Zapotecs, the Otomies, and others speaking their own tongues— formed small islands of separate Indian nations throughout the length and breadth of the land. Dispossessed Aztecs who had once ruled over some of these neighboring Indian groups, were now subjugated serfs tilling the land for their Spanish overlords.

Four centuries after the conquest only occasional vestiges of an ancient nation remained. A few parchments that had escaped the flame were under lock and key in the museums of Europe and the New World. Spanish-speaking rulers were still trying, like Cortez, to obliterate the barbaric jargon represented by the rare parchments. But their speech was all that the conquered Indians had salvaged from the holocaust. They clung to it as their only weapon. Their mother tongue was the lone symbol of an incomplete conquest.

71

In 1521 Cortez had stopped the Aztec clock. That ingenious system of time calculation was replaced by the foreigner's calendar now dictating the tempo of life in the New World.

By 1935 when Townsend arrived in the Aztec village of Tetelcingo, the ancient mode of counting time had been forgotten by all except a handful of scholars. By careful research they were reconstructing events up to the arrival of Cortez in fulfillment of the doleful prophecy.

Had the ancient Aztec calendar still been in force, 1935 would have again marked the close of one fifty-two-year cycle and the beginning of another. But the dawn of the new epoch presaged a brighter future for the Indian peasants of Mexico long since become beasts of burden for their Cortesian overlords. A long night of bondage was soon to pass. In 1934 a new type of ruler held the seat of power in Mexico. He was a product of the revolution that had torn the nation but that had also broken the power of the mighty land owners.

Cárdenas had observed the plight of the peasants whose lives like those of the Israelites under the Egyptian lash were bitter with cruel bondage. These Indians had served the Mexican people well. For centuries they had labored in vain. Today they had nothing, not even poor land—nothing, that is, but their strange Indian tongue. Their ancestors owned everything, and it was taken from them. The time had come for change.

With determination Cárdenas set about to right the wrong of centuries. He would start the long struggle to help the Indians in their fight for life and land. Cárdenas had been battling alongside the Indian peasants of Mexico for about a year when Townsend's complaining old Buick came to a welcome halt in the pig-filled plaza of Tetelcingo.

"Pardon me, Professor, but which do you eat, the roots or the leaves?" asked an Indian of Townsend upon seeing the first radishes harvested from the garden in Tetelcingo. Aztecs of that village lived mostly on tortillas and chili peppers and—if they were lucky—beans. To them these strange plants with edible red roots were a fascinating innovation. And the school children were delighted when one day each was sent home with a head of lettuce and full instructions on how to eat it. The fame of Professor Guillermo's garden, protected from the bulldozer pigs by a cornstalk fence, was spreading beyond the bounds of the village.

But Townsend had more than horticulture in mind when he planted the vegetable seeds. Of the deeper purpose he said:

"Knowing how prevalent the idea was in Mexican revolutionary circles that all religion was an opiate of the people and that priests and their like were but parasites on the back of humanity, I set out to demonstrate that the simple gospel of Jesus Christ is very practical in its effect on men. The Indians knew nothing about vegetables, and I knew that the government was anxious to have them improve their diet. Having been reared on a farm I knew something about vegetables and hence decided to plant a garden in the central square.

"All the good soil had been scraped off to make adobe for the churches and the town hall, but with the help of the Indians, manure piles and ash heaps that were going to waste were carried to the square and spaded into the ground. An irrigation system was made to utilize the waste water from the cistern. We did not dare use more than the waste, for water was at a premium, having been recently brought in from a spring over two miles away. The means by which I made sure that only the waste water would be used was to install a siphon. When the Indians saw that the water would run up over the edge of the cistern and then out to the garden that we were planting they decided that I must be in league with the devil to be able to make water run uphill. Startled at their conclusion, I quickly taught them to do the same things; and then they decided that it was all right.

"We lacked funds to buy plants but Professor Ramírez and others gave us money, and we laid out a park with fruit trees, roses, and gladioli planted here and there with paths leading in different directions. The beds of carrots, lettuce, radishes, beans, and celery were artificially irrigated. The vegetables grew better than any I had ever planted before."

Townsend planted other seed too. It was the seed of God's Word which he knew would bear good fruit, in its season. But the harvest came almost sooner than he had dared to hope. Within a few weeks that seed planted in Mayor Martín's heart began to show signs of germination. Of Martín Méndez' conversion Townsend wrote:

73

"The mayor was a progressive type of Indian who had spent years in the army, first with Zapata and later with the Federal forces. I lent him a New Testament in Spanish since he had learned to speak and read the national language in the army. I explained different portions to him.

"A few weeks later he said to me, 'Professor, what has happened to me? I can't do the bad things I used to do because this Book stops me.' It was not long until he put away the pistol which he carried to shoot his political enemies who had made an attempt on his life. He purchased three New Testaments and sent them to his main enemies with a letter to each. He explained in the letters that through this Book he had learned to forgive them, and he wanted them to read it too so that they could forgive him, and thus they could become friends.

"He quit his drunkenness and the smoking of both marihuana and tobacco. He quit beating his wife who was the twenty-eighth woman with whom he had lived. Each of her predecessors had become weary of his harsh treatment and had left him. He soon began to gather the Indians around him on the porch in front of the town hall and read the New Testament to them for hours at a time, explaining it to them in their own Aztec language."

The gospel soon took deep root in Martín's life, and he saw it as the only answer for his people. One day when Townsend was suggesting some practical ways of effecting social reforms in the village, Martín said:

"No, Professor, that won't work. My people can only be changed through God's Word, and they need it in their own language."

Townsend spent as much time as he could with Martín in study of the Aztec language. The mayor was happy to serve as an informant for he was eager to hasten the day when the Bible could be translated into his mother tongue. After a few months Townsend prepared a primer in the Tetelcingo dialect of Aztec which was published by the University of Mexico and the Ministry of Education. Friends whom he had made at the Inter-American Scientific Congress were happy to help print it as an early demonstration of the projected linguistic program. Townsend organized reading classes for the adults of the town and for the older children who did not attend school.

Gradually the Arkansas trailer was converted into a new-style Aztec home, a source of continual delight and wonder to the villagers. In their transparent and elegant quarters the Townsends were always on display.

"We were like fish in a bowl," they wrote, "and were watched from morning till our light was put out at night. We had built a little shed around two sides of the trailer, and this narrow L-shaped room served as kitchen, dining room, reception room and our niece's bedroom. The bamboo walls were lined with cheese-cloth to keep out the insects, but at night it did not keep out the curious gazes of the men and children who would gather around to watch us in our strange way of life. Our odd custom of brush-ing our teeth never ceased to amaze them.

"Our little shed-room had been erected at a cost of seventy dollars. It seemed a strange coincidence that the cornstalk house in which we had pioneered among the Cakchiquels in Guatemala had also cost seventy dollars. A check for that amount came from Mr. Legters with a note saying that it had been providentially provided for us to get settled in Tetelcingo."

By January, 1936, Townsend was blissfully busy with several projects in Tetelcingo and utterly ignorant of the fact that reports of the success of his lettuce and literacy had reached the ears of President Cárdenas. Having heard of the activities of the foreigner so industriously at work in the Indian village, the alert president decided one warm day in January to make a quick check of the Aztec town.

Gardener Townsend had just given his vegetables a weeding and was plucking a chicken for dinner when he heard an unusual volume of dog-barking over by the school. The square was almost instantly filled with pigs, children, dogs, and men of the village.

"I wonder what all the commotion's about," Townsend said to his wife.

"I hope it's not visitors for lunch again," laughed Evelyn Griset, whose main job was to keep an eye on Aunt Elvira's health while her Uncle Cam made friends with the Indians.

"I think I'll wash my hands and go out to see who it is—and I may bring some visitors for lunch," teased Townsend.

Two black limousines surrounded by dozens of Indians and animals had parked by the school. As Townsend drew near, he

75

saw a well-dressed gentleman shaking hands with great and small in the mob around him. Townsend recognized Lázaro Cárdenas, the president of the republic, and his heart skipped a beat. What in the world had brought Cárdenas to this forlorn Indian village a mile from the highway over a trail of chuck holes?

"*Buenos días, Señor Presidente,*" said Townsend, stepping forward and extending his hand.

"*Buenos días, Señor Townsend,*" replied the president.

Townsend wondered how Cárdenas knew his name and where to find him.

Cárdenas had known for several months. The primer in Aztec made a few months after Townsend's arrival in Tetelcingo had reached his desk in Mexico City. It had been printed by his government. Cárdenas had also seen a report of Townsend's work in the village of Tetelcingo submitted to American Ambassador Josephus Daniels.

Gradually the real purpose of Cárdenas' visit began to dawn on Townsend. The president had come to visit *him.*

"For nearly an hour we had the undreamed-of privilege of entertaining the chief ruler of the land in our tiny quarters. He looked over our linguistic notes with more interest than anyone other than a linguist had ever shown. He expressed appreciation for the primer and for the reading classes that we had organized among the adults and older children.

"He assured us that his government was going to put an end to the persecution of religion. When he looked at the garden, he asked pointedly if the young people we wanted to bring to Mexico to translate the Bible would help the Indians in the practical way we were doing. I assured him that all whom we would bring would be non-sectarian and only desirous of following the example of their Master who had come not to be served but to serve and to give His life for others.

" 'That is just what Mexico needs,' the president replied. 'Bring all that you can get to come.' "

Townsend watched the black car disappear in the distance. Then he looked down at his gardening clothes and laughed. It had all been so sudden and incongruous—but unbelievably wonderful.

76

9. *Covenant in a Castle*

Having seen with his own eyes the humble efforts the Townsends were making to help the Aztec Indians, and having heard first-hand the plans for Bible translation for the tribes, President Cárdenas was convinced that these foreigners would help his country. They had not come to extract oil or silver, but to share a priceless treasure with the spiritually impoverished Indians.

Assured that the material help given Tetelcingo would be fostered and followed through, Cárdenas sent choice plants and animals to improve conditions there.

"Within a week after the president's visit," Townsend wrote, "a truck drove into town loaded with budded fruit trees. Then some thoroughbred pigs and a bull and cow were sent down in an effort to improve the livestock of the village. This was the be-ginning of a long series of efforts on the part of the Federal gov-ernment to improve the forgotten Indian village. Land was acquired for a new school and a fine building erected. More live-stock and modern implements were brought to the school, and agronomists were sent to teach the Indians how to improve their agricultural methods. The water system was greatly improved and two laundry units were installed for the women who had formerly washed their clothes on flat rocks. Three water deposits were built. A large orange grove was planted with its own irriga-tion system. Electric lights were installed throughout the town.

"Mrs. Cárdenas sent down clothing for the women, and the

governor of the state sent a sewing machine so that they could make modern garments. Many eucalyptus trees were sent to the village so that today every home has some in its yard and a large community grove stands near the highway. A children's playground was installed which has been used almost day and night ever since. A mill was given to the community for the grinding of corn into dough for tortillas.

"The new paved highway, a part of the Pan American system, was surveyed to pass through the town of Tetelcingo so that bus service is now available every hour to Cuautla (where the Indian women go to sell tortillas) or to Mexico City where the men go to sell truckloads of produce or to make special purchases of implements and the like.

"The villagers complained to the president that they did not have enough land upon which to make a living, and as a result several hundred acres of fertile soil that had been spared distribution through political maneuvers were divided up among the Indians, and this transformed their standard of living. Whereas most of the homes were made of thatch and cornstalks when we entered the village, today most of them are made of adobe or brick and with roofs of tile or *bóveda* (brick and mortar)."

No wonder Townsend overflowed in a letter to Bill Nyman in California in the spring of 1936 telling of "the most remarkable experience of God's guidance and blessing in Mexico." He wrote him details of the Lord's seal upon the work in Tetelcingo: "Our hearts are simply running over with gratitude to the Lord for the miracles He has performed, for we realize that it is entirely of Him."

His joy sprang not only from having gained entry into Mexico, but from the freedom to do the linguistic work necessary for Bible translation. "We had told the Lord," Townsend wrote, "that we would be willing to become ditchdiggers if He would give us in exchange the privilege of translating the Scriptures into the Indian tongues. But He preferred that we should become linguists, and expert linguists are needed in order to do an expert job of translating that wonderful Book." The few furrows Townsend had dug in the little pig-plowed garden were a good investment of time and labor. Cárdenas was now happy to furnish ditch-

78

diggers and other material help so that Townsend and his "brigade" could devote themselves to the paper work necessary for the analysis of unwritten languages and Bible translation.

The time had come for more translators to enter the tribes which were freely open to the specialized work Cárdenas and his administration invited. But in the spring of 1936 only three tribes had been occupied. In addition to the Townsends and their niece in Tetelcingo, Kenneth Pike was hard at work on the Mixtec language high in the mountains of the state of Oaxaca. In spite of some knotty problems of tone Pike had not yet analyzed, he was making good progress in speaking the language. He had already made valuable notes on the grammar and the phonetics. In Michoacán, the home state of President Cárdenas, Maxwell Lathrop and his bride Elisabeth were happily working with the Tarascan Indians who lived surrounding beautiful Lake Pátzcuaro. Cárdenas was proud to claim some part of Tarascan heritage himself. He took special interest in the assignment of the Lathrops to his home territory. On March 26, 1936, he wrote a cordial letter to Townsend:

"I am very pleased over the attitude of Mr. and Mrs. Lathrop. I am convinced that during the time they carry on their studies the inhabitants of that region will receive teachings as valuable as those which you and Mrs. Townsend have been giving to the town of Tetelcingo, appreciation for which I personally express to you in behalf of Mexico."

Meanwhile Townsend was writing letters, and Legters was speaking far and wide in the States urging prospective translators to enter Mexico. At the Summer Institute of Linguistics in 1936 a group of students gathered on the nail kegs to prepare for the translation of the Scriptures into the Indian languages of Mexico. Among them were two young girls, Eunice Pike, a sister of Kenneth, who had received nurse's training at Massachusetts General Hospital, and Florence Hansen, a Phi Beta Kappa from the University of California at Los Angeles. Florence, a schoolmate of Evelyn Griset, had received encouragement from her to come to Mexico. Another student that year was Eugene Nida, also a Phi Beta Kappa who had just graduated as a Greek major at the University of California at Los Angeles.

79

It was a happy reunion for Townsend and Legters as they began the third session of the Summer Institute of Linguistics—Camp Wycliffe—in the Siloam Springs schoolhouse rented for them by Mr. Thomas Trowbridge.

Legters, however, did not entirely approve of a couple of Townsend's ideas. Having noted Pike's special gift for languages and phonetics, Townsend wanted him to help with the linguistic instruction in the classes at Camp Wycliffe. Legters thought that Pike was too "kiddish" and lacked the maturity desirable in an instructor. He was willing, however, to give him a try. Townsend knew that Legters had not had the opportunity to see Pike's "exceptional possibilities" as he had in Mexico. By the end of the session Pike had proved his ability to teach, and Legters was satisfied.

Eunice Pike and Florence Hansen who were in their early twenties did not impress Legters as appropriate pioneer material. This, he felt, was a job for rugged men. He had not encouraged young women to join the crusade—but these two had turned up. It was evident that Townsend had not discouraged them.

When in the fall of 1936 the Townsends with their party of young pioneers, including two single girls, reached Mexico, several foreigners who had lived in the country for many years were alarmed. Send those young girls to an Indian tribe where no missionaries had ever gone? Unthinkable! was the strong reaction. Recalling the tense situation, Townsend wrote later:

"The opposition was so strong that I felt I should speak to the girls and tell them that this was really a dangerous project. It might be wise for them to abide by the warning of the experienced friends and not go to the difficult place which they had selected. I shall never forget how they looked at me and said in surprise, 'Won't God take care of us?' I answered, 'Well, girls, if you put it that way—go ahead.' "

It was settled that Eunice and Florence should go out to the Mazatec tribe in the state of Oaxaca as Wycliffe's first single women pioneers. In 1936 that tribe was several days of second-class train and first-class muleback travel from Mexico City, up steep cliffs and down rocky chasms. Big brother Ken would accompany them to their village and get them started.

But scarcely had the young pioneers reached the capital when

President Cárdenas learned of their arrival. He immediately sent an official invitation to the group to be his guests at a banquet in their honor at Chapultepec Castle. The imposing edifice which had been the French Emperor Maximilian's palace majestically overlooked Mexico City from Chapultepec, the Aztec name meaning "Grasshopper Hill." The invitation was exciting for the young recruits, but they were unprepared for it—especially the girls who had not yet unpacked their "nice dresses." The dinner was slated for three o'clock in the afternoon of the day when the invitation was extended. A great scurrying and borrowing of finery followed and a few minutes after three the Connecticut Yankees entered King Arthur's Court.

Elvira Townsend wrote that "the presidential car drove up to our apartment to take us to Chapultepec with Colonel Beteta, the president's chief of staff, as our escort. The colonel very graciously took us through the castle and visited with us until the president entered the large salon where we were then seated. After chatting awhile, we were ushered into that stately old dining hall.

"We could scarcely believe our ears when the president told Mr. Townsend and me to sit on his left and right respectively. On the long, magnificent table were bowls and vases of flowers arranged most artistically, as well as large bowls of exquisite fruit. Scattered on the table were baby's-breath, carnations, and maidenhair fern. Above on a mantelpiece stood the largest and most gorgeous bouquet of gladioli I have ever seen.

"Beside our group of twelve, the governor of the state of Michoacán and the governor of the state of Quintana Roo, as well as the under-secretary of foreign affairs, were present. We were served a most deliciously prepared dinner consisting of nine courses. We were at the table until nearly five o'clock and every moment was filled with joy and happy fellowship. The president is a very kindly man, and we were all made to feel perfectly at home."

Townsend said later that "the food was the best we had ever tasted, and was plentiful. . . . Some of our boys were so short of funds that they had been living on fruit, milk shakes and bread, and not too much of these. They made up for lost time at the president's board. I was amazed at how much they could eat. As for myself, I realized that the food was superb, but I had so much to tell the president I spent more time talking than eating and actually got up from the table hungry.

"I told him that our young people believed the Bible from cover to cover. They lived according to its teachings which revealed to them God's love in sending His own Son to serve the needy and to save the lost. 'Our young people,' I said, 'want to follow His example as well as they can by serving the Indians in practical ways, lending whatever assistance to the Mexican government they may and also by translating that wonderful revelation from God to humanity into the Indian languages.'

"The president assured us that his government appreciated our attitude and would help us in every way possible. He asked me if the ten recruits had money enough to live on, and I was forced to reply that only two had their support promised. Immediately he said that small salaries would be assigned the other eight. While these salaries were not adequate to cover living costs, we chose purposely that they should be small, knowing how far the budget of Mexico had to be stretched to carry out the remarkable Indian program."

Within a few weeks after the feast on Grasshopper Hill the flock of pioneers, salaried as rural schoolteachers, scattered to the far corners of Mexico's tribes. In addition to the Aztecs and the Mixtecs and the Tarascans where work had been begun, other tribes were now occupied. Brainerd and Elva Legters settled in the extensive Maya tribe of Yucatán. Eunice Pike and Florence Hansen were allocated by Kenneth Pike among the Mazatecs of Oaxaca. Richmond McKinney chose to work among the Mezquital Otomies, one of the largest tribes of Mexico living in the central plateau. Walter and Vera Miller went to another large tribe of the state of Oaxaca, the Mixes. Eugene Nida went to the high cold isolation of the Chihuahua Mountains where lived the elusive Tarahumaras. Cameron Townsend personally allocated Landis Christiansen among the Totonacs of the state of Puebla.

The work in the tribes was rugged, as President Cárdenas knew that it would be. He was not ignorant of the difficulties necessarily involved in pioneering among the tribes of his land. But the Wycliffe warriors had been prepared for this by Legters and Townsend in the rustic school in the Ozarks.

82

Townsend kept in touch with his young recruits, and regularly informed the president of progress on the languages being investigated, as well as on other phases of the work. Cárdenas constantly encouraged Townsend and his little band of linguists with such letters as this one, written from the Federal District on June 15, 1937:

"Being convinced of the value of the work which you and your group of North American teachers have been carrying on among the Indian peoples of this country, I extend to you the appreciation of the Government over which I preside, hoping that you may continue co-operating with us with the same enthusiasm for the welfare of the Indian races. In that work you will have the satisfaction of having put forth your unselfish endeavor in behalf of these underprivileged groups. You will be rewarded for the discomforts and hardships which you all must encounter frequently in your noble mission by the satisfaction of the people bettered as a result of the great service which you are rendering.

"It gives me pleasure to remain at your orders as your true friend and attentive servant.

"(Signed) Lázaro Cárdenas"

10. The Best of Friends

From the day of their first meeting in Tetelcingo Cárdenas and Townsend became friends. In many ways they were kindred spirits, especially in matters of pioneering. They were explorers, each in his own sphere cutting new trails through the jungle of human relations. They were not afraid to depart from beaten paths that seemed to have reached dead ends. Cárdenas was a trail blazer among democratic Latin-American leaders, a way-shower for other oppressed nations. He succeeded in Mexico and from his example many others were encouraged.

But some, especially Townsend's missionary friends, were skeptical of the "political" alliance which they predicted was doomed to disappear upon the termination in 1940 of Cárdenas' term as president of Mexico. Townsend was always sincerely appreciative of Cárdenas' efforts, and of his help in the Bible translation program for the Indians. He made the following evaluation of his collaboration:

"We have found in President Cárdenas not only a very valuable friend but also a great inspiration as regards his own sterling character and the way he gives himself unreservedly for the people, literally pouring himself out in service. We have been more than convinced of the truth of the statement of the Honorable Josephus Daniels, ambassador of the United States in Mexico, that President Cárdenas is 'one of the most unusual men in the world.'

84

"President Cárdenas has observed with favor the self-sacrificing efforts of our young linguists to help the many Indian tribes in numerous ways including that of giving them in their own languages portions of the greatest Book we have to offer them, not with any sectarian finalities, but as a basic contribution to the solution of the problem which President Cárdenas calls the greatest problem in the world, the human heart."

The comradeship of the former president of Mexico and Townsend has continued and matured through the years. In 1952 Townsend published a biography of the great Mexican whom he loved and admired, entitled *Lázaro Cárdenas, Mexican Democrat.* This account of the life of a man whom John Gunther called "the greatest Mexican since Juárez" has helped citizens of the United States as well as leaders in other nations to evaluate and appreciate Cárdenas' very great contribution to the solution of problems involved in the struggle for democracy. It was also this volume which, according to an aide of the late president of the Philippines, "lit a fire in Magsaysay's soul."

The former president of Mexico pointed up a unique aspect of their association when he once said to Townsend, "Of all the people who come to talk to me, you are the only one who speaks to me about spiritual matters." In conversations and in correspondence Townsend has never failed to communicate to his good friend the matter which is closest to his heart, his love for Christ. In February, 1938, Townsend wrote Cárdenas a letter, originally in Spanish, about his best Friend:

"Dear Friend:
    "Let me review some of the qualities of the best Friend I have.
    "He also was a Ruler, but the most powerful one there possibly could be. He loved His subjects greatly but they, due to their rebelliousness, did not wish to take advantage of His love. Not finding any other way to release them from the dreadful situation into which their rebelliousness had dragged them, He disguised Himself and lived among them as a poor carpenter. He was so poor that He had not where to lay His head. Wherever He went, and He was constantly in contact with the people, He gave assistance to as many needy people as asked for His aid. He never denied help to anyone. His patience was inexhaustible toward all

85

types of people except the hypocritical religious leaders whom He called a 'generation of vipers' (Matt. 12:34). They tried to overcome Him in debate but they could not, for 'never man spake like this man' (Jn. 7:46), though He spoke so simply that the masses could always understand Him.

"My Friend demanded complete self-denial from the ones whom He chose to be His followers, saying: 'Whosoever will come after me, let him deny himself, and take up his cross, and follow me' (Mk. 8:34). His own life was blameless, so much so that even though His enemies were spying upon Him constantly, He was able to challenge them with these words, 'Which of you convinceth me of sin?' (Jn. 8:46) and they were not able to point out a single defect.

"My Friend always spoke the truth; all that He did was just and was carried out in perfect calmness; selfishness was completely foreign to His being; He lifted up the fallen; He blessed those who cursed Him; He was silent before those who judged Him; and He pardoned those who were tearing out His very life. With the humble, my Friend was always humble and He invited them to join with Him in forming a club which might be called, 'THE YOKE OF REST.' I am going to quote the convocation since it illustrates the simple though sublime way in which He expressed Himself: 'Come unto me, all ye that labour and are heavy laden, and I will give you rest. Take my yoke upon you, and learn of me; for I am meek and lowly in heart: and ye shall find rest unto your souls' (Matt. 11:28, 29).

"With all His humility, my Friend was valiant to the extreme that even when His enemies had settled upon killing Him, he continued to go about publicly and even went into their very fortress, the temple, which instead of being a house of prayer as it should have been, had become a den of thieves. There, alone, He drove out the mercenaries. When He had fulfilled all His plan, He turned Himself over voluntarily into the hands of His persecutors in accordance with the statement He had previously made to the people: 'I lay down my life for the sheep. . . . No man taketh it from me, but I lay it down of myself' (Jn. 10:15, 18). Thus it was that He died to save His people, 'the just for the unjust' (1 Pet. 3:18) suffering in their stead the full penalty which their rebelliousness deserved.

86

"Nevertheless, death had to loosen its grip upon Him and let Him go because it was discovered that He was Immortal Love revealing Himself in human form. And so He lives. He is everywhere. It is not necessary to wait for hours to have interviews with Him. He grants long or short audiences at any time and to anyone who asks for them if they enter before Him through the lowly gate of repentance and the broad hall of faith. He accompanies His followers all the time and inspires them to serve humanity in accordance with His own example, which was recorded as follows: 'The Son of man came not to be ministered unto, but to minister, and to give his life a ransom for many' (Mk. 10:45).

"Unfortunately, my Friend has many untrue partisans who hinder His work, but some day He will tell them: 'I never knew you: depart from me, ye that work iniquity' (Matt. 7:23).

"Mr. President, is it any wonder that I have dedicated my life, and pledged my loyalty in a spiritual way to such a Friend? At least I can assure you in the most categorical way that in Him I have found everlasting joy and peace, because He has the faculty of imparting His own abundant and eternal life to His followers as one of His biographers has explained in the following words: 'As many as received him, to them gave he power to become the sons of God, even to them that believe on his name' (Jn. 1:12).

"(Signed) Cameron Townsend"

11. Pike Persuaded

I wonder why it is that I can't always say these words to suit old Nalo? mused Pike. Sometimes I do and sometimes I don't. They seem to change on me. I think I have it, then all of a sudden he shakes his head, and I've missed again. The consonants and the vowels are the same, but there is something fishy about the tone, or the accent, or something—and on Pike struggled. Throughout the winter and into the spring of 1936 until it was time to go up to Camp Wycliffe in the Ozarks, he battled with unsolved problems of the Mixtec language.

In the fall of 1936 after he had finished his first season of teaching phonetics, Pike helped his sister and Florence Hansen get settled in a clammy cold Mazatec village separated from his Mixtec town by several days through rugged mountains. By speaking the little Spanish he knew he rented quarters for the girls in a Mazatec house where they could begin their language work. He helped them to extract the first words from co-operative informants, with further instructions on how to start writing the unanalyzed Mazatec language.

Very early in the language lessons they discovered a pair of words that sounded exactly alike, except for the musical tone of the second syllable. That was the only difference in the words for "shirt" and "pig."

"Watch that tone," warned Pike. "It makes a difference, a difference in the meaning of words." But he hadn't figured out just what difference tone made in his own Mixtec language. He warned them anyway.

Leaving the first two Wycliffe women pioneers on their own to struggle with tone tangles and strange Indian food, Pike made his way down the mountain to the train station where he would take off for his Mixtec country. While waiting for the train, he lent a hand to some Mexican farmers who were loading bags of wheat. Losing his balance under the weight of one of the loads, Pike slipped and broke his leg. Through the help of kind Mexicans he managed to arrive at the Baptist hospital in the city of Puebla where he received first-class medical treatment. His leg was put in traction, and he was safely settled in a clean white hospital bed.

Pike had been impatient to get back to his tribe in the Oaxaca mountains. He was eager to begin a second round with the elusive tone he had not yet conquered. He could hardly wait, but now he had to. It would take a while for the leg to mend.

"I wonder why this had to happen?" was the natural question he frequently asked during the first long days. "What have I done which has displeased the Lord?" But as far as Pike could find his spiritual house was in order. "What *haven't* I done that I should have done?" He began to take another inventory.

There was one thing he hadn't done. He hadn't followed Uncle Cam Townsend's suggestion about *writing* something on phonetics. And he really hadn't wanted to. He was eager to learn the Mixtec language and to translate the Scriptures for the Mixtec people, but he wasn't thrilled at the thought of other writing. Townsend had not been trained linguistically before he went to Guatemala and translated the Cakchiquel New Testament. "He worked it out by the sweat of his brow in prayer and pain as he tore the language apart." Now he was seeking a way to make it easier for other translators and he knew that Pike could help. Townsend had had correspondence with Dr. Edward Sapir, one of the pioneers of descriptive linguistics in the United States who was scheduled to teach at the University of Michigan in the summer of 1937. Townsend had wanted Pike to attend that session and to work out "something to show to Sapir." But Pike hadn't taken the suggestion.

As the days wore on at the hospital Pike decided to follow the request of his leader. Propping his paper on a book before him in bed he began to write phonetic symbols with explanations of them in English. It was difficult at first, but he wrote. He forced himself to write eight hours a day for about three weeks. He could make the sounds, but it was hard to describe them and to make explanations about the system of which they formed a part.

Finally he produced a one hundred and twenty-five-page manuscript.

Within a few weeks after this assignment was finished, Pike's leg mended sufficiently for him to hike the rugged trail back to the Mixtec Indians.

The following summer a limited number of scholarships were to be available for the Linguistic Institute at the University of Michigan. Townsend encouraged Pike to apply for one. By the time correspondence between Pike and Townsend had volleyed over the mountains of Mexico and the application was sent to Michigan, it was too late. The scholarships were all gone.

Townsend felt Pike should go to Michigan anyway, and accordingly made the necessary arrangements. Pike arrived on the campus the last day of registration. He made his way toward the office of Dr. Charles Fries, the professor at Michigan at whose initiative the Linguistic Institute had been brought to the school and who invited Dr. Edward Sapir to give the special summer courses in descriptive linguistics.

In his office Dr. Fries had just hung up the receiver. It was a message from Western Union stating that an emergency would prevent one of the applicants from attending the session. His scholarship was canceled.

"Then there was a knock at the door," Dr. Fries recounts, "and there stood Kenneth. He had arrived without a scholarship but here was one for him."

Ken Pike spent a very profitable summer with Dr. Sapir. And it was through working with him that Pike got a clue which eventually helped him to crack the Mixtec tone puzzle. He had been concentrating on the individual Mixtec words that caused trouble, but Sapir said that pitch, or tone, in language was "a matter of relationships—the pitch of each word should be compared with the pitch of others." With this hint Pike later developed an attack on tone languages helpful to linguists around the world.

Both Fries and Sapir saw the linguistic possibilities of the young missionary, but Pike himself had not yet seen the potentialities of linguistic study. His mind was on Mixtec. He wanted to learn just enough to do a good job of translating the New Testament for a needy tribe.

At the end of the course, "we talked about his going on," said Dr. Fries. "He didn't seem very much interested. He was such an able person that I thought it was a shame that he didn't go on and develop so that he really could make a satisfactory contribution. He showed great ability.

"I tried to persuade him that if you are going to make a contribution you need sound scholarship. I wanted him to be able to fit in what he was doing with what had been done. He didn't know that that was necessary. He got to work, but rather reluctantly. I felt that he became much interested in it and saw the desirability of it. It didn't take him very long—he just needed to get started.

"He had material that was excellent and was a real contribution. It was different from anything else in the field. But he didn't know *how* different, and I wanted him to know how it fitted in. I felt that this was necessary for scholarship. He did it, and he did a good job."

Later J. R. Firth, the eminent British linguist, said of Pike, "Well, there's one American who knows the literature." But it was Dr. Fries who first encouraged him to do "outside reading."

"Pike is one of the linguistic finds of the year," wrote a professor at Yale in 1937 after seeing what he had gathered from his language work in Mexico.

The following summer Pike was back at Michigan for further research. He was invited to address the Linguistic Institute. According to the report of the discourse appearing in the *Michigan Daily* on July 15, 1938, Pike included in it more than pure linguistic information:

"Sleeping on an earth floor, attended by the enthusiastic ministrations of innumerable fleas, and subsisting on a thrice-daily diet of native-prepared garlic and beans were just a few of the many experiences encountered by Kenneth L. Pike, today's Linguistic Institute luncheon speaker, when he began his research in the structure of Mexican Indian languages. Mr. Pike's research is now being made the basis for further study in the preparations of additional investigators to carry on similar linguistic work in Mexico and elsewhere. . . . He has spent the past three years in linguistic study for the purpose of translating the Bible for the Mixtec Indians."

In 1942 Pike received his Ph.D. from the University of Michigan. Dr. Fries, who was one of his examiners, said:

"His doctoral examination was very interesting, for instead of being an examination it was really a seminar. He had control of his material and control of all the scholarship. This was magnificent."

Beginning in 1938, Pike assisted by Eugene Nida had directed the Summer Institute of Linguistics in Arkansas. He also collaborated as research associate in the English Language Institute at the University of Michigan, producing several volumes of material on intonation and pronunciation. His publications coupled with his directing of the Summer Institute of Linguistics have, according to Dr. Fries, exerted a great influence in "shaping" the linguistic program in the United States and abroad.

Back in the tribe in Mexico each year, Pike continued to work on the Mixtec language and the translation of the Bible. He had finally solved the tone problem of the language, not simply by following Dr. Sapir's suggestion nor by dint of hard work. He had spent much time in prayer—whole days—beseeching God to help him and to give him the answer. "Desperate as he was for the answer, concerned as he was for the Mixtecs, he asked that the solution not come to the Mixtec problem until with it he had a technique which he could apply to other language problems and with which he could help his fellow translators."

Following one such day of prayer the answer came as he was working with his informant. That day he established the fact that Mixtec was a three-tone language, but that "certain words exerted an influence upon other surrounding words and caused them to change from one pitch to another." It was that fluctuation that had baffled him, but now the solution was clear.

"The echo of that triumph" crossed the rugged ranges of mountains over to two girls struggling with Mazatec tone. Through

Pike's help the four-tone system of that language was analyzed and the translation of the New Testament later completed.

There were other triumphal echoes through the high hills of Oaxaca as the Word of God in Mixtec began to sink into the ground watered well by prayer. Pike had prayed much that the translation would be more than a good piece of linguistics. He wanted the sharp edge of the Sword to penetrate hearts that needed surgery for sin.

His prayer was answered when old Nalo, the faithful language helper, received Christ as Lord. It was a happy day for Pike when Nalo showed him a man-shaped outcropping of rock he had formerly worshiped. He told Pike it had been some time since he had been up to see "the old man," as he called the rock.

"You see," said Nalo, "it is only recently that my fear of him is gone. The witch doctor in the village says that he serves just as well as the saints in the church for divining diseases, and for other secrets of witchery. But now I know this is nothing but a rock."

Through Nalo's witness, others began to come to the Lord until there was a band of believers in San Miguel. Pike one day felt they were ready to sing the praises of God in their own language, so he attempted the translation of a hymn. In a tonal language this was not without its complications, as described by Pike:

"Four men, our teachers and carpenters, gathered around a folding organ, listened to the tune, giggled and balked at trying to 'fix up the words' of the rough translation I ventured from English into Mixtec. The first line I gave, then sang. They gaped, looked askance, and finally started to sing the 'Jesu . . .' by the time I reached '. . . a friend.'

" 'We don't hit it together,' they said. Several times we went over the first line. I suggested a second.

" 'No, it should be so and so,' said Nalo changing the tone (not tune; this is a tonal language à la Chinese, more or less), cutting out at the same time a syllable vital to the line length and adding a couple more to complete my rout.

" 'He delivers believers'—I departed on an excursion of my own, emphasizing His care of those who believe, since the cleavage has begun between word-believers and saint-believers, as the one or two or four who profess to believe, refuse to offer flowers to hill-top crosses which are said to be watched by spirits, and get called 'Donkey' (and worse) for not kissing the table before pictured saints.

" 'Our fault it is if thus,' I managed. Nalo said that the 'thus' was no good. Lesiu suggested a 'then' to take its place. With a rare flash I found a perfect word for 'indeed' which just finished the notes of the line, a word which they deny exists if you ask them to define the indefinable thing, but which constantly occurs as oral punctuation, exclamation point, underscoring and italics all adding up to a slight 'O.K.—that's-it-of-course-believe-it-or-not-most-assuredly-man!!'

"Over and over it we went, until beaming Nalo said, 'Oh, we're coming out at the same note now!' Then we typed it out and gave copies to three of them. After puzzling through it by word and song they decided to go home since the moon had risen to light the way.

"They know how to wait for the light, moon by night, down here. They have had to wait a long time for light on the path to heaven."

12. Five-Year Ebenezer

In 1935 when Cameron Townsend walked into the Inter-American Scientific Congress meeting in Mexico City the first official to recognize him was a man who had told him and Legters two years before, "You can't translate the Bible. And if you succeed clandestinely, we won't allow you to circulate it."

"So," said Townsend in retrospect, "the Lord made it very plain that the cards were on the table. I walked up to this man and gave him a good old Mexican *abrazo*. He said, 'Hello, Townsend. Delighted to see you.' "

Even through that reserved friendship "we saw the hand of God working." Contacts at that Scientific Congress made possible the publication of Townsend's first Aztec primer for Tetelcingo which, in turn, brought President Cárdenas to the town for a personal visit and opened the door for Bible translation in Mexico.

Five years later, Townsend commemorated the handful of years in Mexico by presenting some New Testaments bound in beautiful leather to a number of officials. One official inadvertently overlooked in the distribution of the gifts spotted Townsend one day in a government building. Running after him he called, "Say, Townsend, you didn't give me one of those little red books!"

In five years the climate had changed. Officials had now been shown the practical effects of the gospel in Indian villages and in the lives of their own circle. They had not seen such religion in

95

action before. A number of them had visited the few believers now meeting in Tetelcingo to study the Word of God as preached by the fiery Aztec apostle, Martín Méndez.

The change that the gospel in their own language was producing was unmistakable, and Townsend invited Mexican officials down to the meetings.

One professor famous in circles of Indian education in Mexico but noted also for his antireligious tendencies visited the Christian meeting in Tetelcingo. He wrote the following report to a friend who was a Mexican general:

"I want to give you an account of New Year's Eve when I was in Tetelcingo with Mr. and Mrs. Townsend who had organized a very interesting program for the Indians there. I was simply astounded at the success that these two real apostles have attained in behalf of the betterment of the Indians. No less than fifty adults, many of them elderly women, took part in the different numbers on the program. I am almost convinced that the power of spiritual faith is greater even than that of education, and that by means of it a more rapid transformation of the Indians can be brought about. This can become the foundation for development in other aspects of life. It is too bad that all who exercise religious influence are not sincere like the Townsends. Too many take advantage of the gullibility of our Indians and make fanatics out of them, then exploit them.

"I report the foregoing to you, my General, because I know how interested you are in all that concerns our Indians and also our friends the Townsends who love and esteem you as the most sincere benefactor of the needy peoples."

At the close of the fifth year in Mexico the Instituto Lingüístico de Verano invited friends in officialdom and in the National University of Mexico to a banquet. Accomplishments in the various fields were reviewed, and plans for the future previewed.

"It was my privilege," said Townsend, "to explain upon this occasion what our motives were in going to the Indians. We had a threefold program: scientific research, practical service in cooperation with the Mexican government's program, and spiritual service through giving the Bible to the Indians in their own tongues. The spokesman for the National University, responding in an eloquent oration, made the statement that our young people had brought a message that was far above Catholicism and far above Protestantism; it was the message of God's love in non-sectarian service, both practical and spiritual. We appreciated such tributes from our Mexican colleagues."

Still, Stateside there was no organization back of the youthful linguists scattered on the backsides of the deserts and mountains of Mexico, learning to speak the Indian languages and pressing forward in the translation of the Scriptures. Legters was speaking in churches and conferences in the States, informing his listeners of the Indians of Latin America and the work of the group of translators. He and Mrs. Legters made it a practice to give the offerings they received at one conference each month to help in the work. It made no difference whether the offering was large or small, they would give all that was received during the week that they had decided upon.

Concerning the matter of financial support Townsend said:

"One of the questions that we were asked by Ambassador Daniels when we first came to Mexico was how our work was supported. Our answer made quite an impression on the Ambassador, and he records it in his book *Shirtsleeve Diplomat*. With no organization on which to depend the only answer that we could give was, 'The Lord will provide.' We had no promises from anyone except Mr. Legters who had assured us that he would do all he could."

But in May, 1940, that strong human prop was knocked from under Townsend. While on a speaking tour in California, Legters had a sudden heart attack and died within a few days. This was a severe blow, but Townsend knew that God would see the Indian project through.

The financial assistance provided through the Mexican government made it possible for "our self-sacrificing young pioneers to carry on in spite of lack of funds." When the young translators would come into Mexico City from the tribes they would crowd into a very limited space, sleeping on cots and on the floor in sleeping bags. "But," said Townsend, "owners of apartment houses in Mexico City did not complain when ten or twelve of our group would occupy the same two- or three-room apartment."

Transportation out to their "jumping-off places" into the tribes was graciously provided through the National Railways of Mexico.

"The manager of the railroad upon learning that our young people were buying second-class tickets and traveling in considerable discomfort gave orders that they should be given first-class tickets at half price. He said that anyone who was in dire need should be given a free pass."

And the number of translators who were "jumping off" at lonely stations on the railways was growing. Single girls, hearing that Eunice Pike and Florence Hansen were surviving notably among the Mazatec Indians of Oaxaca, were finding their way to Mexico. Young fellows from the States who had been inspired by Legters' impelling messages were beating a path down south to the tribes.

Herman Aschmann, a young fellow from New York, had come to work on the Totonac language. The fathers of the Indian town where he had settled had generously offered him quarters in the jail where a room was available. He wrote on March 24, 1940:

"This is Easter, but who would think so here! The big church door was open for the last three days, but today it is closed and all of the people stay at home. They hung Judas' effigy from the church tower on Thursday, and on Saturday they cut him down and burned him amid a torrent of sky rockets. They know that Christ died, but no one seems to know that He is risen and in glory now.

"I have been here now two and a half weeks, and really like the little town. My apartment is in the jail house with a cell on either side of my room. I have had two neighbors. The first made a good informant, but he didn't like his board and 'flew the coop' via the roof. The Indians are as friendly as can be and give me all the language material I want and more."

A young fellow from Kansas, Bill Bentley, had heard the call to the Indian field through Legters when he spoke at Moody Bible Institute. By 1940 he was hard at work among the Tzeltal Indians speaking one of the many Mayan dialects of the state of Chiapas. "There was already an awakening interest in the Word of God in one village as Indians gathered when they heard I was there and that I knew the Word of God. . . . It was a fearful and joyful privilege to give them some of the verses that I have translated experimentally and to sing one chorus. About two hundred

98

must have heard a bit of the Word in their language, or any language, for the first time."

Across a high Chiapas mountain range separating the Tzeltal tribe from another neighboring Mayan dialect two young girls from Pennsylvania were pioneering among the Chol Indians. Marianna Slocum and Evelyn Woodward (later Mrs. Wilbur Aulie) were writing Chol words with one hand while scratching flea bites with the other. Bill Bentley took a brotherly interest in the two city girls nobly adjusting to a very great contrast in surroundings. From time to time he would hike over the hill to give them tips on building wood fires, or ferreting out phonemes of the Chol language. But Bill's trips over the high mountain gradually became more frequent in spite of the fact that Marianna was progressing rapidly in the analysis of Chol. It soon became clear that his hikes had more than linguistic motives.

Having had some orientation in practical nursing Evelyn Woodward was able to meet a dire medical need in the primitive tribe, in addition to her linguistic work. Marianna Slocum wrote of her medical partner:

"The real event of the week was the birthday we celebrated on Thursday as Evelyn, working single-handed on the dirt floor of one corner of a tiny thatched hut, and in a foreign language, brought an Indian baby girl into the world. It was a true triumph for the Lord, for the family, although believers, thought the woman was dying and had called in an old woman *curandera* to practice her rites of witchcraft to sweep the evil spirits away. And she was just about to begin her rites (there was even the smell of burnt feathers in the air) when we arrived and put her out of business. . . . The devil and the old *curandera* had to leave when Evy and the Lord Jesus were there. I met Evy on the trail coming home, radiantly happy, and inordinately proud of her 'fee for services rendered,' four eggs, one live chicken and a bottle of honey. Her true reward was that the Lord was glorified in her and through her by two lives saved and Satan defeated!"

Ken Pike had chinked up some of the holes in his windy log cabin in the Oaxaca Sierras to welcome his bride, Evelyn Griset, who had finished her schooling in California in 1938 and had joined "Uncle Cam's group" in Mexico. Having "batched" for several years in various Indian shelters in San Miguel, Pike was exceedingly grateful for a capable homemaker and linguist as a helpmeet.

Down in Tetelcingo Richard and Kay Pittman had joined the Townsends in the growing Aztec work. Because of his many contacts with officials in Mexico City whose interest in the Indians grew keener each year, Townsend had less time for the Aztec New Testament. Dick Pittman was soon translating with Martín who had become an invaluable language helper. "He is a jewel," wrote Dick. "He is far ahead of any of the rest in thinking out Scriptural terms in Aztec. He seems indispensable to the translation."

Noting Pittman's ability not only in Aztec but also in Spanish when with Mexican educators and officials, Townsend soon began to take Pittman with him to government offices. With the growing number of linguists in Mexico—there were thirty-seven in 1940 —Townsend knew he would need help on the diplomatic level. Pittman was his protégé and he was to fill an important post in the future work.

By 1940 there was a paved highway from Tetelcingo to Mexico City, thanks to Cárdenas, and regular bus service. Pittman would sometimes take an early morning bus for the big city to visit government offices. Once he wrote of such a trip:

"I had to run errands in Mexico City. To get there by nine I had to take a six-fifteen bus. It's dark here at that early hour, and chilly. I stood on the corner watching the dim, muffled figures of Indians going to work in their cornfields, some on foot, some on burros. Among the others there came one striding out the dusty lane opposite me and turned onto the highway. It was too dark to recognize the blanketed figure, but as he went he whistled. And the song that he whistled was, 'At the cross, at the cross, where I first saw the light, and the burden of my heart rolled away; it was there by faith I received my sight, and now I am happy all the day.' "

Down in Tetelcingo many persons were now singing the songs of Zion, chiefly through the witness of the "sawed-off Aztec" who had laid down his pistol at the sound of the gospel.

But the Word of God was also making headway in official circles as well as among humble Indian tribesmen. And Townsend and his colleagues had constant opportunities for witnessing to officials concerning Christ and His Word. One friend in government circles was the director of a Mexican institute for Indian linguistics. According to Townsend he was "an outstanding man of letters, a great friend of the Indians, and tireless in his efforts to have the Indian languages studied and utilized in bridging the gap between illiteracy and learning. On different occasions during the years that we worked together we had spoken to him about our best Friend, the One who had died to pay the penalty for our sins and who had risen again to give us life and joy and peace. He had merely smiled, though, indicating that he wanted to have what he considered a good time while carrying on his humanitarian work."

Pike also had pleasant associations with the same official. He recounts:

"After the director of that Mexican institute invited us to help in some of his problems, I went out on an Otomi trip with him and then wrote up a report on it.

"How I remember that night! After we had walked along all day working with one of the Indian lads, we turned into our hotel very tired. We left the door half open because of the heat, and were lying on our beds with the electric lights above us. We picked up a couple of the Indian boy's slingshots. This Mexican official was dignified and proper, but here we were with slingshots shooting wads of paper at the lights. We started to giggle, and across the way a señorita shouted, 'Let's go to sleep!' So we would quiet down, then it would start all over again."

Some time later when the official became ill with cancer, Townsend and Pike called on him and read portions of the Scripture to him.

"Pike got him to memorize John 3:16," Townsend wrote, "and it was not long before he was resting in the assurance that Christ had taken away his sins. A joy came into his life such as he had never known before. His wife told us later that the last two weeks of his life were the happiest for him. He talked frequently of the mansions that Christ had gone to prepare for His own.

"The last time I read the Word to him and had prayer with him he asked me to wait until his wife and daughters and his sister had been called. His sister was a nun who had been permitted to leave the convent to be at his side during his last illness. As I began to read such verses as 'This is a faithful saying, and worthy of all acceptation, that Christ Jesus came into the world to save sinners, of whom I am chief,' the nun laid aside her rosary and listened attentively. The wife and daughters with tears in their eyes hung on every word. My dear friend sat in a wheel chair with a radiant smile listening as I read and explained verse after verse about God's love.

"Then I led in prayer and said the last good-by to my friend. The nun followed me outside the room, closed the door, threw her arms about my neck and began to sob, 'Sir, you will never know how much we appreciate your coming to expound to us the things of God. Do come often.'"

The dignified director of that Mexican institute died, "talking about the heavenly mansions."

13. Faith for Fifty

"Fifty," Townsend was saying. "Fifty. We must have at least fifty more." He kept repeating the number, half to himself and half as if in conversation with someone else. But there was no one else around.

As Townsend watched the Tarascan fishermen throwing their nets out for an early morning catch, his tone became decided and final. All right, fifty. Then he took his pencil and paper and began to write. It was a letter to his forty-four fellow workers scattered throughout the tribes of Mexico. He would tell them of the step of faith, of the conviction that fifty new workers were needed immediately.

"Will each one of you please make yourself responsible before the Lord for one new recruit for this Bible translation project? That would mean forty-four new workers. I am sure that the Lord would give us six extra ones for good measure."

It was October, 1941, just two months before Pearl Harbor. Cameron and Elvira Townsend had gone to the home of Max and Elisabeth Lathrop on the shore of Lake Pátzcuaro for an overnight visit. But Townsend had something on his mind. He had awakened early in the morning still thinking and praying about what he had recently heard in Mexico City.

For some time he had wondered about sending workers into the smaller tribes of Mexico as well as into the large groups of Indian speakers. Some of the small tribes numbered only a few hundred, or less. How about these? Did the Good Shepherd still care for *one sheep?*

These thoughts had concerned Townsend when one day in the capital out of a clear blue sky a high Mexican official asked him, "Townsend, why don't you send workers to the Lacandóns?" The Lacandóns were the smallest of the Mayan tribes in the state of Chiapas in southern Mexico. There were only a few of them left. Extremely primitive and elusive, they were living in an inaccessible region of the jungle. But a Mexican official was concerned about the welfare of the small group. Another official that fall had mentioned the Seris, a very small group of Indians living on the border of Arizona in the northern state of Sonora.

"I could think of no excuse to give them for not going to these tribes," said Townsend, "even though they are so very small and so inaccessible—nor could I think of any adequate excuse to give my Lord."

It was the question of the officials added to his own preoccupation for small tribes that had brought Townsend to a place of decision. "That morning at the Lathrops' the challenge seemed to be, 'Call upon Me and I will answer you and thrust forth workers into every unreached tribe in Mexico, large or small.' "

Later after World War II had broken out in full fury he wrote to his flock already at work:

"How many of you would be willing to help open up a new station next fall, giving at least one month of your time to this task? Would it not be wonderful to have all the tribes of Mexico occupied now when so many fields are closed due to the war conditions?"

It would be a big jump, from forty-four to almost a hundred workers. It was a leap in the dark in other ways, too.

Legters had raised a good portion of the funds and had recruited many of the workers then in Mexico. Now he was gone. There was no one in the States presenting the need of the tribes as he had done. Where would the fifty new workers and their support come from?

There was another complication, too. Training fifty new workers for Mexico in addition to the number of candidates from other missions who would be taking the summer training in linguistics would require a much larger plant than the farmhouse or the small schoolroom in the Ozarks. Where would a group of a hundred or more students plus staff be housed?

But Townsend was sure that the problems posed by some of his conservative fellow workers would be solved by the God who had given him the assurance for fifty new workers. As if anticipating a sharp incline, wheels had already been in motion north of the Mexican border, wheels of which Townsend was unaware.

14. Cherokee Trail to Oklahoma

"You are the one to do it," the department head had told Della Brunstetter. "Why don't you go to Washington and see what can be done?"

Della Brunstetter was teaching French at the University of Oklahoma but had become fascinated by the Cherokee language spoken by a large number of Indians of Oklahoma. Now there was talk about offering a course in Cherokee at the university. But someone needed to study the language and write it down in modern script before it could be adequately taught. Miss Brunstetter was elected.

In 1838 the Cherokee Indians had been moved from North Carolina to Oklahoma over the painful "trail of tears." At the Cherokee centennial celebration in Oklahoma Miss Brunstetter had learned something of the history of the tribe and the remarkable syllabary of the complicated tonal language invented by Chief Sequoya. She had made attempts at studying the strange tongue and at writing some of it incompletely with French phonetic characters.

On her way to Washington to confer with government authorities Della Brunstetter visited the original Cherokee region of

North Carolina. There she met George Owl, a leader of the tribe, who gave her valuable information about his people. Back again at the University of Oklahoma, she tried to settle down to solid study of the Cherokee language with an informant from the tribe. But French phonetics were not sufficient for all the odd sounds of Cherokee.

In her dilemma Miss Brunstetter heard of the summer session at the University of Michigan where a new method for analyzing all languages was being taught. In the summer of 1940 she attended the classes there but found the technical jargon beyond her. She was unfamiliar with the basic technique used in this new scientific approach to language. Again she seemed to be thwarted in her desire to write the Cherokee language.

Then a companion at the Michigan summer session told her, "I know a group who start from the beginning. You might get a good foundation from them. They've been going at this for a long time, and two of their teachers are here this summer." When Della Brunstetter talked with Kenneth Pike and Eugene Nida she began to get practical suggestions for studying Cherokee. "I knew then that I was going to try to go to the Summer Institute of Linguistics," she said.

In the summer of 1941 the French teacher turned up in the Ozarks with her Cherokee informant, an Indian woman from Oklahoma. She began to learn linguistics "from scratch," for she found that this group of linguists really did start at the beginning. And she was intrigued by the missionary motivation prompting it all. "It was a wonderful summer, spiritually and intellectually," was her comment on the course, and in spite of the rustic living conditions.

As she saw the limitations of the small room in which classes were held for the group now grown to nearly fifty students, and also visualized future expansion, Della Brunstetter decided that the group needed larger quarters. "And we needed them at the University of Oklahoma," she added.

"I returned to Oklahoma that fall with all enthusiasm to find a way for them to come to the university. We proceeded to contact the Board of Regents, making a special trip to the home of President Chambers. We pled the cause and had his ear, so the very next week we heard the good news that the Summer Institute of Linguistics was going to be invited to the campus of the University of Oklahoma. That was a great day in my life."

There was another great day in the life of the Cherokee linguist, for George Owl had made a trip from North Carolina to Oklahoma. And it was Mrs. Della Brunstetter Owl who in the summer of 1942 joined the first staff of the Summer Institute of Linguistics to teach on the campus of the University of Oklahoma at Norman.

The young directors of the Institute, Pike and Nida, were more youthful than would have been gathered from the information circulated about the capable linguistic instructors to head the new session on campus. One day before classes began one of the new students asked, "Where is Dr. Pike?" "There he is down at the end of the hall," he was told. When the student found only a skinny, youngish-looking person who might have been a fellow student, he stuttered, "Are—er—are you Dr. Pike's son?" "Yes, I am," came the answer. When Pike saw the baffled expression of the student, he explained that he was the son of Dr. Pike, for his father was a medical doctor. "But," he added with a laugh, "I am also Dr. Pike."

In the summer of 1942 the new approach to language study created a sensation on the Oklahoma campus. The classes were often attended by curious newspaper reporters and interested citizens. The unacademic antics of the two young linguists giving the main lectures were good entertainment, as well as good teaching. It was a refreshing surprise to find the new type of professors successfully conveying the impression that languages could be exciting.

"Who said phonetics was a dull study?" wrote one of the reporters of the *Oklahoma Daily,* the campus news sheet, on June 26, 1942. "A speech sound is like a pumpkin pie. We don't mean to imply that the study of linguistics is as easy as eating pie. What we mean is that one of the most scholarly young phoneticians in the country, and one of the most skilful teachers of linguistics, used the figure of a pie very effectively in explaining to a class the other morning what a speech sound is like. . . .

"And his big roomful of students sit on the edge of their seats, gurgle with delight at every fresh comparison and seize every

108

opportunity to make their contribution. It's a safe bet that there isn't a livelier class on the campus, or any campus, than this 9 o'clock class in Phonetics and Phonemics. Ask Dr. Pike the difference between these two imposing terms, and he'll wake you up with some audacious but perfectly accurate comparison. . . .

"Their classes are open to the public, and they have visitors every day.

"They are worth listening to," concluded the write-up.

And many visitors came to the Institute, especially when demonstrations of actual work with Indian informants began. Surrounded by a battery of blackboards Pike would scribble symbols for the strange sounds extracted from unsuspecting Indian speakers. And when he would scrawl at lightning speed a series of symbols for an innocent Shawnee word of twelve syllables meaning "their cats," the aspiring young linguistic students would gasp in admiration. But many of the same students would sigh with satisfaction when a few weeks later they were doing the same thing, perhaps less rapidly, but with assurance and accuracy. Pike had not only performed, but he had taught them how to do it.

The University of Oklahoma was ideal for the use of Indian informants from many tribes in the state. It was also centrally located in the United States. The courses were given full university accreditation, with the further advantage that graduate credit could be transferred to other universities in partial fulfillment of requirements for higher degrees.

The University became the academic home of the Summer Institute of Linguistics, especially as an increasing number of textbooks and linguistic articles on American Indian languages were published in scientific journals in the United States and abroad. Contracts for co-operation in tribal work under foreign governments bear the names of the University of Oklahoma and the Summer Institute of Linguistics. The summer courses first held on the campus at Norman, Oklahoma, became the model for similar studies offered later by the Universities of North Dakota and Washington where SIL was invited to hold branch institutes.

In 1942 one hundred and thirty students attended the ninth session of the Summer Institute of Linguistics which had graduated from the Ozark farmhouse to a state university campus.

Where did the one hundred and thirty students come from? No one was quite sure how word had reached them all but there they were, gathered from thirty-two states and twelve foreign countries. Among those from other lands were missionaries of various boards who had been struggling with languages and wanted help. They had heard and had come.

It was a wonderful summer, with fifty-one responding to the call for workers for Mexico. Townsend's faith had again been rewarded, plus "one for good measure."

15. Lumber and Linguistics

Suddenly Townsend had a Topsy on his hands. The influx of new translators from Oklahoma more than doubled the group working in Mexico. But even before, the leaders of the Pioneer Mission Agency that had forwarded "emergency" funds for Townsend's group had advised him to organize on his own.

Townsend and Legters had not originally planned to organize another mission. Rather they aimed to train translators who would serve under other established mission boards. But now Operation Translation had taken a different turn in Mexico and friends of the work strongly recommended the formation of a board.

But where would Townsend turn for help?

"I put out a fleece in three directions," recounts Townsend. "One letter went to Pennsylvania, one to Illinois, and one to California."

From Pennsylvania came the answer that headquarters for the enterprise in the States would cost a minimum of fifteen thousand dollars a year, and that was "too much for us to undertake."

A puzzled letter came from Illinois asking Townsend "to explain just what I was driving at."

The old-time friend from California, Bill Nyman, responded with one of his typically encouraging letters written on May 12, 1942:

"First, last and always, I am prayerfully anxious that the 'Bible Translation Movement' continue its God-given task of giving the Bible to every creature in his own language, and to this end I am willing and ready to do all I can to further this until the job is done. . . .

"If you and your associates are agreed that a council should be organized here in Los Angeles, and desire that I should serve as a member I shall be glad to do so. . . . With a competent secretary I would be glad to give the time should you decide on Los Angeles as headquarters. As to my health, that is another matter. . . ."

Since 1939, when he was stricken with a serious heart ailment, Nyman had been under the constant care of a doctor who treated him as a semi-invalid. He had been warned to stop his strenuous Christian activities, if he wanted to live. This had been a brutal blow, for serving missions and missionaries filled his life for a number of years. It had not always been so with Nyman, however.

Back in Chicago he had been successful in business. At thirty years of age he was secretary-treasurer of a lumber mill which he later owned. He was riding high financially but was spiritually bankrupt. At the height of his success he heard a Bible message from a man who "presented the Word of God dynamically." Afterward the same man had a conversation with Nyman on a street corner in a Chicago suburb. That night Nyman couldn't sleep.

Early the following morning the lumberman knelt beside his bed and gave his life to Christ.

The next day Nyman called a meeting of his staff and told them of his conversion. He announced that a new partner had joined the business, and now Jesus Christ would have a big say in operations. Some of the men laughed, others called Nyman a fanatic. But the new convert was unshaken.

In time his business dropped off until Nyman was in desperate straits. His fair-weather friends had forsaken him, and he was going downhill fast. Finally he was without workmen for projects needing completion. In desperation he sought out an Italian carpenter recommended as a prospective helper. But when he arrived at the home, the father was so overwrought by the condition of a sick son that he couldn't talk business. He only mumbled something about thirty-five dollars and getting his son to heaven. "The man say he have to have thirty-five dollar . . ."

"But your boy can get into heaven for nothing!" said Nyman. By using some Bible verses he had recently learned, Nyman told the dying boy of the sacrifice of Christ for his sins. The boy listened to every word. Nyman was not a skilled clergyman, but he made the way to heaven through the shed blood of Christ very plain. With radiant assurance, the boy died, leaving behind a comforted father who soon found the Savior with Nyman's help.

The Italian was transformed, and began telling the world about his Lord—and about the Swedish lumberman who had been a real friend in need. Soon the carpenter's friends were loading Nyman with business. They knew they could trust him, and through them his business was more than rebuilt. He finally prayed the Lord not to send any new customers.

Not only did many Italians in Chicago come to know Christ through Nyman's witness, but a number of his other business associates were thoroughly converted. When in 1930 he moved to California, he left a large scattered parish composed of those who had found Christ through the lumber business.

Soon after his conversion Nyman had learned about foreign missions. His desire to spread the gospel to the ends of the earth grew until he was supporting several foreign missionaries. In California he joined the Church of the Open Door which supported Cameron Townsend in Guatemala. Through the years the friendship of Nyman and Townsend, begun through correspondence, ripened into a mission partnership. On furlough the Townsends would visit the Nymans and spend time in their "prophet's chamber" in the garage apartment of their Glendale home.

It was to that upper room that Cameron and Elvira Townsend had been invited after Townsend's health broke in 1932. For almost six months the Townsends rested in the Nyman home, a convalescent period which, added to the recuperation commenced at his sister's home in Santa Ana, put Townsend on his feet.

During his stay with the Nymans, Townsend's vision of the need of the Indians of Mexico had led him to formulate a plan of attack as soon as he was well enough to move. He had enlisted Nyman to pray with him daily for a way to enter the closed door to the south. It was during that time that Nyman came to a "real understanding of the life of faith." The prospect of entering Mexico was absolutely hopeless—and Nyman was a hardheaded businessman. There seemed to be no way through the walls of Jericho which kept the Word of God from the Mexican Indian tribes. But here was a modern Joshua persistently plodding around the uncracked walls, through prayer, assured that they must fall.

Nyman watched, and wondered. Sure enough the day came when Townsend set out for Mexico. But the ever-practical Nyman asked about funds. Did he have enough money for the trip?

Nyman didn't have to wonder long. "The mailman was coming up the walk. He handed Townsend an envelope. In it was a check for three hundred dollars from an unexpected source."

"See?" said Townsend calmly. "The Lord always provides."

Nyman had seen. And he had seen that God "had the use of funds other than mine." But, he concluded, "if I would yield to Him in my way, as my intrepid missionary friend yielded to Him in his way, both of us would see the Lord do wonderful things."

After Nyman's health broke he had written Townsend, whose work by that time was well under way in Mexico:

"If there is anything I can do for you here at home, Cam, I'll be glad to. But it won't be much. I'm virtually a dead man."

But it was this virtually dead man who had responded to Townsend's call for help in organizing a home base. And when in 1942 the Wycliffe Bible Translators, Inc., was officially formed and its headquarters established in California, it was the little garage apartment of the Nyman home that became the base on which the fast-growing mission planted its spreading feet. The nearly dead man organized the mission with the same business know-how that had spelled success in Chicago. Now he wasn't interested in making money, but in saving it—saving money for a mission with a big job where every penny was needed for the work and the workers on the field.

Nyman took no salary and donated the headquarters, so that all the intake of funds went directly to the field—all, that is, except five per cent, voted by workers on the field, which was needed for the salary of an office secretary and a minimum of supplies. That was the principle when there were less than a hundred members of the translation group. But even when it had grown to almost nine hundred members the original blueprint remained. Through the years Nyman has kept the money matters of Wycliffe Bible Translators on an even keel, giving to the limit of his mental and physical ability to make the dollars stretch.

And the dollars have stretched around the world, into inaccessible jungles where aircraft and radios are needed to carry the gospel to primitive tribesmen. Nyman has kept his eye on that goal, and his hand on the sacrificial dimes and dollars of the hardworking Christians co-operating in reaching the last of the two thousand Bibleless tribes.

Several years ago when he realized his heart had been pushed to the limit as secretary-treasurer and his doctor had already washed his hands of his impossible patient, Nyman had asked for an understudy. Kenneth Watters, who was happily translating for the Cocama Indians in Peru but who had had considerable business experience in the United States Navy, was picked for the job. Nyman's mantle has fallen on him, but the senior partner as secretary still gives valuable advice and counsel.

Beside his work at headquarters, now a three-room office in a Glendale store building, Nyman has made a number of trips to Mexico and the jungles of Peru, and one to the Philippines on official SIL business with the late President Magsaysay. Once told that he shouldn't fly or climb steps, Nyman has been flying for years and is still thriving.

It is a mystery to many what has kept Nyman going years beyond medical predictions. It is no mystery to Townsend. He knows that the God who raised him from a bed of tuberculosis gave Bill Nyman a new heart to do a job which He wanted done.

16. Mayan Miracles

"Gu morin," said the burly old Indian to Bill Bentley who had just arrived in his village. That's not like any Tzeltal I ever heard, thought Bill. It bore a faint resemblance to English so Bill took a chance.

"Good morning," he replied.

Delighted, the old Indian broke into a broad smile and said in Tzeltal, "That's all the English I know." As a young man he had been forced to join the Mexican army which took him north to the Texas border where he learned a little English. Now he was back in Bachajón, an isolated village in southern Mexico where the softening influences of civilization had scarcely reached, and where murder was common.

"When I was in the north," the old Indian continued, "I heard of a Book that tells about God. Do you know about that Book?"

"Yes," said Bill, "I have that Book. If you will let me build a hut here in your village, I'll come and give you the Book—in your own language. I am to be married soon, and I could bring my wife. She knows the Book too."

The old man was pleased. After consulting the other old men of the village it was agreed that Bill should be given a spot for a home in Bachajón. It was spring of 1941, and about time for the torrential tropical rains to begin. Bill said that he and his bride would return in the fall after the rainy season when the trails were not so muddy.

116

Bill sang more than usual on the trail back to the coffee hacienda near Yajalón in the state of Chiapas where he had been living since 1938. At last an invitation to live in a Tzeltal village —and with Marianna!

First I'll write Jean about this wonderful answer to her prayers, then I'll hike over the hill and tell Marianna—so ran Bill's thoughts as he panted up the last long hot hill to the hacienda. It would be a long climb over rugged trails to the Chol tribe where Marianna Slocum was working, but he could hardly wait to share the good news.

When Mrs. Jean McGrew received the letter from Bill back in Topeka, Kansas, she felt like singing too. Once Bill hadn't been concerned about foreign missions. He was handsome, happy, and popular. He had a good voice, and played in a dance orchestra to help earn his way through medical college. When he was home in Topeka he would often drop into the home of his good friends Jean and Carl McGrew to chat and play the piano. During one such visit Jean and a friend were discussing the fulfillment of Bible prophecy and the Lord's return to earth. On overhearing the conversation Bill broke in, "Well, if that's going to happen, what's the use of sending out missionaries?"

"I told him he had it all wrong," Jean said, "and I explained what the use is." And in the following days Jean taught Bill much from the Bible concerning God's plan for reaching the world with His message.

Within a shockingly short time for his family and friends Bill had canceled his plans for a medical future. He was saved and knew it, and now he wanted to share this knowledge with those who had not had a chance to hear. He had decided to train for missionary service at the Moody Bible Institute. It was while studying there that he heard Legters plead the cause of neglected Indian tribes of Latin America.

In the summer of 1938 Bill attended Camp Wycliffe in the Ozarks. In the fall he went to Mexico and began work in the Tzeltal tribe of Chiapas, the largest of the twelve or more Mayan-speaking groups of that backward area of Mexico. Two years later he helped to allocate a pair of workers, Marianna Slocum and Evelyn Woodward, in the neighboring Chol tribe.

And now, in the spring of 1941, Bill and Marianna had made

117

plans to translate together for the Tzeltal tribe. With the opening in Bachajón, Bill's heart was even lighter than usual. And in the summer the happy engaged couple were on their way to the Slocum home in Philadelphia.

By the end of August all was in readiness for the wedding. The last tucks had been taken on Marianna's bridal gown, and the last invitation was in the mail. Florist and caterer were arranging details for the big event only six days away.

Bill was an early riser so Dr. Slocum was a bit concerned when his future son-in-law did not appear for breakfast on that Sunday before the wedding. He slipped upstairs to give a last call for breakfast, but there was no response.

Quietly, sometime before daybreak, Bill had died in his sleep.

A few hours later Marianna was talking on the phone with Cameron Townsend in Arkansas.

"May I go to Bill's tribe and finish the work he began?" she asked in a calm voice.

"Yes," Townsend said, "of course you may, Marianna." Later he said, "Who would have had the heart to say no to such a request!"

But by the time Marianna and her partner reached Bachajón in November, the villagers had been warned against the foreigners. No, they couldn't come to live there because they would steal their pigs—and their language!

Marianna reminded them of the promise they had made to Bill. Well, she could come if she insisted, but they would tie her house shut and set fire to it!

Marianna decided to work patiently in another part of the tribe. She learned the language, translated portions of the Bible, and prepared a hymnal for the Tzeltals who had come to know the Lord. A number of records in the tribal language were prepared with the help of Gospel Recordings, Inc., of Los Angeles, and these were sounding forth the gospel message on victrolas scattered throughout the tribe.

In 1947 Florence Gerdel, a trained nurse from California, joined Marianna to help in the heavy medical work. She established a clinic in the mountain village of Yochib where many Tzeltals came for treatment. Marianna had just finished translating the Gospel of Mark and was working on the book of Acts. A number of Indians in Yochib had turned from their idols and wanted to build a chapel where they could worship the Lord without "two-sided hearts."

Martín Gourd, one of the Yochib believers, had been traveling around on foot throughout the highlands of the tribe playing the records and telling the gospel to his people who had not heard it. In the settlement of Corralito, hearts were ready for the good news, and five families turned to the Lord. The group began to grow and soon sent a letter to the translators in Yochib, saying, "Thirty-three of us men believe the Word of God. Also women. In all there are perhaps seventy of us. All the time we play the victrola. Each Sunday all the time we gather together. The men and women say: 'Can you come and teach us more of the Word of God?' "

In November, 1949, Marianna and Florence set out for Corralito "with seven of the brand-new believers to carry our duffels and to show us the way. On the afternoon of the second day, as we neared the place, the believers came to meet us on the trail. From there they led us to a thatch-roofed hut they had especially prepared for us.

"And to welcome us, seventy of them stood in a circle outside our hut and very reverently sang most of the hymns in the Tzeltal hymn book! Sunday about two hundred gathered in the little clearing in front of the hut, and without a single exception were intent upon every word of the flannelgraph of the death and resurrection of our Lord.

"With 'one heart' as we say in Tzeltal they begged us to stay and teach them God's Word. They had already started gathering poles to make us a house of our own, and were only waiting for us to choose the site we liked best. We chose a wooded hillside with a rushing stream nearby and a view of mountains all around. Thirty men or more are spending all this week working on our house while we make the ten-hour trip over the terrific trail to Yochib to pack all our belongings. As soon as our new house is ready the believers are coming over that trail to carry our things back for us. Our thanks to the Lord are limitless for this band of men whose hearts God has touched!"

The highland area of the Tzeltal tribe was steeped in witchcraft, and several prominent Mexican educators and officials predicted the Indians would "never change." But by the end of 1949 "more than four hundred, counting the children of believers, had their names listed as wanting to profess their faith in their new-found Lord in this place where a little over a year ago there wasn't one believer.

"One of the most faithful of the believers is former witch doctor Tomás who was one of the first to throw his idol in the fire as evidence of his faith in the living God." He had prepared to burn candles before the idol when someone came to his hut with a victrola and gospel records. According to old Tomás' testimony, "The instant I heard God's Word, I believed it with all my heart." From that day on he had nothing further to do with witchcraft or drunkenness.

The first Christian funeral in Corralito was that of a former witch doctor who had turned to the Lord. One Sunday a half hour after he had left the meeting with the believers, he was ambushed on the trail and shot by his enemies. Marianna wrote:

"Without a word from us we found when we went to the hut where the dead man lay that the believers had gathered of their own accord from far and near to stand with the family in their hut. While watching over the dead they sang hymns all night, except when they were praying."

By the end of 1950 the group of believers had grown to more than a thousand, and smaller gatherings of believers were springing up throughout the mountainous area around Corralito. Still the Tzeltals came over the long rugged trails to the clinic in Corralito where Florence was doctoring from morning until night, and praying with the patients as well. As many were cured by prayer as by medicine, but Florence used both.

"Because of the constant press of people around us from morning till night," wrote Marianna, "it was hard to get much translation done. So the believers themselves decided that since they wanted all of God's Word translated into the words of their language they would free Juan Mucha, the president of the congregation, to help me with the translation, and they would take turns helping make his cornfield. Now the translation is going forward better than it ever has before."

And replacing the pagan festivals at the planting of crops was a special corn-planting ceremony consisting of Scripture reading and special prayer for crops.

At the first "collective marriage ceremony" more than two hundred couples were legally united according to Mexican civil law. The government regional secretary had performed only one marriage during the previous year, and "was stunned at the idea of two hundred!"

In spite of the statement by the Mexican government official of the area that the Constitution gave freedom of worship to all, severe persecution of the Tzeltal believers came from their own tribesmen. Although hundreds continued to turn to God from idols, they paid a price for their faith. The believers built a large chapel ninety feet long in which to worship. On the day of prayer when the chapel was dedicated they remained on their knees before God "from nine in the morning until five in the afternoon, with only two brief intermissions."

Not long afterward the same believers knelt in the smoldering ruins of the chapel destroyed by the enemies of the gospel, and prayed for them. In the following months and years many of the enemies joined the congregation as soundly converted members.

Chapels were soon built in other parts of the Oxchuc area of which Corralito became the Christian center. It was a happy day in 1953 when a caravan of translators, a Mexican Presbyterian pastor, and a large company of Tzeltals from Corralito went to the village of Mud-Walled Hut to dedicate the new building which the believers of that settlement had made. "See, that is what we worshiped before God's Word came to us," the believers said as they passed over a high mountain with a cave gaping on one side. It was "The Black Lord," a sacred mountaintop where all the Oxchuc Indians once worshiped. Now the cave was dark, and crude candleholders stood empty where incense was once offered to pagan gods.

By 1954 when the manuscript of the Tzeltal New Testament was finished there were thousands of Indians worshiping in twelve chapels throughout the highland area, and a hundred and fifty "preacher boys" were gathering regularly for instruction in how to teach their people the Word of God. "Lord, we put into Thy hands the whole New Testament in our language. Use Thy Word to bring many more to Thyself, as Thou hast already used it to bring us to Thee," prayed the humble Indian Christian in the crowded church at Corralito, as he dedicated the final portion of the Tzeltal New Testament to the Lord.

It was on the night of August 10, 1955, that Sebastián Tsul, the leader of a growing group of believers in the town of Tenango, was martyred for the sake of the gospel. He had taken the victrola and records to the house of believers to play them, and to pray for a sick member of the family. As he raised his head from praying, his enemies who had been watching through a half-open doorway shot him. A few minutes later, as he lay dying, he raised up on one elbow and said, "It is for God's sake that this has happened."

"I've noticed that in places where believers are being persecuted the Word of God seems to prosper in a wonderful way," observed Manuel Osorio the following year in Tenango. He had just been counting up the great number of Indians who had turned to the Lord in that place since the murder of Sebastián. And Manuel together with his family had just been driven from his home by a crowd of men with machetes, whips, and sticks.

Back in Corralito the healing of bodies and souls continued at a hearteningly busy pace. Florence Gerdel had been joined in the clinic by another nurse, Avis Crowder of California. When the facilities of the clinic were taxed sometimes with eighteen hundred patients a month, much-needed help came from another quarter. Dr. and Mrs. John Kempers, pioneer missionaries of the Reformed Church in Chiapas, who had assisted the Tzeltal and Chol translators from the beginning of the tribal work, saw the need for more adequate medical facilities. By 1957 a spacious clinic was erected under Dr. Kempers' supervision to replace the rustic building in Corralito. There Tzeltal male nurses are now being trained to do simple medical work and teach hygiene along with the preaching of the Word of God.

But Florence and Avis did more than dispense medicines and bind up wounds. The treasurer of the Corralito congregation came regularly to Avis for help in keeping his books straight. Often she was so busy that he had to wait for her. During these waits in the clinic he spent his time learning to do various tasks including seeing "those little specks" in the microscope. Later he even learned to extract teeth. Now he is a full-time worker in the Corralito clinic.

On Sunday morning, August 5, 1956, pilot E. W. Hatcher of the Missionary Aviation Fellowship serving Wycliffe in Mexico, circled the small airstrip cut out of a mountainside cornfield near Corralito. In the yellow plane he was carrying precious cargo, the first shipment of the Tzeltal New Testament, hot off the American Bible Society press. On that notable day more than twelve hundred Tzeltal Indians filled the trails for miles around and finally overflowed the chapel at Corralito decorated for the occasion with arches of wild palm and flowers from the forest. After a full day of joyful celebration as the Book was dedicated to the service of the One who gave it, a barefoot Indian elder who had helped to translate every word of it into his language prayed:

"Lord, may we not only have Thy Word written down on paper in our language; may we also have it written in our hearts."

Meanwhile good news was coming from the lowland country of Bachajón where the seed of the Word was changing many lives. In the summer of 1956 a new group of forty-eight Christians in a settlement near Bachajón asked for someone to come and teach them more of the Word. The Indians of the area where Bill Bentley had first taken the gospel in Tzeltal were now beginning to turn to God in large numbers, despite constant opposition. Tzeltals of that part of the tribe killed those who deviated from the accustomed pattern of life. Santiago Gómez, a leader of a group of believers of the area, had refused to appease the gods of earth and sky, and late rains had spoiled the corn crops. He was to blame, his fellow tribesmen said, and they threatened his life many times. Such killing "is not murder to them but rather self-defense against those who bring disaster to the whole community." Another believer lived in constant danger because he was blamed for the death of an unbeliever struck by lightning.

In the summer of 1957 Marianna and Florence started out for Bachajón territory, leaving Avis in charge of the work in Corralito. Several congregations were now meeting in the lowlands, so that a revision of the New Testament in that dialect was needed. They hung their hammocks in Domingo Méndez' hut and began

123

teaching in the cane-thatched chapel built by the Bachajón believers. Soon those whom they had taught were out preaching in four other chapels in the Bachajón area.

Florence set up her clinic among the Bachajón Indians. One day she treated a patient who had been expecting to die for seven years. He brought with him his "burying mat" in which was rolled a new brightly-colored suit of clothes for the occasion. Slowly, painfully, he had made his way to the clinic with the aid of two canes. It had taken him a day to travel the distance ordinarily covered in half an hour.

Florence saw immediately that her patient had some very bad teeth. She pulled one. To her horror a portion of the jaw came out with it. This proved to be the seat of the infection and after treatment the man recovered rapidly. For the first time in seven years he planted his cornfield. And now he comes regularly to the services in the chapel—dressed gaily in the clothes he had kept for the day of his death.

By the end of 1958 more than five thousand Tzeltals in Corralito and Bachajón and in twenty other villages in the tribe were walking in newness of life, raised from spiritual death through the power of the Word in their own language.

When Marianna Slocum and Evelyn Woodward began working in the Chol tribe of Chiapas, there was already a small group of believers meeting in the village of Tumbalá, under the supervision of the Mexican National Presbyterian Church. A Mexican believer who also spoke the Chol dialect had been evangelizing in the area and a number of Chols forsook their idols to worship the living God. But they desperately needed the Word in their own language. Some who professed faith in Christ were still following the rites prescribed by the witch doctor.

Describing a Chol cure, Marianna and Evelyn wrote in 1940:

"The Indians tried their own method of curing a man the other night in a hut very near here. Believing that the power of the witch doctor had made the man sick, they got an old woman to get the power out of the man. They killed a pig on top of his chest, let the blood run over him, and gave him some of the hot blood to drink. The intestines were taken out and put on his head. The meat was cooked and feasted on all night long. The bones will be kept hanging in a bag above the fire for several months to be sure the witch doctor's power will stay away."

The relatives of Nicolás in the Chol village of Amado Nervo had urged him to become a witch doctor, but God chose him for another purpose. Although quiet and retiring, he had a strong desire to read the Word of God now being translated into his language. Each evening he went to the translators' home for the reading class, and later was used occasionally as a translation helper. His spiritual growth at the translation table was very marked, and he became a valuable leader among the local believers. Through his Spirit-filled ministry, many of his companions found the Lord, and others who had backslidden were restored to fellowship.

"Had you not translated the Word of God and taught us from its pages," he said one day to a translator, "we would still be fighting one another and living in superstition and sin."

Wilbur and Evelyn Woodward Aulie were steadily pushing ahead in the Chol translation when John and Elaine Beekman joined them. The number of Chol believers was rapidly increasing and instruction in the Chol language was essential, for the Indians understood practically no Spanish. In an isolated part of the state of Chiapas where roads had not yet penetrated, culture remained practically unchanged for hundreds of years. The Chols still spoke their Mayan dialect and drank hot pig's blood at the command of the witch doctor.

But soon small congregations were being formed in several villages of the tribe where the gospel had been taken. Translators were living in the rainy mountainous terrain where fifteen thousand Chols were scattered. The Aulies traveled "a steep, muddy trail up the mountainside to its very summit," with Chol Indians carrying little Aulies in baskets on their backs, to reach their tribal home. The Beekmans lived over the high mountain in another direction in the village of Amado Nervo. In addition to his translation work John Beekman also served in lieu of a doctor for throngs of Indians who came to him for treatment.

Finally, when the rigors of the rugged trail had taxed their strength to the limit, the Beekmans left their home until John, with the aid of Chol Christians, had carved an airstrip out of a mountainous ledge nearby. Pilot E. W. Hatcher, affectionately known throughout Chiapas as "Hatch," has through the years serviced the Chol field as well as the neighboring Tzeltal area. In early 1950 when John Beekman had been struggling with the construction of the airstrip, he wrote:

"The most important bit of news perhaps is that the airstrip I think is in landable shape. As yet Hatch has not seen it, but I think he could safely land on it.

"Believers from distant villages have voluntarily offered their services to complete this strip so that Elaine might return. When offered pay for their service, many of them remarked that if it were not for the medicine we had given them they would not now be here at all, but in the ground. Others from Xpaktun mentioned when offered pay that their new life was found through our witness and they wanted to show a bit of gratitude. In my first week here I saw thirty men leave their beds of sickness to return to their coffee fields."

By 1949 more than half of Amado Nervo had become Christian, with a congregation of three hundred bulging out of the local chapel. In many other surrounding villages, Chols by twos and tens and twenties were turning to the Lord. And Arabelle Anderson (later Mrs. Morgan Whittaker) had joined the translation team in the heavy task of making an unlettered tribe literate. In addition to language work she helped with the constant medical treatment that was a necessary part of the Chol translation project. Once during an epidemic of smallpox she assisted a Mexican doctor in vaccinating over two hundred Chols, in addition to treating many more stricken with the disease.

Soon Chol Christians numbering in the thousands were meeting in dozens of chapels large and small throughout the tribe. They became known as the "singing Chols" because of their happy habit of singing not only for hours in their services but also on the trails and at work in their cornfields. On approaching Chol villages, many of which were predominantly Christian, one could hear singing from quite a distance.

The word of God in Chol became not only a powerful magnet drawing the tribesmen to Christ, but also a sharp scalpel. In one of the villages, for example, six brothers, all Christians, fell to feuding over some coveted property. Bitter words and actual fighting broke out and the testimony of the whole group of be-

126

lievers was being nullified. The Chol elders of the local church called the brothers in and talked with them, but to no avail.

Finally, the sad group of frustrated elders and feuding brothers knocked on the door of the translator who had just finished putting the book of James into the Chol language. What would he do with this church mess? As a foreigner he hesitated to handle such a delicate tribal matter involving many intricacies of Indian culture.

Before him lay the handwritten manuscript of the Epistle of James. At a loss to know what to say, he picked it up and began reading aloud. He read it all the way through. Still unsure of what to say to the brothers, he read the book through again, aloud.

Soon the Word had done its work. The brothers, melted in contrition, became reconciled, and the church was restored to joy and happiness. The next day turkeys were killed and a love feast spread—and the translator was among the invited guests!

When the Chol Testament was finished, there were more than five thousand believers in the tribe, in thirty congregations. One hundred young men had been trained to teach and preach, and a number trained to do medical work. Mexican government officials visiting the area and comparing it with the state of the tribe two decades earlier, recognized a complete transformation in the physical and social condition of the Chol Indians.

One of the by-products of the gospel in Chol has been the economic change in the tribe. Says John Beekman:

"Formerly these Indians were indebted to the Mexican ranchers who lived in the area holding large coffee plantations. They also sold liquor. The Indians before conversion were habitual drunkards, in debt to these landholders. To pay off their debts the landowners forced them to work on their plantations whenever they needed work. After the Indians became Christians, they stopped their drinking, paid off their debts, and began to plant their own coffee plantations. The coffee of the ranchers was left unharvested. As a result the Mexican ranchers have been forced to sell the land to the Indians and are moving out of the area."

Completing the translation of the Chol New Testament under difficult field circumstances had taken a heavy toll on the health of the whole team. A heart condition that had been slowing John Beekman's activities finally stopped him. In 1955 he underwent a serious operation in which an artificial valve was successfully installed in his heart. This resulted, however, in a prominent ticking sound. When after a long absence from the Chols he was finally able to return to them with his "ticking" heart, they were curious about what had happened. John recounted his return to the Indians who had prayed so long for him:

"As the plane circled late in the afternoon, we could see men, women, and children streaming out of their homes to converge on the airstrip. As I left the plane, the fellows took my bags and I started walking toward the house. Then one of the fellows began to blow a whistle, the method used for calling people together for meetings.

" 'Has the time of the midweek service been changed?' I asked.

" 'No,' they said. 'We have prayed for you, now we hear your heart ticking, and we are going to gather together for a praise service. We also have many questions concerning some of the difficult parts of First Corinthians, and we can do two things at the same time.'

"After the service was over I was a little anxious to go into the house to get things set up. As I made a move toward the door, the church leader said, 'No, we've heard your heart tick, we've prayed for you, we've had a praise service, and you have given us instruction from the Word. Now we want to see it.'

"So I sat on a stone and bared my back as first the women all passed by shyly to look at the scar. Then the men filed by—not so shyly, for they were not satisfied just to look. They passed their fingers over the scar tissue beginning at the back and all the way around to the front. It was a ticklish experience.

"After this was over the Indians opened the door to my house which they had cleaned and swept, purely out of love and gratitude. They did not realize that anyone with a heart condition has to have limited physical activity, but they hung up my net and announced that I was not to prepare my own meals. For the weeks that I stayed with them the deacons brought my meals which their wives had prepared, set the table, did the dishes, and accompanied me all the time."

128

17. Manuscripts and Medicine

The gun had gone off accidentally, but it did considerable damage —five holes, to be exact. To make matters worse the bullet had passed through the arm of an innocent Seri girl, through the baby she was holding, then into the side of the older girl.

"The baby reminded us of a shot rabbit with the bullet going through near the stomach," wrote Mary Moser, Wycliffe worker among the Seri Indians of Mexico. "Trying to keep calm in the midst of wailing women, Ed and I dressed the wounds. Within half an hour he had begun the seven-hour trip into Hermosillo with the victims and two women to accompany them. Both of us prayed hard that the relatives of the girls would not seek revenge against Roberto. We knew that a murder or two in this setting would not be out of place in their culture pattern.

"The next night Ed returned with the good news that both would recover. A number of Indians gathered together to drink coffee and celebrate, and Roberto took the opportunity to witness to them. He thanked God for permitting the children to live, and he exhorted the people to believe on the God of the Bible and to turn to His Son as their Savior."

It was more than a physical victory for the translators who in 1952 had gone to the tribe of fishing peasants just south of the Arizona border. Some thought that it was a waste of time and talent for Edward and Mary Moser to settle down among two hundred Seri Indians and learn their language under very difficult living conditions. But the Mosers were sure from the very beginning that God wanted a witness among those isolated, forgotten remnants of a tribe. Their faith has been rewarded as they have seen Roberto, their faithful informant whose gun had gone off accidentally, and other Seris respond to the gospel they are translating. Medical work, particularly the rescuing of victims of the dreaded lethal scorpions of the area, has given them a wide entrance into the hearts of the Seris.

Townsend, too, is gratified with the Seri work. It is palpable proof to the Mexican officials who in 1940 asked him for Seri workers, that he and his team care for the tribes, for a few hundred Seris in the northern desert of Mexico as well as thousands of Tzeltals in the mountains to the south.

Upon entering Mexico, Townsend assured officials that the Scripture translated into Indian dialects, buttressed on the one hand by solid scientific language research and on the other by practical projects such as literacy and medicine, would transform the tribes. Twenty-five years later even the most skeptical accepted the widespread evidence in Mexico as eloquent fulfillment of the prediction.

In 1958 Dr. Benjamin Elson, director of Wycliffe's Mexican Branch, reported that there were two hundred and twenty-five members of the organization reaching seventy-three languages and dialects of the country. Twenty-five years earlier when Legters and Townsend first crossed the Rio Grande to investigate possibilities of translation, they were told that there were about thirty-five groups of Indians in the country who spoke their own languages, or at the most, fifty. As translators occupied more and more of the larger tribes they discovered many speakers of subdialects, tucked away in the mountains and deserts, who could not understand translations in the main dialects. As a result, more workers were required to translate for divergent language groups meriting separate translations.

Headquarters for the workers in the tribes is an old gray building in downtown Mexico City, long since inadequate for the enlarged family continually bulging from its strained seams. Affectionately known as "the Kettle"—a tourist's corruption of "Quetzalcoatl," its original Aztec name as a hotel—the decrepit edifice is home to hundreds of translators who either work in

Mexico, or come for jungle training, or stop over en route to a South American assignment. It is Wycliffe's outmoded Grand Central Station in Latin America.

Ben Elson, assisted by Howard Klassen, directs the heavy traffic, by paper or in person, funneling through the teeming headquarters. The English "paper work" of Wycliffe, in addition to the publications in Spanish and the Indian languages, involves a fantastic amount of round-the-clock dedication to the job. Almost any time of the night, and sometimes in the early hours of Mexico City's gray awakening, the fluorescent lights on the third floor of the Kettle signal activity. The modern glassed-in top layer of the old building was added as an incongruous afterthought to accommodate the prodigious Publications Department in Mexico, where everything from alphabet picture books for beginning readers to portions of the Bible are produced.

At odd hours a Wycliffe artist may be found putting the finishing touches on illustrations for a primer that must be ready for printing *today* when the faithful Mexican operators start the machines. Or it may be a translator in from the tribe for his health, stealing some precious early morning quietness to check the Greek on his translation of the Gospel of John. Or it may be a near-Ph.D. waiting for the copies of his dissertation that must get off on the morning plane to make a deadline at some university in the United States.

"I feel just as I did the day Roberta was born," said Bob Longacre as he paced the floor waiting for the last sheet of his "Proto-Mixtecan" to roll out of the typewriter. Sure enough, thanks to the co-operation of the Wycliffe family, the "baby" was delivered on schedule, bundled, and weighed in at the airport in time to catch the plane for a January deadline at the University of Pennsylvania. Dr. Robert Longacre, the happy father, was profuse in his gratitude to all who helped.

The multiangled activities of the Wycliffe family grow basically out of the translation of the Scriptures into seventy or so languages in which they are working in Mexico. But as they translate, the workers collect information that may come out in the form of a Ph.D. dissertation, or an article on some phase of the ethnology of the tribe, or a good-sized bilingual dictionary. All of these scientific productions delight Mexican officials and foreign

131

scholars who find in the published materials a gold mine of information. A cross section of the work in process at any time in the Publications Department points up the fused activities of a hybrid organization. Stacked beside a pile of dictionaries in Tarahumara may be a shipment of the Gospel of Luke in the same language, produced by the same individual who is simultaneously a linguistic investigator and a Wycliffe translator.

As early as 1948 the Summer Institute of Linguistics, the academic side of the Wycliffe Bible Translators coin, received a high commendation from the Linguistic Society of America for its scientific publications. The first staff members of the summer session at Norman, Oklahoma, were called from Mexico where they were doing field work in linguistics and producing tribal translations. By 1948 a number of monographs and articles as well as textbooks had been published and commended as an "impressive series of publications appearing from the pens of its staff members." It was stated that work done by the Summer Institute of Linguistics under the direction of Dr. Kenneth L. Pike "should be strongly commended by our Society and welcomed as one of the most promising developments in applied linguistics in this country."

As of 1955, the date of the last published bibliography of the Summer Institute of Linguistics, two hundred and fifty technical papers had been published by one hundred and sixty authors, based on research in more than seventy languages. Most of these concerned Mexican Indian languages, although investigators in other fields also contributed appreciably.

In 1957 C. F. Voegelin, editor of the *International Journal of American Linguistics,* stated that the Summer Institute of Linguistics, "a whole army . . . led by Kenneth Pike . . . covers more territory than that occupied by the combined forces of all other linguists." Although Mexico, the first field occupied, still led in the number of linguists, by 1957 members in Peru had published a number of noteworthy linguistic studies.

Mexican Branch director Elson received his Ph.D. on the basis of a grammar of the Popoluca language of the state of Vera Cruz. Cornell University conferred his degree in 1956. The first grammar published under the Summer Institute of Linguistics was that of the Zoque language of the state of Chiapas, analyzed by

Dr. William Wonderly. His degree was granted by the University of Michigan. Dr. Wonderly and Dr. Eugene Nida, among the earliest Institute members in Mexico, now spend their full time with the American Bible Society which publishes most of the translations of Wycliffe workers.

In addition to scientific and Biblical publications, a constant stream of literacy materials issues from Wycliffe's presses atop the ancient Kettle. Readers, story books, and graded helps for literacy workers in dozens of dialects are always piled high on the long tables in the Publications Department where they are assembled for mailing to remote Indian villages.

Clinics manned by personnel of the Instituto Lingüístico de Verano reinforce the spiritual and educational activities in many Mexican locations. Nurses dedicated to relieving Indian ailments free translators for concentrated work on the New Testament.

Iva Chizek, a Navy nurse stationed in California, heard of the need and went to the Zapotec village of Atepec where Jane and Neil Nellis were translating. Iva established a clinic for the needy area, aided by her co-worker Dorothy Wright. They were able to treat not only the hundreds of Indians who came to the dispensary but to make "house calls" on horseback throughout the rocky mountains of the region where all of the villages angle down the sides of pine-covered slopes.

The father of a boy who had been cured by the girls came one day to thank them for their help. During his visit he heard the gospel story for the first time, as Jane and Neil Nellis evangelized him in his own language.

"God forgives murderers?" Arcardio asked in wonder. "And there is no fee to pay for eternal life? Our witch doctors tell us only of demons and evil spirits. Our whole town fears them."

Arcardio accepted Christ and later became one of the leaders in the fast-growing Zapotec church. In 1950 when the United States issued a call for agricultural laborers from Mexico to help harvest crops, Arcardio heard of the opportunity and ventured out to the States with a number of other bilingual Indians from his village. When he arrived at a labor camp in Arkansas, he found that he was the only Christian among the laborers, and was constantly taunted and ridiculed for his faith in Christ.

Desiring fellowship with others of like faith, even in the

133

foreign English language, he dressed up one Sunday in his clean blue work clothes and went looking for a church. He carefully placed his Spanish Bible in a brown paper bag, a custom he had followed in rural Mexico.

He found a likely-looking church, but as he entered he noticed hostile glances cast his way. The people of the church motioned him to move on.

Bewildered, Arcardio looked further for a church where he could worship. He tried another, and remained in the vestibule with his head bowed reverently during the entire service. In his hand he clutched the cherished Bible in the brown bag.

"Come, let's look for an interpreter," said the pastor to Arcardio at the close of the service when he saw that communication was impossible.

"All I want is a temple where I can worship God," Arcardio told the pastor.

From then on this devout Indian attended the services carrying his brown paper bag. His silent testimony of love for God and His Word spread conviction and challenge to the members of the church. There had been dissension and talk of the church splitting into two groups. The people began to sense their lack of love for God and one another. They became convicted of their sin. In one service forty of them rose one by one confessing their sins, and some accepted Christ.

"The sight of that faithful Indian brother and his effect on this congregation here in Arkansas," stated the pastor, "has been the greatest blessing of my life."

By 1959 the Nellises were polishing their translation before delivering it to the American Bible Society for publication.

Translations of the New Testament in other Mexican Indian languages had already been completed. With the aid of their co-workers Donald and Ruth Stark from Wheaton College, Kenneth and Evelyn Pike finished the Mixtec New Testament. Although completed in 1947, it was not published until 1951. Because of Pike's heavy duties in directing the Summer Institute of Linguistics in Oklahoma and his part-time teaching at the University of Michigan, the checking of the translation for printing was delayed. One of the faithful Mixtec believers, Angel, had helped Pike and Stark with the translation from the early stages. In the

134

final checking of the translation Angel became very weary. Unaccustomed to long hours of sitting, he stood for the final stint before the New Testament in his language went to the press.

"It speaks good!" was his comment in Mixtec when at last he held the printed product. And it has spoken "good" to his fellow Mixtecs living in porous pine log cabins in the Oaxaca mountains where Pike first pioneered.

In 1956 Pike's sister Eunice and her co-workers George and Florence Cowan finished the Mazatec New Testament. Another Mazatec worker, Sarah Gudschinsky, was studying for her Ph.D. at the University of Pennsylvania in preparation for assisting in Wycliffe's advance in Brazil. The three Cowan children completed the team that finally produced the precious manuscript for the American Bible Society printer. In the fall of 1956 as Florence Cowan was typing the last pages, the younger Cowans became as eager as the parents to see the job through.

"Mother, how much did you get typed on the Testament today?" became a daily query as the children came home from school in Sulphur Springs, Arkansas, where the family was located for the final stages of the work. "How soon will it be done?"

"On Wednesday, December 12, 1956," wrote Florence Cowan, "I had the last sheet of the last chapter at the last line to be typed waiting in the typewriter when the children came home from school. We all gathered around the typewriter to write the final phrase. Esther typed the next to the last word, and Paul the last, and Ruthie punched the final period to end it all. We sang the doxology, and knelt to thank the Lord that the Testament was typed."

Back in Mexico in remote mountain villages thousands of Mazatec Indians were reading gospel portions already in print in their language. And those who had turned from idols—including the Sacred Mushroom—were longing for the day when they would hold in their hands the completed Book telling them that Jesus Christ was the living Son of God. The Mushroom had not changed their hearts, but the living Christ revealed in the living Word in Mazatec had already delivered many from sin.*

---

* The story of the translation of the Mazatec New Testament is told by Eunice Pike in *Not Alone* and *Words Wanted* (Chicago: Moody Press, 1956 and 1958 respectively).

135

By the spring of 1956, the Totonac New Testament was also completed, a major victory for the vigorous tribe covering a large area in the states of Vera Cruz and Puebla. As allies of Cortez, the Totonacs had helped to subdue the powerful Aztec nation. But they themselves became servants of the conquerors. It was more than four hundred years later that Herman and Bessie Aschmann completed the translation of the Book that was bringing light and liberation to a tribe long bound by sin and superstition.

After Herman had submitted the final manuscript of the Totonac New Testament to the American Bible Society, some of his Wycliffe family members at the Kettle wanted to help him celebrate. But Herman had disappeared. Someone finally detected a light on the third floor, and heard Herman's habitually happy whistle.

"Herman—what are you doing here *tonight*? Let's celebrate!" exclaimed one of his friends.

"Well," chuckled Herman, the indefatigable worker with a built-in smile, "I thought I'd celebrate by starting to revise our Totonac dictionary."

Meanwhile, in the Tarascan tribe in the state of Michoacán where Max and Elisabeth Lathrop were pressing toward the completion of the New Testament, the gospel had made an appreciable impact on the tribe. On Lake Pátzcuaro and in the hill town of Cherán the dissemination of the gospel was being aided considerably by medical and literacy work. Three nurses, Phyllis and Julia Burpee and Mary Smith, were daily doctoring hundreds of Tarascan patients who with the physical relief always received a balm for their souls. Max Lathrop has been responsible for the preparation of Tarascan literature and of a government training program that has transformed the Tarascans into a near-literate tribe. The Lathrops have received high official commendation for the outstanding educational contribution they have made. The presses operated by Tarascan Indians whom Max has trained produce quantities of secular and Scriptural reading matter for the tribe. Alice Thomas, a faithful helper of the Lathrops, has taught many Tarascans to read in their own language, and has prepared numerous manuscripts of Scripture portions and supplementary reading material for printing.

The blessings resulting from the translation of the Scriptures into the Tarascan language have been accompanied by many trials. In 1954 the heaviest blow fell when the youngest of the Lathrops' four children, Theodore, was drowned in Lake Pátzcuaro on Easter eve. The faith and rejoicing of the stricken parents in the face of such a trial greatly strengthened the Tarascan believers mourning the loss of the thirteen-year-old boy who was to have been baptized along with a number of them the following day.

During those days of testing Elisabeth wrote:

"Among the superstitious Indians, it is believed that a witch who put a spell on us last year has caused this. She is taking large credit, and says this is only the beginning. Our Christians need to learn not to fear these witches; so often their threats seem to take effect, as in this case. We have had a number of narrow escapes in the last month. Just for instance, the other day a squirrel hunter's stray bullet cracked the window by our dining table, exactly in line with my head. It was spent, so did no damage. I would like to be in heaven, but I would also like to give the lie to the threats of this old woman who claims to have bewitched me!"

Since 1942 Milton and Clara Warkentin have been translating the Bible for the Huave Indians who live by fishing near the Isthmus of Tehuantepec. Extremely suspicious of outsiders, the Huaves uncordially tolerated the Warkentins during their first months in the tribe. However, as the foreigners began to speak the Huave language all barriers fell and the Warkentins became a part of the community. Finally, the day came when they had to leave the tribe for a brief period.

"Do you have enough money to return?" asked the mayor of their village anxiously.

"No, sir," was Milton Warkentin's honest reply.

"Isn't it pretty far to your country?" continued the mayor.

"Yes," said Milton, "it takes several days by bus."

"Listen, my friend," said the mayor, "it looks doubtful to us that you will return if you don't have money. The people want you to come back. They have authorized me to advance you enough money to buy return tickets now."

The Warkentins returned and continued their work of translation as well as medical treatment of the ailing Indians. They wrote:

"We even thought that we were running a baby clinic as a half dozen or more mothers would be sitting all over our floor with their children, while they were waiting for Clara to tell them what was wrong with their children and then pronounce a perfect cure.

"One day a mother and father came over with their little girl just two months old. They said that the baby had a sore mouth; but when they unwrapped it, we were horrified to see nothing but skin and bones. They said that the sore mouth was caused by sucking on empty breasts, since the mother had no milk. They had tried to give it goat's milk, but the baby would not drink it. We fed the baby some powdered milk with an eye dropper. The little thing just drank and drank till it fell sound asleep in its mother's arms. When we asked the parents why they hadn't brought the baby sooner, they said that they first had had to ask pardon of their 'saints' for the mother who had no milk. In the meantime the baby had almost starved to death. But we praise the Lord that the baby is living today, and that we had a wonderful opportunity to tell the parents for the first time of God's pardon for them through Jesus Christ."

Later the Huave team was augmented by Glenn Stairs and his wife Emily, a capable nurse who was able to carry the growing medical load. Glenn has ably followed through the literacy efforts begun by Milton Warkentin who is now free to devote his whole time to the completion of the Huave New Testament. One of Milton's first pupils was an old man who came to him wanting to learn to "find letters." When first handed a primer he held it upside down. Milton demonstrated the use of the reading book which had appropriate captions under the pictures when held right side up. The old man was delighted. He stayed several hours and went through the whole primer. Then he asked to take it home where he would have leisure to study it more carefully for the next few days, because he was "celebrating" the death of a relative and would not be working. He came back later, having mastered all but a few words of the book. He wanted more so he bought the Huave-Spanish dictionary the Warkentins had prepared.

"For several mornings after that," they wrote, "we saw him sitting in his back yard very diligently reading his dictionary. In less than a week, he was able to read both of the primers and the dictionary without help. So we praise the Lord that some have begun to read in their own language."

Today there are many Huaves who can read the Scripture portions printed for them, and who are eagerly awaiting the completion of the entire New Testament. One of the Huaves who will be most grateful when the Book is done is Juan, the Warkentins' first informant and believer. He has recently been elected pastor of the organized Huave church which now has several thriving branch groups. With Milton Warkentin, Juan began translating by lamplight in the village of San Mateo, after the crowd of the day had retired. His careful attention to detail in translation, and his eagerness to put the words of God into his own language, have been responsible in good measure for the progress on the Huave New Testament.

From the Pacific coast of Mexico to the Gulf on the east, and from the Texas border to Guatemala on the south, the darkness is giving way to the light of the Scriptures. Educated Mexicans who two decades earlier objected to Bible translation because the Indians had had "too much religion" are now saying, "This is what every tribe in Mexico needs."

18. Roughing It

"No matter what we dream up, Cam is always ten years ahead of us," said Nyman recently of plans for advance concerning which Townsend had written him.

And back in 1944 when Townsend searched for a site for a jungle training camp in southern Mexico some of his fellow workers thought it premature. The work was well under way in Mexico, but the tribes were not all occupied. However, an invitation had come for translators to go to Peru and Townsend recognized the need for preparing recruits for the rugged jungles of the Amazon.

A United States government rubber hunter from Peru had once told Townsend he would not employ an American. He had been raised on an Iowa farm and went to Firestone's rubber plantations in Africa where he learned the rugged life of the jungle. "If I had to use an American," he had said, "I would take only one who had been raised on a farm. Our American way of life is too easy and doesn't fit a man for jungle hardships."

Townsend knew that his language hunters would go to live in the jungle for longer periods of time than rubber hunters would. He knew also that most of the volunteers for the mission field were from crowded cities. A jungle setting in southern Mexico would be just the place to toughen them up.

"It will also give an opportunity for them to decide whether they are really cut out for this type of work," concluded the jungle trainer as he trekked the trails in search of a suitable location for the camp.

He found the perfect spot on the edge of the jungle in the state of Chiapas, bordering Guatemala. Located at the margin of the actual forest area, there was enough space for a landing strip that would provide a link with civilization. The city-bred trainees would be taken farther into the jungle itself to complete their training after first being "broken in" halfway from human habitations. Around the spot selected for the Main Base of Jungle Camp lived the Tzeltal Indians who were more communicative than the very primitive Lacandón Indians farther in the jungle. Practice with the Tzeltal language and Indians would be good preparation, too, thought Townsend, for the strange tongues to come in the Amazonian jungles.

Earl Adams, one of the early trainees who later supervised the jungle training program, wrote of his four months' training:

"Jungle Camp is located in a beautiful spot on the edge of the jungle and beside a large river. We have been very busy here with Dr. Pike at the helm. Camp goals are techniques in improvising for comfortable, healthy, efficient living and working in the jungle, and techniques in jungle travel. Classes thus far have included house-building, furniture-making, first aid, Spanish, informant work with the local Tzeltal Indians, linguistics, hiking, canoeing, camping on the trail, cooking, eating and liking native food, target practice, soap-making, hominy-making, dye-making, butchering, meat-preserving, riding, using common carpenter tools, repairing lanterns, as well as other practical instruction.

"The biggest event since coming here was a nine-day hike into the jungle, surveying a river valley with some mahogany lumbermen. It is good training to travel and live with those who know the jungle and its ways. The trip was most interesting with the novelty of the real jungle—big trees, climbing vines, snakes, big birds, parrots, rivers, daily rains, tapirs, monkeys, butterflies and all. One highlight of the trip was taking part in the initial excavations of a Maya pyramid and finding carved designs and clay pots filled with bones."

In 1947 Townsend's dream had become a reality as twenty-three young people were busy learning how to live in the Lacandón jungle.

141

"Educated, refined, used to the type of life you live in the United States and Canada," he wrote, "these young people are planning to go to live in dense forests. There the sunlight breaks through only in clearings or on the rivers. Mud lies everywhere during the rainy season. Biting insects are legion, causing almost constant irritation of the skin, and often sores. Poisonous snakes abound. Supplies trickle through from the outside world only irregularly and at great expense.

"What are these young people thinking about? Are they going to make a lot of money prospecting for gold, or exploring for some well-endowed geographical society, or hunting rubber? No! They have left good salaries to receive only enough to cover their expenses. They go in quest of souls, long-neglected Indian souls, and one soul outweighs the world in value. The love of Christ constrains them. They are full of joy."

Girls as well as fellows were learning many skills that would be useful in the isolated tribes where they would work. Not only from the United States but from Canada and England came recruits to weather the jungle training period. Constance Naish, a British trainee, wrote:

"Have you ever slept in a pool? Neither had I till I lay in a jungle hammock last week-end and listened to the steady downpour and felt the water engulfing me on all sides! Life is full of the unexpected here at Jungle Camp and the surprises are nearly all pleasant ones—that one *can* understand the mysteries of an engine's insides, that it is not impossible to make a table that will stand on its own four legs, that mule-riding is fun, and that capsizing in a canoe over the rapids is not the end."

But for one of the young pioneers a canoe experience threatened to be the end. Wayne Nicholes, assisting Earl Adams in the jungle training program, wrote:

"We had just started back upriver on the return half of the canoe trip. We arrived at the second rapids upriver from the waterfalls. Here the current makes a turn directly across the river and bounces against a big rock on one bank. One of the canoes got swept against the rock and pinned there by the current. Then a paddle fell overboard. Melba Carson, always an eager volunteer, jumped into the water to retrieve the paddle. She had a sudden lesson in the force of moving water as she was swept underneath the canoe. She would probably have been swept on down the river, but many arms from the canoe grabbed for her and someone managed to get hold of her arm. Soon they had pulled her back into the canoe. She left her glasses in the water, but Melba was still with us. When we had gotten all the canoes safely up through the rapids, we stopped to give the Lord our thanks."

By the time Jungle Camp got under way in 1944, a Wycliffe couple had already pioneered in the heart of the Lacandón jungle, and had learned some of the language spoken by the few hundred remaining Lacandóns, a remote residue of the ancient Mayans. Phil and Mary Baer answered the challenge to take the gospel to this isolated, primitive group. Visits out to that Wycliffe station, which later became famous as the "Baer trip," provided a finishing touch to this part of the jungle training program.

Here the firsthand observation of primitive Indian customs is a sobering picture of what lies ahead. Watching the Lacandón Indians pray earnestly to their clay gods is an unforgettable experience. One camper reported:

"The god house was a thatched hut covering an area of about twenty by thirty feet. It had no walls, just a roof. Along the west side and facing east, was a line of about thirteen clay gods. These gods were sitting on a carpet of palm leaves and looking like big soup bowls with gruesome faces.

"Originally these gods had been gaily painted, but now they were black from the burning pitch pine that is offered for incense. I watched as new pitch was set on top of these gods and set afire. It would sparkle and crackle, throwing up a dense black smoke. The pitch would melt and run down over the sides of the bowl until the whole was a mass of yellow flames.

"The one offering the sacrifice moved back and forth behind the gods, chanting and waving sacred palm leaves in the smoke. With these he would touch his own shoulders, or take them to touch a sick child outside the hut, for this ceremony was for the healing of the sick. It was sad to watch, knowing the folly of it all, and knowing the mercy and healing that were theirs if they would only accept them."

When the half-toughened campers have completed their work at the relatively accessible Main Base, they move on into the

143

jungle to Advance Base where living more nearly resembles conditions to be encountered in virgin jungles of unreached tribal areas. There they learn to build a shelter from material available in the forest, adequate enough to keep out the rain and where they might hang their hammocks and build their fire. Rations are limited, and they learn to forage in the forest for game and birds to eat. One of the highlights of the stiffer training period is the "Survival Hike." Campers must have a "survival kit" packed and ready at all times. They may be asked on a half-hour's notice —or none at all—to go out into the jungle for four days, then make their way back to the main camp unaided by staff members. Those who survive the ordeal feel ready to tackle almost anything Amazonia has to offer. Jungle campers, and especially those who have gone to isolated areas, have been high in their praises of such a preparatory program.

Having selected a spot for Jungle Camp and a staff to initiate the first session in 1944, Townsend returned to California for Christmas with his family. On Christmas Eve Elvira Townsend succumbed to the heart ailment that had threatened her for years. She had lived twelve years beyond the most optimistic estimates of her endurance.

For Townsend it was a time of rededication to the task of reaching the lost tribes of the world. As he laid away "the frail girl who had pioneered in two Indian tribes," he said:

"If I have permitted hardships, dangers, pleasures, or the powerful cords of human love to swerve me at times from full obedience, henceforth 'none of these things move me.'

"This pledge is not taken lightly. It has been burned into my soul, and though the branding processes have not been easy, the pain now seems like nothing as I visualize the fruit and joy of a truly all-out effort for my Savior and the unevangelized tribes that need Him so."

19. Back to Guatemala

By 1950 all of the major Mayan dialects of Guatemala had received the New Testament, complete or in part, after the initial thrust of the Cakchiquel work many years before. Thousands of tribesmen had turned from their idols and were now reading God's will for them in their own languages.

Edward Sywulka, the first Wycliffe-trained translator to work in a tribe, had already helped the Pecks of the Presbyterian Mission complete the translation of the Mam New Testament. Now he and his wife Pauline, members of the Central American Mission under which Townsend had served, were teaching the Word to thousands of Mam Indians.

In 1951 three evangelical missions working in Guatemala asked the Wycliffe Bible Translators to send linguists to the smaller dialects of Indian languages. Thus linguistic work was undertaken in eight tribes where translation was needed. Two women workers, Francis Eachus and Ruth Carlson, went to a tribe already occupied to help in the final stages of completing a translation.

The first small Mayan tribe to receive Wycliffe translators was the Aguacatec. The tribe had been much prayed for by missionaries working nearby in Spanish, but the Aguacatecs were beyond the reach of that language. Thus when Harry and Lucille McArthur began to translate the Word for them, there was almost immediate response to the message they could now understand.

By 1958 there was a large group of believers in the central

Aguacatec town of Aguacatán, and several groups meeting in other villages. Of one recent experience Harry McArthur wrote:

"Last Sunday I hiked out to a believer's home for a sunrise service. Monday came news that the witch doctors were taking advantage of the fact that one of the newer believers had not yet thrown out his idol. One of our stronger believers organized a counterattack. We were all to go up to Manzanilla, hold a meeting and stay all night to strengthen the believers there while the witch doctors would be burning their candles and incense and shooting sky rockets as well as getting powerfully drunk.

"What a night! We were all in the same house with the idol and his crew. There were eighteen believers and about the same number of the witch doctors. Old Chico tried to keep things from getting too wild, and I was amazed that there wasn't open war. The witch doctors had a violin and banjo. We had an accordion and eighteen lusty voices. When the violin quit, we would strike up the band with a gospel hymn. Then when we were finished they would take over. They heard much of the Word read to them in their own tongue.

"We all left before things got too wild and slept in another house about fifty yards up the mountain. I was quite pleased at the strength of the believers in the face of the head witch doctor of Aguacatán. I must say, though, that I was happy to trek down the mountain the next day." *

Among the first Wycliffe workers in Guatemala were Marvin and Marilyn Mayers who began work with the Pocomchí Indians at the request of the Nazarene Mission. Christian informants were available, so that immediate progress was made on translation. Within a few years the Gospel of Mark was published, to the delight of Pocomchí Christians eager to read the Word in their own tongue. Marvin Mayers also prepared a volume entitled *Pocomchí Texts with Grammatical Notes* published in 1958 by the University of Oklahoma.

Wycliffe in Mexico, which has supplied several workers for Guatemala, recently provided the Guatemalan Branch with a director when Earl Adams, who had initiated the work, was called

* The story of the formation of the Aguacatec church as a result of early translation work is pictured in the Wycliffe film *Unsheathed* produced by John Meredith.

to help with the advance into New Guinea. John and Elaine Beekman, having helped to complete the Chol Testament in Mexico, willingly moved south to fill the gap left by Earl and Betty Adams. Assisted in the office by Eunice Anderson, the Beekmans are capably supervising the work in progress in eight tribes.

The Black Carib tribe on Guatemala's eastern coast, the only indigenous group of the country speaking a non-Mayan dialect, was one of the earliest occupied. Because of the linguistic and cultural differences of the tribe, the experiences there varied greatly from life in the seven other tribes where Wycliffe translators are working.

In the spring of 1952 a double column of women in white dresses with green crepe paper sashes paraded through the streets of a town on the shore of the Caribbean. They were led by their queen, who was wearing a gold paper crown. Drums were beating, horns playing, and the marchers came along two by two shuffling out rhythm with their feet. They were Black Caribs celebrating one hundred and fifty years of being civilized. Among the spectators were two spellbound girls who had come to explore the need of these people for Bible translation. As they became better acquainted with the Indians and the advisability of translation, they knew that this was the place the Lord had chosen for them. Lillian Howland from Maine and Ilah Fleming from Florida went back to Guatemala City to pack and return to Livingston to take up their work among the Caribs.

The language of these people is challenging and intriguing. Lil and Ilah were faced with an Arawakan language of South American origin. Long before the discovery of America, apparently, its original speakers migrated from South America to the Lesser Antilles. Later, but still before the discovery, a group of Carib men made an expedition into the islands. Perhaps not expecting to stay, they had brought no women with them; but they did stay on, killing off the Arawak men and occupying the islands with the Arawak women.

The children first learned Arawak from their mothers. Then the boys, to preserve the prestige of the men's Carib language, substituted Carib roots while retaining Arawak structure. This combination of the principal language families of South America

147

led, within a few generations, to the present linguistic lines: Arawak in grammatical structure and with a large predominance of Arawak roots, there is yet a mixture of Carib roots. In addition, the gender of many abstract nouns will differ, depending on whether men or women are speaking.

The cultural characteristics of the Black Caribs are also an interesting mixture. In the late 1700's Arawak and Carib were further combined with African blood when escaped slaves settled among them. There is even a story of a slave ship from Africa wrecked off the coast. These slaves contributed African physical characteristics and some aspects of the culture, especially the built-in rhythm in the hands and feet of young and old alike. But they had no appreciable influence on the language or food customs. The basic foods are still yucca (rather than the corn of the Central American culture), fish, and coconuts.

The town of Livingston is accessible only by boat from Puerto Barrios, itself about two hundred miles overland from Guatemala City on the Caribbean coast. At first Lil and Ilah lived in a Ladino section of town, surrounded by Spanish speakers. But they went out walking to hear Carib and to try out the words they had picked up. By scheduling their walks they gradually covered the whole town. Their attempts at using Carib met with varied reactions. Some of the people were frankly scornful and resentful, thinking the two translators were showing off or making sport of them. Some were embarrassed or scared or amused, and overcome by laughter and giggles. One woman carrying a tub of water on her head almost giggled it off. But others, pleased that their language was of interest to the newcomers, would stop and talk away not realizing how little the girls could understand. As they kept walking and smiling and talking, barriers were broken down and contacts made. It was a time of preparing the soil for planting, an effort that proved well worth while.

Lil and Ilah soon discovered where the Caribs of the town really lived. Out of a population of three thousand, there were only two hundred Ladinos in town—and their house was in the midst of them! They moved to a Carib house believed to be occupied by evil spirits ever since a man had died there some time before. Their landlady afterward told them the Lord had sent them to rid the house of the spirits.

148

Now informants were plentiful. Carib children were on the porch and in the house day and night. The girls enjoyed them but in self-defense made half doors to "slow them down a bit," as Ilah said. At night they let them in and they came in droves. The house was small but often as many as forty children of assorted sizes were in it. To keep them under control Lil and Ilah decided to teach them.

But the translators were not advancing toward the work they had come to do. They stopped to take stock of the local educational situation. There were Spanish schools in the town; and although many Carib children soon dropped out of them, the teachers were willing to use the primer already available and were asking for more Carib material. However, investigation showed that those who had learned to read Spanish and who might not understand much of what they read in that language, could easily transfer to reading Carib. Therefore the girls felt that in concentrating on translation and the language analysis necessary for that they were not being unfair to those who were anxious to learn to read.

They had not expected to have enough control of the language for possibly several years to be able to do any translation or intelligible witnessing. However, they heard of a Christian Carib called John the Evangelist, a carpenter who had worked elsewhere but returned to Livingston at some economic sacrifice in order to reach his townsmen with the gospel. Encouraged by his presence, the girls attempted gospel records by using John to translate through Spanish. But his misinterpretation soon forced them to delay translation and to concentrate on language work.

Analysis, however, was hampered by lack of knowledge. After a year and a half of gathering material and studying Carib, the girls returned to the Summer Institute of Linguistics at Norman, Oklahoma, for a second summer of study there. In the two years since their first summer, new procedures had been developed for language analysis. When again they worked with the tribe, real progress was made.

Meanwhile John, who had been disappointed at the gospel record failure, was encouraged to write Carib hymns. With great care he selected hymn tunes impossible to dance to and fitted words to the music. The two did not match exactly, but with some hurrying here and slowing down there they could be sung,

149

and with practice most of the congregation hurried and slowed down in the same places. In the Spanish meetings the Caribs were sometimes asked to sing.

Before Christmas, 1956, four years after coming to the Caribs, Ilah had a Scripture verse translated and ready to be tried out on the group. She introduced John 14:27 during a pause in a rehearsal for the Christmas program and a brief study of the text. The reaction was as unexpected as it was instantaneous; the people requested Bible studies four nights a week.

Lil had gone to Guatemala City temporarily and Ilah, alone and with a very limited knowledge of the language, would be overburdened. Therefore, the meetings were postponed until after Christmas and then reduced to two a week. It was enough to translate for that number of meetings. She herself had to read and discuss the passages translated. With no time to work far enough ahead to teach them to someone else to introduce, she just made it to each meeting with a rough draft.

She was relieved to welcome Lil back from Guatemala City. Now there were two to translate, and soon the verses were taught to the few who could read and who in turn introduced the translations in the meetings. Leading the meetings was rotated among all, men and women alike.

In Carib culture women are quite independent. They own fields and houses and are largely self-supporting. On Sunday afternoons the women of Livingston hold what the girls have dubbed the Ladies' Meeting. The organization owns a rice field which the members co-operate in cultivating for the benefit of all. They also help one another with their individual field work. It is in many ways a mutual aid society. At the meetings sixty to a hundred women are present and every officer from the queen down, about twenty in all, makes a speech each Sunday. After the girls were accepted by the group as regular attendants and were called on also to participate, it became an excellent opportunity for language listening and speaking up in public.

After four and a half years with the Caribs, furlough time came for Lil and Ilah. Much had been accomplished in that first term. The confidence of the people had been won; a good start had been made on language learning and analysis; a group was gathering to study the verses already translated. Furlough was used for further linguistic study and in November, 1958, the girls went back to Livingston to an enthusiastic welcome.

Of the return Ilah writes:

"It really is wonderful to be working on the Carib translation again and we aren't the only ones who think so. Lil's informant Cándida went all the way to Puerto Barrios to try to meet us the day before we arrived. That meant getting up at 4:00 A.M. to catch the boat and not getting home until about 1:00 P.M. She met us at the Livingston dock the next day though, and it surely was good to see her again, as well as all the others. For the last six months Cándida has been keeping a close check with Hencha our landlady as to when we might come.

"By the time Lil made her first visit with her to begin checking translation materials again, she was more than delighted to be helping once more and learning more about the Lord. As she said it: 'This is what I have been hungering for.' The native pastor of the Nazarene church here in Livingston told us of several times when a Sunday school lesson or sermon had been finished in Spanish only to have one of the Caribs say he or she was still 'hungry,' or ask just what he had meant to say once more. He is so convinced of their need to be taught in their own language that he has already asked us to begin teaching a Sunday school class in Carib.

"Not only is there the need for translation work, teaching and leading in Bible studies, preparing primers, etc. here in Livingston, but we are also concerned about the Caribs of British Honduras and Honduras. They need the same things. In the Lord's timing, a Carib man from British Honduras was in Livingston for several days this week.

"I encouraged him to try to read some of the mimeographed portions we have put out in Carib. When he began to realize that here was some of God's Word written in Carib, his face lit up and *then* he said he had often wanted to try to help his own people in the Carib language but he never knew quite how to. With his own spiritual vocabulary limited to English, he did not know how to translate it into Carib. Now with some of the Word already translated, he felt he might really be able to work with

151

some in their own Carib language. There is evidence that the Lord has begun to raise up believers in scattered areas, such as this man, who can be potential sowers of the seed. But they need the Word in Carib, and it is a real opportunity to supply them with the Word and to train them in it to be able to teach others."

20. Peru: Unraveling the Knot

"Lord, this is it. So far as I know this is my only chance, these two days. If I muff it here, I'm through with it, I'm afraid. Please Lord, do something today . . ."

Kenneth Pike was praying rather desperately in his hotel room in Lima, Peru, where he had gone in response to a request of the American Bible Society for assistance on a linguistic problem in the Quichua language. At Townsend's suggestion Pike was also to call on government officials and investigate the possibility of translation work with the jungle tribes.

"I'd never done anything like this, and I was frightened. I'm not very courageous in such matters, but the 'Chief' had asked me to do it.

"I opened up my Testament to the book of Timothy where we are told to pray for all those in authority, for kings, and all in high places. I said, 'Where is the God of Elijah?' For a minute I was in that spot."

Pike had not relished the idea of going to Peru, although Townsend suggested it even before this 1943 trip. Townsend was eager for Wycliffe to get on with the job of translating for the countless tribes in Amazonia, but Pike felt "we were not ready for it." When, therefore, the request came for Pike to go to Peru, he remembered his former reluctance and thought, "This looks like the hand of God."

It was wartime and Pike was of draft age. Dr. Fries, with

whom he had been writing textbooks for teaching English as a foreign language at the University of Michigan, helped obtain permission for him to leave the United States. He gave him a letter to the chief of cultural relations for Latin-American affairs in Washington, D.C.

"You helped write Fries' book?" the official asked Pike in the Washington office.

"Yes, I did," he answered.

The official then swung around in his chair and, removing the book in question from the shelf behind him, read in the preface where Dr. Fries had included his co-author's name on a line reading, "Pronunciation—Pike." The official closed the book.

"Your passport has to come across my desk, and when it does I will okay it," he said.

Now in his hotel room Pike finished praying.

"Then I went over to the Ministry of Education," he said, "walked up the stairs to the second floor, found the minister, and gave him my card. He had studied in the United States. I handed him my book entitled *Phonetics* published by the University of Michigan Press. That was my credential, and he was interested in it. I talked with him about my work with Fries on teaching English as a foreign language. He asked me if I would give a series of fifteen lectures to all teachers of high school English in Peru in the summer session.

"He asked me about our work in Mexico. I told him of our language investigation and our practical projects, and how we helped the Indians spiritually by translating the Bible."

"Well, why don't you do that here?" he said.

"We haven't been asked," Pike replied.

The minister turned to his adviser, chatted a moment, then said to Pike:

"What do they pay you?"

Pike replied that President Cárdenas had paid the very first workers in Mexico schoolteachers' salaries amounting to about twelve dollars a month. The government had facilitated entrance for workers and their residence in the country, as well as the bringing in of necessary equipment duty free.

"Well, do come in then," said the minister, "and just let me know if there is anything I can do for you."

154

He breathed a prayer to the Lord and said to the minister, "There is one thing. Sometimes your consular officials are slow to give us visas. If you could just put your invitation in writing, it would help."

"Come back tomorrow and we'll take care of it," he answered.

He prayed much that day, Pike recalls. He knew that he could not give that oral invitation to Townsend and say, "You go on from here." The next day in the corridor at the Ministry of Education he met a young Peruvian with a brisk stride holding a letter in his hand.

"Well, hello Pike!" he exclaimed.

"Hello," replied Pike vaguely.

"Pike! You lectured to us at the University of Michigan!" continued the young fellow enthusiastically.

"Well, so I did," said Pike.

"Look what I've got in my hand. The minister asked me to write a letter for you. Come along with me." And Pike followed his friend into the office of the director of education. He handed the official the letter for the minister's signature and said, "This is Pike. He lectured to us at the University of Michigan."

"Oh, you know him?" asked the official.

"That's right," replied Pike's former student proudly.

He took the letter to the minister, came back with his signature, handed it to Pike—and entrance was assured. This was the hand of God.

But it was not until 1945 that Townsend made the follow-up trip to Peru. At that time he signed an agreement with the Ministry of Education providing for the occupation of the jungle Indian tribes, the study of their languages, and the translation of the Scriptures. Under government auspices, he made extensive surveys of the vast Amazon region to determine where the young pioneers would be located. He flew to remote areas near the Ecuadorian border, and into the heart of the jungle facing into Brazil and Colombia. It was a staggering panorama.

"Groups of the so-called savages speaking scores of languages dot the entire inland empire that is Amazonia. Some are on the big rivers and can be reached by a journey of a few days by steamer or launch. Most of them are harder to reach. I inquired about one of the tribes that was nearest to civilization.

"My informant, a seasoned Peruvian frontiersman, smiled and said: 'That tribe is easy to reach. You go down the Amazon from here to the Nanay by launch, then up the Nanay for two days by motor boat (if you can get one), then two days more by canoe, and from there a day over land by trail. It's quite near.'

"As a matter of fact," commented Townsend, "the tribe was near Iquitos by air—just a few minutes in a good airplane."

As Townsend flew up the Napo River from Iquitos over the vast expanse of dark green jungle, broken here and there by clearings and Indian settlements, he knew that aviation was a must. It would be impossible for young women translators and families with small children to live and work in the tribes without air service. As he flew over the forty or more tribes of Indians buried in the dense jungle, he envisioned a network of two-way radios linking the remote locations to a central base where planes would be available in time of need. Canoe or land travel was out of the question.

"I saw why missionary work has been so hard in the jungle," Townsend said. "One missionary told me that she and her husband and daughter had spent twenty-five days on a raft to cover a stretch which by government plane took us only two hours. If forty tribes in those jungles were to receive the Scriptures, it would be necessary to ameliorate the trials with ample modern equipment."

He recalled what Carlton Beals had written in 1934 of the problems facing a country which was eighty per cent Indian, and where most of the tribes were geographically and linguistically beyond the reach of Spanish culture:

"Peru is the hard unraveled knot of South America. No genius has yet arisen great enough to untangle that knot, to solve its major problems. Here is the uncut umbilical cord of South America's future. Here a new world is being born." *

Townsend wrote on the eve of initiating translation work in Peru:

"No one organization, nor a single group of workers, no matter

* *Fire on the Andes* (Philadelphia: J. B. Lippincott Co., 1934).

how consecrated, well-supported and gifted they may be, can cope with the situation. Ours is to be a ministry of service and co-operation in the spirit of Christ. We shall serve the government of Peru which is concerned about the welfare of those tribes, and we shall serve the handful of valiant missionaries now laboring in some sections of the jungle. We shall serve all who want to help the Indians."

In 1946 twenty-five eager pioneers fresh from their jungle training period in Mexico arrived in Peru. Within a year workers were located in seven tribes that had been surveyed, and a temporary base was set up in the jungle on the Aguaytía River.

The first Wycliffe translators in Peru went to their posts without radios and without planes because they were eager to locate their tribes and get on with the long job of language learning. The first pair of girls to go up the treacherous Urubamba River to the Machiguenga tribe spent seventeen days in a canoe, traveling through water inhabited by boa constrictors and alligators.

Finally, help came in the form of a military surplus Grumman Duck, the first Wycliffe plane in Peru. But one plane was insufficient for the many needs in the wide jungle.

Titus and Florence Nickel went to the Aguaruna tribe on the Marañón River in northern Peru near the Ecuadorian border, expecting the plane to make occasional trips out to them with food and mail. However, repairs on the Duck became necessary and the trips could not be made. After eight months in the tribe, food supplies were exhausted. Florence Nickel also needed medical attention as she was expecting her first child. They would have to get out by land and canoe.

"We tried to find some Indians who would take us upriver to the place where the trail began," Florence related, "but they didn't want to go because it was the rainy season, and the river was high and hard to travel. Besides, they don't like to go very far away from home because they can never tell when they are going to run into some enemy and meet a sudden death. But the Lord intervened for us. He sent a Peruvian trader up our way, which is something quite rare. This trader had a large canoe with a motor on it. He agreed to take us with him up the river to the place where the trail started.

"The second day out, the river which had been swollen by rains began to rise and the boatman got drunk. That was a bad combination. He wasn't handling the canoe very well. About four-thirty in the afternoon the motor ran out of gas. We stopped to refill it, and the propeller fell off and down to the bottom of the river, so we couldn't go any farther. A kind Indian woman in a little, dirty hut took us in. We stayed there until the boatman went down the river where he had another propeller, and then he took us on.

"We reached a place where the river is forced through a narrow, rocky gorge, and the water was just roaring through. We could see whirlpools forming, and big trees and logs were dashing down in the water, being tossed around like matches. Titus and the boatman decided that we would walk around the spot—and the boatman and two Indians went through the whirlpool in the canoe.

"After two weeks we got to the place where the trail started, and I thought the worst part of our trip was over. But I didn't know what was ahead of me. We had four days of jungle hiking to do. At the end of the first day we were both very tired, and at night we were so stiff that we could hardly turn over on our air mattresses.

"At the end of the third day my legs were so stiff that it didn't seem possible to crawl over the trees and up and down the hills and wade through the streams any more.

"When we got to the end of the walking trail, we were able to get mules to ride for a day and a half—a luxury to us. After that we came to the road where we got a truck that took us to the coast. We arrived on the coast the afternoon of Christmas Day. It was a very strange Christmas Day to us, but a very happy one because we had reached our destination. We had been traveling twenty-one days."

When the Nickels went back to the tribe with their first-born baby John, Wycliffe pilot Lawrence Montgomery flew the family to their jungle home in one hour and fifty-five minutes!

After hearing of their grueling experience, Townsend said with tears in his eyes, "No more of our translators should go into the jungles of Peru until they can be assured of adequate transportation service."

A Wycliffe trainee at Jungle Camp in Mexico loads his
duffel on an improvised balsa raft for
a camp-out downriver. (Chap. 18)

Trainees must learn to build quickly the durable,
leak-proof shelters used in the southern Mexico jungle
where monkeys, mosquitoes, and mahogany abound.

Although modern tribal witch doctors of Guatemala
still burn incense and chant like their pre-Columbian
ancestors (above), the gospel is now heard through
the work of translators such as Harry McArthur
who teaches among the Aguacatec Indians (below).
(pp. 145–46)

Named for the Mexican educator and official who first invited Townsend to Mexico, the Catalina PBY *Moisés Sáenz* is presented by Mexican President Alemán to Peruvian government officials in Mexico City in April, 1951. (pp. 40–43)

The *Moisés Sáenz,* being received here by the Republic of Peru, operates out of Yarinacocha, the jungle base of the Summer Institute of Linguistics.

Aerial view of Yarinacocha, a crossroads for SIL workers in the farthest corners of Peru.

Technicians Bevensee and Shanks at Yarinacocha help to maintain a network of communication with 29 tribal stations, planes in flight, and headquarters in Lima, Peru.

Westminster Films Phot

Unloading after a flight bringing Piro Indians to Bilingual Teacher
Training School at Yarinacocha.

David Beasley translating with the aid of his Huambisa
language informant, Yampiki, in the Peruvian jungle. (p. 201)

A Shipibo woman of Peru, with traditional face paint and jewelry, whose tribe is receiving the New Testament through the work of James and Hettie Lauriault.

Larry Montgomery, a former U.S. Air Force captain stationed in Peru, saw the desperate need of air aid for missionaries and joined Townsend in 1948 to build Wycliffe's Jungle Aviation and Radio Service. (pp. 175–176) Here he is greeted by Secoyah Indians in Ecuador.

A group of Piro Indians are taught by Esther Matteson (left, back to camera), whose translation of the New Testament brought many of them to Christianity. (pp. 177–83)

A Campa lad beams at a Polaroid picture of himself and companions taken by pilot Montgomery in the isolated area of Peru where Willard and Lee Kindberg are translating the Scriptures.

Amuesha children of central Peru learn reading, writing,
and Peruvian history in a bilingual government school, using
textbooks written by Wycliffe translators Martha Duff
and Mary Ruth Wise. (pp. 187–90)

Yagua pupils study in northern Peru with teacher trained at Yarinacocha.

One of 19 bilingual Aguaruna schools in Peru using materials prepared by members of the Summer Institute of Linguistics.

The fierce Amarakaeri tribe in the Andean foothills of southern Peru
was hostile to outsiders until 1957, when a delegation of nine painted
men clutching bows and arrows emerged from the woods to invite
translators Charles Peck and Ray Hart to live among them. Since that
time, rapid progress has been made with the language of this remote
and primitive people. A traditional tobacco-blowing
ceremony (above) is a special custom among Amarakaeri men.

The crude but sturdy dwellings of the Amarakaeri have been built according to the same pattern for generations.

An Aguaruna Indian on his first visit to the Peruvian capital dislodges sugar in his coffee cup.

Painted Colorados of western Ecuador, noted for their independence and colorful dress, stand beside a hollow log vessel used for hulling rice.

Cofan tribesman of Ecuador's Oriente Province.

Rachel Saint, translator to the savage Auca Indians of
Ecuador, appeared on the television program *This Is Your
Life* in June, 1957. Surprise feature was the visit of
Tariri, converted head-hunter of the Shapra tribe of Peru
where Rachel had previously worked. (Left to right) Ralph
Edwards, Tariri, his wife and child, Rachel Saint, and
Dayuma, converted Auca. (Chap. 25)

A Bororo Indian of Brazil wears characteristic tribal
decorations: feather headdress, face paint,
and jungle kapok on his body.

Chacobo Indians use feet as well as hands to spin kapok fiber. Gilbert and Marian Prost are making rapid progress with the language of this isolated tribe of northern Bolivia.

Chacobos wear bark cloth dresses and bright-colored feather crowns to match their gaudy pet toucans.

When the Jungle Aviation and Radio Service—JAARS—was organized in 1948 to meet Peru's urgent and growing needs Captain Montgomery, former combat flier, appeared in answer to Townsend's prayer for a superintendent of the gigantic operation. Skilled and experienced in aviation and spiritually seasoned, Montgomery immediately sensed the needs of the struggling pioneers and came to the rescue. Having served in the United States Air Force in Peru, where he trained national pilots, he was familiar with the terrain and flying hazards involved. Townsend's faith and Montgomery's know-how and vision have resulted in an amazing outfit of twenty planes and twenty-one pilots who in a decade have helped loosen the core of the hard jungle knot.

JAARS planes are based at Yarinacocha, a lake site six miles through jungle from the town of Pucallpa at the end of the trans-Andean truck road. Jungle Base Yarinacocha is the hub of the Summer Institute of Linguistics' outreach to twenty-nine jungle tribes.

This fleet of planes, ranging from a Piper Super Cub to a PBY-5A Catalina amphibian, paces Wycliffe's outreach in the Amazonian jungle. Advance into primitive areas cannot exceed the limits of JAARS operations, lifeline of jungle translators. Top-rated plane of the JAARS fleet is the Helio Courier, a five-place high performance craft "proven with exceptional short takeoff and landing capabilities, practical useful load and safe flying characteristics."

Before the production of the Helio Courier, Townsend had been praying for a plane that would cruise at varying speeds for use in jungle surveys as well as fast emergency flights, and would land on a small muddy field.

"But there *is* no such plane," one of his friends objected.

Townsend prayed on for his dream plane. One day in 1955 as he was driving through Tulsa he saw banners advertising the demonstration of a new type plane on a field just off the highway. He arrived in time to see a Helio Courier, his prayer answered to specifications, take off at a breathtakingly sharp angle.

Now seven Helios have enabled Wycliffe to press the advance in South American countries and more recently in the Philippines.

JAARS serves not only the personnel of the Summer Institute

175

of Linguistics but also others laboring in the jungle. The South American governments under which the linguists operate call upon JAARS personnel for many emergency flights or rescue missions. Missionaries of various religious organizations are also served by JAARS. Commercial enterprise is grateful for the dependable air service offered impartially to all who need aid in penetrating the formidable Amazon jungle. The executive of an oil company appreciative of JAARS service said of its planes, "They are excellently maintained and the pilots are real jungle veterans."

Careful maintenance of the planes is credited to the skill, ingenuity, and ceaseless activity of an efficient ground crew at Yarinacocha.

There is another explanation, however, for the exceptional record of the fleet that has served in the jungle for over a decade without serious injury or fatality. The personnel at the base is alerted by phone hookup when a plane is in flight over the jungle, and a volume of prayer ascends to God for its safety.

For the year ending March, 1958, JAARS planes had flown 1,652:31 hours, making 2,562 safe flights. For this record Wycliffe translators praise the God whom they serve, whose "faithfulness reacheth unto the clouds."

21. Of Planes and Piros

Esther Matteson, translator to the Piro Indians living in the isolation of the upper Urubamba River area, remembers the time before JAARS when a shipment of food sent to her by truck, launch, and canoe had taken six months to arrive, and all perishables had been dampened en route and thrown out. Later when help came by air "we were able to forget the hectic problem of transportation and spend all our time with the Indians and the work we had come to do."

Within eight years she had translated the Piro New Testament, and witnessed the complete transformation of a tribe where the gospel is now preached in twelve locations. Grateful for the help of airmen and jungle base personnel in the gigantic feat, Esther says:

"I wonder if we might not have taken twenty years instead of eight for the translation, and if we might not have failed altogether to reach the scattered communities, without the planes and radios and all the staff of supporting workers." She added that the Piro Indians pray, too, for the planes. "Keep the plane, Lord," they pray. "She's the one that brings your Word."

But in 1946 when Esther first went to the Piro tribe,* she traveled by foot and canoe. When her partner became ill and returned to the coast, she stayed on, living fourteen months in a

* The Piro story is portrayed in the Wycliffe film *White Condor* produced by Westminster Films.

sordid spot in the jungle with no radio communication or air service. She had found a desperately needy tribe of Indians, degraded by contact with the worst type of "civilization."

Mrs. Lois Schneider, who with her husband Robert were among the first Wycliffe workers in Peru, relates a conversation with Esther after her first fourteen months among the Piros:

"Do you have a comfortable house in the tribe, Esther?" Lois asked.

"No," she said with a smile, "the Indians let me have an abandoned hut that leans at a dangerous angle and the roof leaks like a sieve."

Esther reported that drunkenness and immorality prevailed, so that often there was confusion as to the paternity of the children. Even the small children thought only in immoral terms. Although she had changed informants three times, not a single folk story could be printed in a children's reader. Nor could she rescue a plot from the mountain of Piro text she had gathered.

"Esther, that can't be true," Lois countered. "We were taught that every tribe has its interesting folk legends. Perhaps you are asking for too high a standard, an unnatural standard."

"All right," she said, accepting the challenge, "I'll translate at random for you." Five minutes later Lois begged her to stop. The sordid immorality of the stories obtained from a twelve-year-old girl was indescribable.

"I'm afraid I would have come limping back long ago throwing up my hands and saying the Piros are hopeless," Lois said. But Esther's immediate reply was, "Just think how wonderful it will be when they have Christ!"

In 1947 Esther began a preliminary translation of the life of Christ for "a woman who was dying of tuberculosis, and an aged couple found sick and alone in a temporary lean-to shelter on a creek. The three obviously could not wait until the language work was far enough advanced for regular translation."

But it was difficult to tell the story of salvation when so many key words were yet unknown. Further study would be necessary. Early in 1948 Esther decided to take her informant to the jungle base in the Wycliffe plane "Amauta." It was Hortensia's first trip out of the tribe—and in a plane! Upon arriving Hortensia sent a letter home telling of the fantastic ride in the plane: "They didn't throw us out. Everyone in the plane arrived in Pucallpa." Wheels were new to her, too, so the ride in a truck from Pucallpa to Jungle Base was just as strange.

Regarding her progress in language study, Esther wrote:

"Here at Jungle Base Hortensia and I have our own little hut with floor and thatch of palm, and walls of cane. The birds and insects whose language she knows live close by us in the jungle, and help to make her feel at home. I am praying that in these two months apart with her I will somehow be able to find the necessary words to bring her to know our Lord. Many of the essential words are still lacking.

"Just yesterday I found a word which will probably translate 'peace.' The Piros have a way of expressing extremes by opposites. In a story, a huge boa constrictor had just swallowed a man, and a terrified onlooker told his friends, 'I didn't have peace.' So you see something of the way in which we hunt out the words we will need for translating."

Back in the tribe, and with greater assurance, Esther resumed the translation of a brief account of the life of Christ and a series of Bible verses explaining the way of salvation. Hishonki, the informant who had helped in this preliminary translation, was himself a first-fruit of the Word in his own language. A visitor in the tribe in February, 1949, described the effect of the first words of Scripture to be read to a group of Piros crowded into the translator's hut:

"It was a special joy to be in on the first reading of the Scriptures in Piro at Huau. Manuel and his wife Clarita and their two children had been invited and a few other children gathered around to hear. Esther sat down on the floor with the book in front of her, using an Indian lamp to read by, and they gathered around. I just sat behind in the shadows to watch the expressions on their faces. They listened intently as Esther took them through the story of the cross and the resurrection, quoting other pertinent Scripture verses, explaining along the way and then reading a list of salvation verses at the end. They were all touched, especially at the portion telling of Christ on the cross, and the women's eyes were filled with tears. This scene has been repeated over and over throughout these days in Huau."

By the first of May, 1949, fifty Piros had put their faith in

179

Christ. "And their need for the Word was so acute that regular translation of Mark was undertaken," wrote Esther.

In 1949 the Schneiders, while entertaining an official from a penal colony in the jungle, heard of an "almost unbelievable experience" he had had in the Piro area. It was his job to buy food for the colony, and in his travels he had come to know the Piros and their ways. According to him, they were about the lowest type of human life in the jungle. They never had anything to sell and very little to eat, since most of them were habitually drunk and neglected their crops and banana groves. He usually just ignored them.

But one day as he was passing the Piro village of Huau he saw something that made him stop and investigate. There were new houses, cultivated and cared-for fields, and people walking about on steady feet! Everyone was busy, and industry and happiness were in the air. He ordered his boatman to pull over to the bank. To his amazement there was a school in the village, and Piros were reading. He learned that a "Señorita Esther" had taught them, and that people in many other villages were also reading now. The Piros told him that the señorita had translated some of the Bible for them, and that she would be back soon. Like a man in a dream, the Peruvian official went to other villages up the river, and sure enough, it was just as the villagers of Huau had told him—the Piros had changed.

The Schneiders were happy to tell the amazed official that Señorita Esther Matteson was a member of their linguistic group.

"What you have seen," they said, "has been brought about by the Christ revealed in the pages of the Book she is translating."

"By April, 1950, there were over one hundred and seventy Piros living who had professed Christ. Those first three for whom the initial translation was made had died in Christ, as had a few others," wrote Esther.

Early in 1950 the Gospel of Mark was ready for publication, but even in the process of translation many Piros had found Christ—and the number was growing daily. The conversion of Chomawari, a chief of the Piros, after hearing the Word in his own language, was rewarding. Of the entrance of the Word into Chomawari's village, Esther wrote:

"The chief, Chomawari, had called in his family and friends

180

to listen with him to the story of the Lord and His cross. The chief had heard before, and his strong face showed obvious conviction and anxiety. He was given an opportunity to receive Christ, and as he bowed his head and began to pray, his wife laughed aloud with embarrassment and walked out of the room with some others. His face flushed, but his voice was firm and clear as he owned Christ as Lord before his people.

"A night or two later a crowd had gathered in an open hut, and this time the chief's wife was under such conviction it seemed she could not wait for the story to end and the invitation to be given. Remembering her embarrassment, I said, 'When the closing prayer has ended, then any who want to receive Him may come to me alone.'

"She spoke out in a loud voice before all the crowd, 'I want to receive Him.'

" 'Good. After the prayer you come to me,' I said. I began to pray, but the conviction was so strong she could not wait, but began to repeat after me the words of the prayer. Her children in loud whispers told her to wait. She stopped for a minute, but could not wait, and so began again to repeat the prayer audibly. As soon as she was saved, she wrote a chorus of praise.

"Some months later I stopped for a brief visit in Chomawari's village. When the morning of our departure arrived, instead of loading our canoe, the chief went about visiting his people and then asked me to come to the main hut. There he had summoned certain of his people, and it was quite obvious that he had told each what he was to hear. They sat down on the floor along the wall, and Chomawari said to me, 'Now give us the lesson on marriage and on sin.' It was from Mark 10:2–12, and Mark 9:43–48 ('If thy hand cause thee to sin, cut it off . . .'). It was very evident for whom this lesson was intended. The guilty pair hid their faces, and their eyes were red before the Scripture reading ended.

"Then the chief said, 'Tell us what God's Word says about keeping the seventh day, and about the law.' The chief's older brother slid out from the wall and sat up straight, acknowledging openly by nods and exclamations that this lesson was for him. I had wondered why he would not receive the Lord Jesus after hearing so much of Him. At the close, before a time of silent prayer when they were told they might receive the Lord right then, he nodded agreement, but he did not afterward confess Him. After the Scriptures on the law, the chief asked what the Bible said about drunkenness. A young man opposite began to squirm, and could hardly keep his seat during that lesson.

"Chomawari is new in the faith, but he seems to have determined to govern his village by the Word of God."

Within the next few years, several other villages had turned to Christ and their chiefs were leading them in the way of righteousness, as patterned in the Book. Piros were now wanting to read so they could see for themselves what God had to say. Suddenly there seemed to be a burst of motivation for literacy in the tribe.

With the faithful assistance of Joyce Nies, Jeanne Forrer, and Anne Shaw, bilingual teachers were trained and textbooks prepared for ten schools where today hundreds of Piros are learning to read and write. There is also an intensive program of training the Piros to evangelize their own tribe scattered throughout a broad expanse of the Urubamba jungle area.

The conversion of White Condor gave the Piro Christians a strong leader. He set the pace in living the gospel and preaching it to other Piros. He was also Esther's right arm in the translation of the New Testament. The Word of God which had brought conviction of sin to his heart was his constant guide for living.

White Condor's son-in-law Antlers acquired a fervent missionary vision simultaneous with his conversion to the gospel. As he also helped Esther in the translation of the New Testament, the desire to reach others with the Word grew. When the translation was completed in 1955, he said:

"Just now, this year, we finally have the message of Jesus. Since then I am sad because of those who live around me, those who speak other languages, those who need to hear about Jesus. They cry in their souls!"

Antlers thought, too, of his old father who had died without having heard the Word. He said:

"I think of my father who is dead. He kept searching for God's Word. He went far in his search for God's Word. This is the way he would talk when he told us about it. He said he was waiting, wanting to know God. 'Is God the sun, or a star, or a stone?' he would say. And then he told us that he went far off where there was a vine called *ayahuasca,* which was said to cause one to see God. He pressed out its juice and drank it, because he wanted to see God. That's the way he told it to us."

White Condor had a burning desire to preach the Word not only to his own tribe but to the neighboring Machiguengas whose language he also spoke. Taking with him his teen-age granddaughter Mamisha, he made the long trip upriver to Timpia. He had not expected the severe trials awaiting them. He found on his arrival among the Machiguengas that a rival group in the tribe had just killed some of the Indians, and that the adults had fled in fear. A large group of orphans became his immediate responsibility. Poverty abounded in the area.

After several months Mamisha was discouraged. She and her grandfather paddled several days downstream to ask one of the Piros to help them. At the translator's home Mamisha talked by radio with her mother who was at the jungle base. She wanted to leave the Machiguengas, she said, and go to a place where it would be safer and easier to live.

"Timpia is a place of suffering," she related sadly. "There are only children there, and food is lacking. They don't understand us, and are not receiving the Word from us, and the killer said he would go there and kill us and the babies."

Mamisha's Christian mother listened before the microphone at the base. Her eyes were red and she was choking with emotion, but she spoke clearly and firmly.

"Mamisha, suffering does not matter. Death does not matter. We'll see each other again in heaven. You ought to go back upstream. You go with your grandfather and help him with the Machiguengas. Read Romans 8, First and Second Corinthians, and Luke, and the others, and help the Machiguengas to hear it."

"Thank you, Mama," said Mamisha at the other end. "I have heard your word. I will go back with my grandfather."

183

22. Jungle Bookworms

Little Mamisha and her grandfather were not the only missionaries valiantly battling in the "place of suffering." For several years Wycliffe translators Wayne and Betty Snell had been working among the Machiguengas and steadily gaining ground for Christ as they translated His Word for a tribe once hostile to them.

Wayne Snell had come to know Christ as Savior during World War II. As a gunner's mate he served in the Pacific and traveled widely in the islands of that area. He saw what the gospel had done for many groups of native peoples "who were better Christians than I was." It was through the testimony and follow-up of Dawson Trotman's "Navigators"—a dynamic group of Christian service men—that Wayne Snell gave his life to the Lord. After hearing of Cameron Townsend and the Wycliffe Bible Translators, he subsequently decided to go to the jungles of Peru to translate the gospel that had so radically changed his life.

It was while Betty was struggling to speak the language that she learned much about the sordid, tragic lives of the Machiguenga women who were teaching her. One of the greatest conflicts in the first years was her inability to explain in Machiguenga the way of Life to some who needed it desperately—and who died before she could communicate adequately with them. Those days were later eclipsed by the joy of free expression, and fluency in pointing many to Christ. Betty in a series of short vicarious autobiographical sketches tells of what women's life was like in the days before the gospel had taken root:

"My name is Tsikeri. I am a Machiguenga woman who used to be the wife of the head man of our communal house at the Timpia. When the Gringos first came about four low waters ago, I was the first to try to teach the Señora my language. Later I began to call her my sister and my husband Victor called the Gringo his brother. But we didn't have much confidence in them then. Finally, one time when they were away at Yarinacocha I died— probably of tuberculosis. I didn't live long enough to find out just what it was the Gringos wanted to tell us when they learned our language. . . ."

"My name is Sebastiana. Victor took me as a wife, too. I was very different from my sister Tsikeri who was serious, hard-working, and almost witchlike and sinister at times. I was plump and lazy and loved to tease the Gringos. I'll never forget the time I saw my sister coming down the trail alone and I hid behind a tree and jumped out at her. I laughed and laughed because I scared her so. But I was often dreadfully unhappy and jealous of Victor's other women. I used to tell my sister that some time I would poison myself. The Señora tried to talk to me but she didn't know very much of my language yet. Finally Victor gave me to Pablo to be his wife and I was so happy—until Pablo suddenly died. I ran off and killed myself. When they found my body on the beach, the Machiguengas were afraid to bury me or to throw me in the water as they usually do so the buzzards disposed of me. Now I know what happens to people when they die. . . ."

"My name is Rosa. When I first saw the Gringos at the Timpia I was very unhappy. A white man who was the father of my baby girl was trying to take her away from me. I didn't have much confidence in these new strangers but I finally went to them for help. At least they could speak a little of my language. But then my baby died. And the Gringo even helped me bury her. Why he even dug the grave and laid her in it. Then the Señora and I began to treat each other as sisters and even went on a few excursions together. I used to tell her about the things I believed—like the sting ray that lives in the Milky Way. (Skin River is really the

185

right name for it because it's there that the immortals bathe and get their new skin.) She tried to tell me about God's Son but she didn't know quite enough of my language yet."

"My name is María. I was the Señora's little sister. How happy she was the day I received Jesus. I was the first girl at the Timpia to receive Him. We used to pray and sing together. She was thoroughly happy when Arturo, who had received Jesus at Yarina-cocha, took me for his wife. For two weeks Arturo and I lived together in the little house he had built for me. But no one knew the sadness I was hiding in my soul. Only I knew that the child that would some day be born was not Arturo's. And I was determined that he would never know. And the mother of the father of my child scolded me every day and I used to threaten to run away. I tried to pinch my child to death but I couldn't so I drank strong herbs. I only meant to throw away the child but in one day I was dying. As I lay twisting and turning on the ground, I said to my sister, 'True I will go up high?' I never heard her answer but mine was the first Christian funeral in Machiguenga land and many were the tears that were shed both for sorrow and for joy the day that I died."

Death is a menace that constantly threatens the Machiguenga and dogs his steps. Ordinary conversations will often end with the pessimistic parting words, "I'll die." It is believed that all the birds, animals, fish, snakes, and evil spirits of the jungle are dedicated to haunting the Machiguenga, and finally catching and killing him.

"At last, after a lifetime of narrow escapes, the dying Machiguenga is lying on his mat on the ground. He has rapidly become emaciated. As his fever rises higher he attempts to go bathe himself in the chilly water of the mountain stream he is near, believing that this helps him because it makes him cool again. By one means or another he gets himself back to his mat and perhaps now he is chilling. He warms a few stones in the fire and puts them at his feet. He's thirsty and asks for a little sweet *masato*, a drink made by masticating the starchy root of the sweet manioc and mixing it with water. If he is old, or has been sick for some time, or the signs indicate that death is certain, the members of the family are doubtless making every effort to starve him to hasten the end. If there is anyone who cares for him, on seeing that the patient is dying, he will begin a type of chanting, repeating a single word with each respiration of the dying man. *Nomanchaki . . . nomanchaki . . . nomanchaki . . .* hour after hour.

"Death strikes. He is then tied up in his mat and carried in a canoe to be taken for burial either in the earth or in the waters of the river itself. It becomes the duty of the nearest of kin to care for the disposal of the corpse, even if it means that a mother must bury her child alone.

"Rituals following the burial include cutting the hair of each member of the immediate family, cropping it as close to the head as possible; scalding themselves with hot water to prevent any ugly skin disease; and the gathering of bamboo or cane which will be painted with bright red figures. These same grotesque replicas of human beings will also be painted on the door posts and on the trees along the trails leading to the house, all in an effort to thwart the attempts of the deceased or the demons to bother them in the night."

After the Snells had learned the Machiguenga language and translated substantial portions of the New Testament, they faced the need for teaching an illiterate tribe to read.

Providentially timed, an educational movement propelled by the government of Peru was already beginning to affect the jungle tribes. Desirous of incorporating the unlearned and non-Spanish-speaking Indians into Peruvian culture, officials were seeking to integrate the tribesmen beyond the Andes into the life of the republic.

They chose the jungle base at Yarinacocha as the center from which a system of bilingual education would radiate to remote tribal areas. As a link in the educational chain, members of the Instituto Lingüístico de Verano speaking the indigenous languages were asked to help in the writing of primary readers and other textbooks needed.

Personnel of the Instituto already trained in pedagogy and linguistics welcomed the opportunity to serve the republic that had been their cordial host through the years.

At the Jungle Base the full-scale governmental Bilingual Training School that Cameron Townsend had envisioned for Amazonian Indians sprang to life with the aid of his wife Elaine Mielke Townsend.

Cameron and Elaine Townsend had been married in Mexico in 1946, prior to leaving for Peru with Wycliffe's first contingent of workers. Elaine was uniquely prepared for the tremendous job confronting her. Before going to Mexico to help in Indian literacy, she had occupied a highly specialized position in the Chicago school system supervising a number of schools devoted to the training of handicapped children.

Through Elaine Townsend's capable guidance primers were prepared and bilingual teachers trained for several dozen tribal schools throughout Peru's jungle area. Teachers trained at Yarinacocha and commissioned by the government of Peru are salaried through the Ministry of Education.

Bible translation and bilingual education are gradually transforming the Machiguengas into a peace-loving tribe, devoted to a life of education and obedience to the gospel. Thatched schoolhouses now dot the jungle where Machiguengas learn the three R's plus a fourth, righteousness, through the powerful written Word. Humble teachers daily hold forth the Word of Life along with the patient teaching of letters and numbers. Although books are still few, the Machiguengas are lapping up every opportunity for learning. Starved and deprived of light for centuries, they are now being satisfied by the fare of literate richness.

Clarence Hall * tells of his trip to a Machiguenga village where a converted chief had enthusiastically espoused the cause of literacy, and was energetically acting as head of the "board of education":

"The next morning before dawn I was bonged awake by someone beating on a hollow log. It was the bell announcing school's start an hour later. The Indians were already assembled outside the one-room schoolhouse; they'd been up, I found, since three-thirty.

"Chief Shironkama was herding the students, ranging from very small to near-manhood, into the building whose thatched roof was still dripping from the night's torrential rains. When they

---

* *Adventurers for God* (New York: Harper & Brothers, 1959), pp. 142–43.

were all in, the rough benches behind rude desks filled, Shironkama himself sat on the floor, leaning against the bamboo-pole wall.

"School began with a Bible reading. The lesson dealt with John the Baptist's manful defiance of Herod. As it was explained in fluent Machiguenga, I watched the chief's face. It was alight with understanding. With every point Snell made, Shironkama nodded thoughtfully, and from his throat came the murmuring assent, 'Mmm-mmm-mmm.'

"Instruction was then taken over by a young Indian named Mario, whom the Snells had carefully developed into teacher and village Christian leader. While Mario's voice droned on, the chief's sharp eyes searched the faces of the students to see if they were listening. They were—intently.

"These students, Mario told me later, wanted to have classes all day. They scorned recesses, barely taking time out to eat. At dismissal of school they gathered in small groups to compete in display of their new knowledge. I noticed one youngster, about fourteen, saunter off to the river bank, a primer under his arm. He seated himself on a log and began to read loudly. His pose was one of elaborate indifference to the kids who came to catch the performance. But, behind the lifted book, I saw his eyes dart up from the page now and then to note his erudition's effect on his awestruck audience.

"The scene was, in a way, comical; in another, strangely pathetic. I turned away, feeling not a laugh but a catch in the throat."

In another part of the Machiguenga tribe a new teacher was tackling a tough assignment. As a tribesman who had just received his teacher's diploma from the Bilingual School at Yarinacocha, Silverio was eager to teach the Indians on the Camisea River, a tributary of the upper Urubamba. He arrived at a spot on the river where a handful of Machiguengas were living in temporary shelters and where fishing was good. But the people of the hidden jungle were scared of him.

"I am not a white man," Silverio said persuasively, "but one of you. I haven't come to take you away but to live with you and help you." Praying fervently to the Lord for help, he was able to round up some of the nomads and start a school of twenty pupils whose

189

enterprising parents permitted them to attend the new house of learning. Interest in books grew and soon thirty-three eager pupils were overcrowding the temporary building with its makeshift benches and desks.

Through the help of interested Machiguenga fathers Silverio began enlarging the metropolis of education in the virgin Camisea jungle. Once fearful of intrusions from the outside, by the end of 1958 a group of more than one hundred Machiguengas in this new area had come to live in the clearing where Silverio's teaching was attracting illiterate Machiguengas from their forest hiding.

The chief of the new village is as eager to learn as the children. Unable as yet to read, he listens attentively to the Scriptures taught in his language.

It was while observing the home life of the Snells who had come to live among his people that the chief became curious about grace before meals. After Wayne explained the custom to him, the chief stated that he wanted to learn to pray.

Two days later the chief came to accept Christ as his Savior. Within a short time he brought a friend who wanted to follow Christ also. Wayne served his Machiguenga guests fish and fowl. Upon leaving the men to their meal Wayne heard the chief say to his friend, "Let's pray before we eat."

By twos and by twenties Machiguengas throughout the Urubamba area are giving thanks to God not only for their food but for the Word of God in their own tongue which satisfies a deeper hunger.

23. Transmitters

In eastern Peru bordering Brazil live the Culina Indians and their Marinahua neighbors, tribes in which Wycliffe workers live. The translators' only link with the outside world, except for an occasional trader on the river, is their scheduled radio call to the base every other day. Contact with one another has to be arranged through the base when they call in. Sometimes for months the only news to reach their anxious parents at home is relayed out of the jungle by radio.

Back at Yarinacocha, Operation Radio is supervised by John Shanks, JAARS chief radio technician. When John became a Christian at the age of twenty-one, he never dreamed the Lord would use his first love, radio. So great had been his interest in radio that he felt he must resolutely put it behind him if he were to go on with the Lord. He says his "childhood had almost not been normal because of the great absorption in the family garage 'radio shop.' I felt that this thing would stand between me and my Lord, that it would interfere with Bible study, and that it was a part of the old way of life, not to be part of this wonderful new life in Christ." But as so often happens, the Lord gave it back to him to use in His service.

During World War II, he was placed in the army signal corps because of his radio background. After basic training, he applied to go overseas as a chaplain's assistant. But after further training in radio and radar, he was shipped to the South Pacific for two and a half years in the New Hebrides Islands and in Guadalcanal and the Philippines in radio maintenance and repair. He writes:

"The Lord showed me that this training, knowledge, and talent was not a thing to be put behind as a part of the old self and life, but something which He could use to His own glory. There I saw the difficulties facing two missionary couples as they tried to service approximately forty islands, evangelizing, pastoring, teaching, and realized how much their work would have been helped and expedited if only they had the advantages of modern means of communication.

"From there on the road was clear. I knew the Lord wanted me as a radio technician on the foreign mission field. After discharge from the army came three and a half years at Moody Bible Institute, and just two months before graduation came the wonderful day when W. Cameron Townsend spoke to the South American Prayer Band. A short discussion with him revealed that our place was with the Wycliffe Bible Translators. Three years of preparation and service with Wycliffe in Mexico preceded service in Peru."

With this background and training John Shanks and his team of technicians operate a radio service at the jungle base on which translators in the tribe can depend. It has seldom been put to more dramatic use than early one morning when Eugene Scott and Kenneth Kensinger returned to their Marinahua village at the mouth of the Curanja River in the Peruvian jungle. The Indian chief with all his braves came to their hut and announced they were off on a revenge killing raid that very hour. He excitedly explained that word had arrived of their relative, Campelo's, murder by the Culina Indians downriver by their magic method of shooting a seed into a person's stomach. "For that reason we're going down to the Culina village right now and kill every Culina in the area." Scotty asked if they weren't afraid they'd kill the two white girls studying the Culina language there. They planned to be careful, the chief assured him, but they were going to kill the Culinas as there wasn't a good one in the bunch.

Scotty prayed silently. Then he had a bright idea. He suggested to the chief that they radio the linguists at the Culina village to verify the report. But the chief insisted this was no false rumor, and he with all his tribesmen were leaving to take the villagers by surprise. Finally, owing to Scotty's persistence, he agreed to wait, and the fellows cranked up their generator.

At once Wycliffe Jungle Base responded. The girls, they were told, usually called on alternate days, but it "so happened" they had asked for a special schedule that morning. At nine o'clock the girls called in and Scotty spoke to Patsy Adams as she listened on her small receiver in the Culina village.

"Why no, Campelo's very much alive," she replied. "Shall I call him to the radio?" With that she hurriedly summoned Campelo and as he talked to his tribesmen, they became convinced the murder story was false.

Plans for the revenge massacre were canceled. The Marinahua chief was so relieved that he invited the Culinas up to his village for a fiesta. A strengthening of friendly ties resulted between these two villages accustomed down through the years to inter-group wars.

Initial translation for the Culinas is now under way. Patsy, who is a nurse, also ministers to them through medical work. They come to her with varied problems.

" 'Erase this white stuff from my eyes.' Alula was talking about an infection which comes quite often in Indian villages where living and working is done so close to the soil. I put in a salve just before she went to sleep so it would have time to take effect during the night. The process was repeated for two or three more nights, and Alula was well; but by that time her baby sister, her father, her little cousin and half a dozen other Culinas had eye infections, so we found ourselves busy every night just before they slung their hammocks for sleeping.

" 'Could you give me something for these stripes on my back and side?' I choked back the tears. I had left her house only an hour earlier. They were having a wedding at which it is their custom to beat one another with a whip made from raw hide of the tapir. Unable to bear the scene I had left to go home and pray."

Brutality and violence prevail among the primitive tribes in this area. One of the first believers among the neighboring Amahuacas where Robert and Dolores Russell are located is a woman who had strangled two or three of her babies at birth. The killing

193

of newborn infants is quite customary among the Amahuacas, especially if they already have children and another one comes along while the mother is still nursing the last baby. There are few Amahuaca women who have not strangled at least one of their children, more commonly a girl. They seem to realize that killing an adult is wrong, but strangling a baby at birth does not bother them.

When an Amahuaca woman is ready to give birth, she usually goes out into the jungle alone and has the baby unassisted. Then if she decides to kill the baby, she immediately strangles it with a piece of vine tied around its neck and throws the infant out into the brush.

"They tell us quite freely of the children they have strangled," Dolores Russell says. "It is very hard to find out how many a woman has killed because they have a poor system of counting. It is based on ones and twos and anything over four becomes very cumbersome. Then they just hold up a hand. You are never quite sure how many fingers are up. And when they say, 'this whole hand,' you're never sure it is exactly five, or more or less. When our informant Shikina was telling us about strangling babies she said to her daughter standing beside her, 'I would have strangled this one also, but my mother-in-law said no.' And turning to the girl she continued with a smile, 'You know I would have strangled you but your grandmother wouldn't let me.'"

But the greatest barrier encountered is a lack of communication among the tribespeople themselves. High walls of hostility have separated families and groups for years.

"Even among friends and relatives," the Russells report, "the Amahuacas are reserved and undemonstrative. They ignore visitors for easily half an hour before they acknowledge their presence. When nearby families are visiting us and Amahuacas from another river come in, our Indians stand with their backs to the visitors with bows and arrows in hand. They might not speak at all that day or even the next day, although the two groups may be related. The enmity might date back to a time when someone in one group was supposed to have killed a person in the other group by witchcraft or by bow and arrow. Perhaps there has been revenge killing and the animosity may have lasted for years. Visitors have stayed at our house for a number of days and never said a word to the other people who live there. They will talk to us but not to their own people.

"This is a great hindrance to us in our language study. The men don't seem to think it is ever dignified to do much talking. Sometimes two men alone will laugh and joke, but if others are present they do not converse."

The Russells began learning the language with such phrases as: "What is this? What are you doing? Say it again. Speak more slowly." It was difficult to find words to express Biblical concepts foreign to Amahuaca thinking. Bob tells of the search for a satisfactory word for "forgiveness":

"In Amahuaca, if you do something against another person, even a minor offense like stepping on a person's foot, you say 'I stepped on your foot. Speak to me.' That is, prove to me we're still on speaking terms. I asked how I would ask his forgiveness if I had killed my informant's brother. The answer was, 'Speak to me.' If one Amahuaca offends another, they just don't talk. They might not speak for years and years. But if a person comes and says, 'Speak to me,' that means he wants forgiveness.

"Finally we found another word for forgiveness. During reading classes, a certain word was used for erasing the blackboard. It was an expression the people used for smoothing over dirt when marks or drawings had been made in it. It meant wiping off dust in which marks had been made, or wiping off writing on the blackboard. To wipe off the slate, to erase, to take completely away—it has a very wide meaning and applies very well to God's wiping away sins, removing them from the record, taking them away."

Macobo and Julia were among the first believers in the Amahuaca tribe. Macobo became concerned not only for the salvation of his family, but also for his former enemies.

"It was a thrill to us," says Bob, "to hear him shortly after his conversion praying for the salvation of those that just a short time before he had planned to kill. He was praying that God would save them."

Freely translated into English, passages of the Bible which are changing Amahuaca hearts sound like this:

"The sky is high above the earth. Like this God greatly loves

195

those who do not refuse Him. It is really far from where the sun comes to where it falls. Like this God has thrown our evil far away" (Ps. 103:11, 12).

"When you believe, God looses you. Without pay he looses you. It is not something you have done or are doing. It is God's gift. It is not a man's work. The man might talk big" (Eph. 2:8, 9).

As the Russells labor on problems of linguistic communication in Amahuaca, they are grateful for a dependable mechanical link with the base. They know that their teammates there, skilled in electronic communication, are prepared to cope with emergencies. Translators and radio technicians teamed with them are driving toward a common goal: the accurate transmission of an urgent message from God to jungle Indians.

24. Modern Medicine Men

Since 1950 David and Nancy Beasley have been living among the Huambisas in a north Peruvian jungle hideaway near the Morona River. It is a two-day canoe trip up a tributary stream to their settlement.

They have a novel signaling arrangement with their Indians. The JAARS plane flies upstream to the Beasleys' village, circles, and thus the Huambisas know they are to come to the mouth of the stream with dugout canoes. Then the plane returns to the banks of the Morona where there is space to land. If it is late in the afternoon, the plane stays overnight and Nancy and the four children have a cozy shelter in which to sleep. "The pilots are gracious enough," says Nancy, "to vacate the plane and sleep on the sand with Dave so we can sleep in the plane."

The next morning the family with their belongings and food supply for at least six months start off on the two-day canoe trip upstream. It is necessary to spend a night in the open, exposed to the elements and possibly animals.

Because of the loose sand on the banks of the river it is difficult to drive even temporary posts into the ground to hold up mosquito nets. One night Nancy kept fighting off some large "moths" fluttering around her baby girl sleeping beside her on the sand. In the early morning light she made an inspection and—

"I saw my baby—the most horrible sight I'd ever seen—blood all over! She was covered with blood—her hair, her face, her

197

blanket. She had rolled off the blanket into the sand which had stuck to the blood. I couldn't imagine what had happened to her until I saw that a bat had bitten her little finger and she had sucked it, and had got blood all over her face. Bat bites bleed very freely, because the bats have an anti-coagulant which they inject with the saliva. But I washed her up in the river and she was perfectly all right."

Bat bites do not usually produce serious illness, but the Beasleys, like all their fellow translators in the jungle, are grateful for radio contact with competent doctors at the base who can prescribe for the relief of more serious symptoms relayed to them. Drs. Kenneth Altig and Ralph Eichenberger assisted by Wycliffe nurses minister not only to translators but to tribesmen coming to the base for treatment. A regular schedule of clinics has also been set up in several tribes where the doctors are flown to give concentrated medical treatment.

In addition to their regular duties the modern "medicine men" have their ears tuned for emergency calls from remote jungle locations.

Another night when the Beasleys were out on the banks of the stream a rainstorm came up suddenly. Their return to the village had been delayed by the illness of little Stanley who for nearly four days ran a fever of 105 degrees. Finally, they set up the radio, which they were taking to their home in the Huambisa tribe, and talked with the doctor at the base. He prescribed regular dosages of aureomycin to be given day and night.

"We were so dead tired," said Nancy, "that we were afraid we wouldn't wake up to give Stanley his medicine and to sponge him off as the doctor had ordered. I can remember asking the Lord to *somehow* wake me up to sponge him off to keep the fever down— and He did!

"In the middle of the night the Indians woke us and told us that the rain was coming. There was nothing that we could do when the storm hit but to spread our tarpaulins over us like blankets. They didn't do much good and we got drenched. We were all soaking wet and pretty soon we couldn't tell the beach from the river. It was just like a flood. We missed Trudy Ann, and couldn't find her. We hunted frantically, fearing that she had been washed into the river. Finally, we found her at the bottom of the heap—stark naked and scared to death! Her little hands were clenched, and she was too frightened to cry.

"In the morning Stanley's temperature was down, and it never came back. He got his bath which really cooled him off!"

The early days of language learning in the tribe brought many trials of patience as the Beasleys ferreted out expressions in Huambisa by pointing to objects, or through transactions basic to living. They first compiled a short word list, mostly of things to eat—chicken, yucca, bananas. If the Indians repeated the words after them, they could see where they were off in their pronunciation.

For several years the Beasleys were not sure the Word was getting across. There was no response from the people. Then through a believer from the Shapra tribe to the south the first clear shaft of light broke through the Huambisa darkness. A number of Shapra Indians had turned to the Lord following the conversion of their head-hunting chief, Tariri. Antonio was one who had been changed by the Word translated into the Shapra language by Loretta Anderson and Doris Cox.

Antonio had married a woman from the Huambisa tribe and spoke both his own and his wife's tribal language. Once when their radio was not functioning Loretta and Doris sent Antonio to the Beasleys' station several days through the jungle with a message to be transmitted by them to the base at Yarinacocha.

"When Antonio had delivered his message," said Beasley, "I thought that he would go on home, but he lingered. After a while he said to me in Huambisa, 'Do these people know God's Word?' I thought I understood him but I asked him again, and he repeated the question. I told him no, that they didn't know God's Word. Then the happy thought struck me, would *you* like to tell them?

"We were building a new addition to our house, and there were many people around. It was a providential time. We started up the generator because we wanted to get his testimony on tape. Everybody dropped his work and came around to listen. But the chief treated the whole thing as a big joke. He was rude to Antonio. He laughed at him, and was very insulting. He made it very plain that he had no use for it. But Antonio gave his testimony and preached.

199

"We checked what we had translated—the Ten Commandments and some Bible stories—with Antonio, and found that we were pretty close. That was the first time that we were *sure* that the gospel was being preached in a way that the Huambisas could understand.

"Antonio was an Indian, and that fact, added to what we had already told them, gave force to his message. Our people knew about the conversions that had taken place among the Shapras, and how the people had changed, but now the message was really reaching them."

The Beasleys, having gained confidence that they were on the right track, played Antonio's taped message, and continued translating the life of Christ in the Huambisa language.

A few weeks before Christmas, 1955, Beasley asked Juan and Julio, the chief's sons who had been listening to a gospel explanation, if they wouldn't like to accept Christ. "We already have," was the happy reply.

Dave and Nancy Beasley looked at each other. "Can it be?" they said. "Are you sure we heard right?"

"Finally, the Lord began to convict both of us," said Nancy. "We had prayed for this. The Lord seemed to say, 'I have given you the answer and you are not believing me.' So we made up our minds that the next opportunity we had we were going to tell someone that there were two believers among the Huambisas.

"The radio schedules at the base were very full and we didn't have a chance until Christmas morning. The folks at the base gathered in the radio shack and sang carols and sent their greetings to all the folks who were in their tribes. Then they asked each of us to say something, and we told them."

After that, Huambisas began turning to the Lord "by twos" as the Beasleys would explain the Way to them. But the first believers were men and boys. There had been no sign of repentance among the women.

"Among the Huambisas," said Beasley, "the very worst sin is stinginess, or to refuse a person a request. Murder, immorality, and other sins take second place." The chief's favorite wife had come to the Beasleys with many "nameless aches and pains," wondering if there was any cure for her. "God wouldn't do anything about my aches, would He?" she said one day, testing

200

Beasley. "Look," he said boldly, "you go on refusing God, and you know what? God is going to keep on refusing you."

The next Sunday she and several other women accepted Christ, a miracle for which the Beasleys had prayed. The Huambisas believe that only the men have souls, and so at first did not entertain the possibility that the women could be saved. It was a miracle demonstrating the power of the Holy Spirit when these unlikely women—including the chief's favorite and very arrogant wife—accepted Christ.

Beasley's first informant, Yampiki, had shown no interest in the gospel. He had moved away from the settlement, and Beasley had not expected to hear from him again. One time when the Beasleys were at the base, they received a radio message from the girls at the Shapra station stating that a Huambisa Indian evidently in the last stages of tuberculosis had come to them for help. Beasley talked with the patient—who turned out to be Yampiki—and persuaded him to go to the base for treatment. Although frightened at the sight of the plane, he was flown to the base where Dr. Eichenberger treated him.

"When Yampiki was settled, I asked him if he didn't want to accept the Lord—and he was really ready. He was more ready than I thought he would be. He realized how close to death he had been. The nurse who saw him said that she had never seen anything so much like living death. He was a skeleton, and couldn't walk. After having tried all the witch doctors, he had finally gone down to the girls for help. He had three large draining holes, and through one of them you could actually see the wall of the lung. Dr. Eichenberger said that he had never seen anything like it.

"He was thoroughly faced with eternity, and had turned to us for help as a last resort. So his heart had been prepared before he showed up at the base, and it was just a matter of leading him to the Lord. And he was so changed! He was eager then to help us with the language so that we could tell him more about God. He wanted to help us with the translation. It was the difference between night and day, and since that time he has been our faithful translation helper."

Neighboring the Huambisas in the northern jungles of Peru

the Aguaruna tribe, where Titus and Florence Nickel had pioneered some years before, was also feeling a powerful gospel impact. Mildred Larson, assisted by her nurse partner Jeanne Grover, was pressing forward on translation. In addition to the work of evangelism and literacy a large medical ministry was under way. In July, 1958, Dr. Eichenberger reported a medical mission to the Aguaruna tribe:

"For several days I had been having at least one radio consultation a day with nurse-linguist Jeanne Grover out among the Aguaruna Indians with her temporary partner Lila Wistrand. On Monday morning before leaving there was an urgent schedule with them. They had been having some cases of intestinal flu in which two influential men of the tribe had already died. But over the weekend it broke out into epidemic proportions and their supply of medicines dwindled to nothing in one day. Inasmuch as we were going to be in the area conducting a Shapra clinic, would I come over and help them with some of their problem cases, and bring medicines?

"We took off at noon in the Norseman and because of the extra supplies of medicines for the Aguarunas had to throw off a drum of gasoline before the plane would take off. To make a long trip short (still four and a half hours flying), we arrived just under the margin of six o'clock at Capirona.

"It was just a half-hour hop from Capirona to Borja where we had to take on gasoline. We have our own gas dump there at the army post on the river just as it emerges from a pass in the foothills of the Andes. As always in the early morning there was a storm front rising straight up over the hills. And we took off into it to fly up the pass because we could see clear skies and sunshine through the rain in the broad valley of the Alto Marañon River on the other side. It was an hour's flight up to the far end of the valley to the Aguaruna village of Chikais.

"This is an unusual place. There are four schools here with four Aguaruna teachers and one hundred and seventy-two pupils. It is also the center for a rubber co-operative the Indians are forming as these, too, are getting away from the old trader system of economy. But it has also shown up to us and to the Indians the real problems of public health when such a congregation suddenly moves into a new area. We are going to have to work out solutions this year.

"Jeanne, knowing that we had exactly an hour and a half to spend there, had the situation well in hand and we saw only her problem cases. I wish I had had time for pictures. What a priceless collection it would have been! We saw over thirty cases of the ugly ulcers of the skin and nose of the tropical disease leishmaniasis. We had talked about these over the radio so all I had to do was a quick check to confirm the diagnosis and indicate the length of treatment for each one.

"We had brought medicines for the treatment of the intestinal flu epidemic, and there were over fifty patients treated by the girls, Jeanne and Lila, after we left.

"There is always a feeling of satisfaction in having a small part in God's great program of calling out a people unto Himself. . . ."

And Jeanne Grover wrote:

"This month will be a very busy time as we treat some thirty Indians for leishmaniasis, one of the scourges of the jungle. They need twenty to sixty injections each, depending upon the stage of the disease. Most often it attacks the tissues of the nose, causing enlargement and grotesque disfiguration. There are many more Aguarunas suffering with this disease whom we want to help spiritually as well as physically."

203

25. Auca Spears

"When the Auca spears struck out in the forest killing my own young brother and four of our friends, someone wrote to me and referred to the Aucas as 'the murderers of those missionaries.'

"I stopped and thought about it," Rachel Saint continued. "Murderers? Yes, in one sense of the word. With their spears they had kept the white man out of their territory.

"But I wondered who has the greater responsibility before God, those who are called murderers for taking life, or those who through the years have *withheld* life eternal from those who know it not? Thirty years ago the Auca tribe was open, and who went in? It was commercial enterprise. . . . Shell Oil lost at least ten men, killed by Auca spears, but they didn't stop. They went on until their search for oil was finished, then they moved out. And the Christian church did not go in—"

Not until 1956, when a down payment of five lives was made for occupation, in Christ's name, of Auca territory. . . .

In January of that year Pilot Nate Saint of the Missionary Aviation Fellowship and four other missionaries fell under Auca spears on "Palm Beach" just as their hands seemed to be on the knob of an opening door. On New Year's Day as the five men were making final plans for Operation Auca, Nate's sister Rachel was praying for the tribe her younger brother was about to enter.

But Rachel was unaware of her brother's plans. She had been working on the Auca language with Dayuma, a girl who had fled the spear-studded jungle nine years before. Some progress had been made on the language but none on occupation of the tribal area itself. Rachel had to be content to study the language on an Ecuadorian hacienda at the edge of the Auca jungle.

"Lord, I don't know what the future holds," prayed Rachel on January 1. "Reach the tribe with me or without me, but reach the tribe." And so far as she knew she was alone in the Auca enterprise.

"The next day was the last day I saw the five fellows who went down the Curaray River," Rachel recounted. "And God wrote a chapter that the world knows now. And I wasn't alone."

Sorrow over the death of her brother increased her concern for the Aucas who now seemed more unreachable than ever. For years Rachel had wanted to give the gospel to them, even while working in Peru.

"But you can't work in Ecuador," her Wycliffe friends had told her at Yarinacocha Base in 1952. "We aren't working in the tribes of Ecuador."

But before the end of the meal that day Cameron Townsend was making an announcement.

"Word has just come from Ecuador," he said, "inviting us to work in the tribes of that country."

"I knew then that the Lord was opening the way for me to work in the tribe that was 'over the border,'" and that settled it for Rachel.

But it was not until 1955 that Rachel met Dayuma on Don Carlos Sevilla's hacienda. Because of the Ecuadorian government agreement under which the Instituto Lingüístico de Verano works in his country, Don Carlos gave Rachel permission to study the Auca language. Dayuma, whom Don Carlos had protected and given employment, worked all day in the fields. Then at night before a flickering kerosene lantern she sat cross-legged on the floor and taught Rachel the Auca language. Rachel's notebooks began to fill with the queer phonetics of a language never before committed to writing. Dayuma giggled in amusement as she saw Rachel puzzling out an alphabet. She soon understood, however, and was offering ideas for new words to be written down in the notebook.

"Dayuma is an excellent language informant," wrote Rachel.

205

"If I ask her for the Auca words for moon and sun, she gives me the word also for stars! If I ask her for the name of the Napo and Curaray Rivers, she goes right on and names all the other rivers she knows. I feel like singing the doxology. She even told me a story in the language the second day."

And as Rachel learned more of her language Dayuma began to speak of her life in the jungle, of the wild animals, and the gay noisy birds, and the wild Indians—her own tribesmen—who still lived there.

"But why did you leave your home in the jungle?" Rachel asked after they had been studying a long time together.

It was a sad story, punctuated by many Auca spears.

Nine years before, Dayuma related, her father Tyaento returned from the forest one day where he had been hunting monkey. Carrying his blowgun, he came to his big thatch-roofed house in the Auca jungle. The monkey he had hit with a poisoned dart had escaped, and Tyaento was apprehensive.

"Now Moipa will spear me and I will die," he said. "I have been cursed." Moipa, the feared killer of the tribe, had already threatened to wipe out Tyaento's entire family.

The next morning at dawn Tyaento was off to the forest again. "In four days, returning, I will come," were his parting words. But by the fifth day he had not returned.

"Perhaps Moipa has speared him," thought Dayuma. "Oh, when will my father come home?" Soon a relative arrived with a message confirming her fears. "Now our father has been speared and he will die. Oh, why did they spear my father!"

The fifteen-year-old Indian girl was grief-stricken. She knew, too, the pattern of revenge in the jungle. She had seen violent death many times in her young life and she herself would not be spared.

"Now Moipa will come here. Tomorrow he will come! My father is dead, and my mother is crying. I will go to a foreigner's house. I will not stay here!" The brave young Indian girl had made her decision.

"Let's go! Hurry!" she encouraged several companions who had agreed to flee with her out of their jungle home and down the Curaray River. Dayuma led the expedition. When the others wanted to turn back she spurred them on. They traveled downstream in a canoe. Neither rain nor hunger nor even the threat that the foreigners might kill her could turn her from her purpose. Nothing, that is, until her cousin Dawa caught up with them. She had traveled by foot through the forest with her baby on her back.

Weeping, Dawa told of Moipa's attack. Both men and women had been killed with spears, and Dayuma's baby sister hacked to death with a machete.

"And my mother?" asked Dayuma.

"I do not know whether your mother Akawo is dead or alive," Dawa replied.

This was too much for Dayuma. She must know about her mother. Sadly, the Indian girl turned the party back, and for three days they poled the long distance upriver. Finally they arrived at the mouth of her own river, a branch of the Curaray.

Her sharp brown eyes searched every beach for signs of her mother. Suddenly she cried out:

"My mother's footprints! My mother is alive! She lives!"

On the sand she had seen the familiar sign. Weeping, shaking with emotion, Dayuma followed the footprints from the beach into the forest.

"Come with me, Mother," Dayuma pleaded upon finding her. "Let us go to the foreigner's house and live well. They will spear you here."

But Akawo refused to leave her jungle home. Her husband had already been killed, and hadn't the fearsome foreigners killed the Aucas, too, years before?

Dayuma set off again without her for the unknown world beyond. She was accompanied by an older cousin, Umi, and a Quichua Indian girl whom the Aucas had captured six years before.

As they poled their way down the long winding Curaray River, Umi detailed the bloody attack. Umi had been with Dayuma's father Tyaento when Moipa's spears struck.

"Your father tried to escape to the river," Umi said, "but he was badly wounded. He had been speared through the knee and he suffered much."

The wound would not heal and Tyaento burned with fever. He had no food. He was unconscious at times and groaned in agony. Finally he faced the greatest of all Auca fears, that of death without a burial. Yes, he was going to die alone in the jungle.

"Dig a hole for me," he said. "Entering it I will die. Cover me over and I will die."

Some protested, but others, fearing that his body would rot in the jungle, dug a hole. Then placing Tyaento in it, they covered him over with split bamboo and packed the hole tight with dirt.

"Later in the night we heard your father groaning," continued Umi. "We heard him moaning 'mmm-mmm' like that, and we said, 'When will he die?'

"We wondered about digging him up, but we waited until the morning, then we said, 'He will not now recover.' The next morning and the next night we heard nothing.

"I saw it," Umi concluded. "Your father is dead."

The teen-age Auca girl, sad and bitter, poled her way out of the jungle into the clearing of the foreigner's hacienda.

But nine long years of daily toil under a hot jungle sun elapsed before Rachel found the runaway Auca girl. Nine years away from her mother, and away from the dreaded spears.

Memories of her jungle home were ever-present with Dayuma. Although there were more fears and feuding than fun, she recalled for Rachel the happy experiences of her childhood. The Auca children's swings made of jungle vines were dropped from trees towering two hundred feet overhead. Four at a time the wild little Aucas, shrieking with joy and delight, would swing out over the forest.

Rachel learned that the Aucas love pets and each one has his own. One time Dayuma and her companions took a huge howler monkey, a pet in the home, and tied his front paws behind his back. Then they cut off his tail, pulled out his teeth, and tied an Auca headband of red toucan feathers around his head. They laughed with glee when he went walking off into the forest on his two hind feet, "just like an Auca." When he came to the river he dived in and swam to the other side. "Just like an Auca, he did," laughed Dayuma, "and at sunset, returning, he came." Everybody laughed with great delight—everybody except the uncle whose pet monkey it was. He wanted to know who had cut his monkey's tail!

Dayuma loved the stories her old grandfather had told from his hammock at night as the family huddled around the jungle fire. He had many tales about the god who created three Auca men and then three women and the animals. He told how scared those Aucas had been of the ugly black tapir, but the god just laughed at them!

Grandfather knew many things, and no one doubted his word. He spoke of people who dwell under the earth, people who have tongues and teeth but who have no openings for mouths.

"They cook the manioc and wild boar," the old man said, "but just sniff the fumes and throw the food away. They do not speak distinctly, but they can be understood." And he knew many of the oracles which they spoke without opening their mouths.

One of Dayuma's greatest fears was of the *winae,* the unseen little devil of the forest who, roaming around constantly, enters the jungle houses at night, grabs the Aucas and sucks their blood. Grandfather named many Aucas who had perished in this way.

As Rachel heard more and more of the Auca beliefs, and of the fears gripping their hearts, she knew that only faith in God's Word could free Dayuma. Although she laughed gaily at the funny stories of her childhood, and seemed to enjoy life at the hacienda, Dayuma was afraid. At night she feared the forest devil would come and grab her and often told Rachel she heard him wherever she was.

There was also the fear of the witch doctor who was called in when an Auca was sick. One time, Dayuma reported, a young girl lay dying and the witch doctor was summoned. He said the girl needed a new heart and that he had brought one with him. But it was not to be seen by other people for it belonged to the patient. He kept it guarded. "Just a little bit of red showed as he clasped it in his fist," Dayuma said, "and I saw it." Everyone was sent out while the young Auca girl swallowed it.

Rachel began to tell Dayuma Bible stories as soon as she had built a sufficient Auca vocabulary. She related one of a young girl who had passed through death's door before Jesus came and said, "Fear not. Believe only, and she shall be made whole." "That was the first Bible story that I was able to tell Dayuma, and it is still one of her favorites.

"I'll never forget the first Christmas when I thought, 'This year I can tell Dayuma in her own Auca language the story of the birth of Christ,' " Rachel recalls. "And so I wrote it out word for word. She listened, but when I finished telling her there seemed to be no reaction. My heart was sad. She had nothing to say, so I thought that somewhere I had failed to make God's Word clear.

"But I was overanxious. I know now that the thing that impresses her the most is the thing about which she says the least. After a long time she looked up at me and very sweetly said, 'Did all the angels sing what the first one said?' How my heart rejoiced!

"From the very first Dayuma's heart was wide open. She wanted to hear about the living God in heaven. She wanted to go to heaven but I didn't know whether she really understood what pardon was. As I tried to analyze this gap in her teaching I realized that I had not been able to find an adequate word for pardon, for it wasn't in the tribal thinking. There is an Auca word *waeti* which means 'reciprocal.' As I prayed about it the Lord put it in my mind to try to use that word to explain pardon. I was only partially successful. Then one day Dayuma told me in her own words what pardon is. She put it this way: 'We, when we did not do well, Jesus *waeti* (reciprocal, in exchange) He died for us.' "

In June, 1957, Townsend asked Rachel to take Dayuma to the United States where the television program "This Is Your Life" directed by Ralph Edwards in Hollywood, California, was to feature the life of Rachel Saint. He arranged for her to fly from Ecuador with her Auca informant. The long ride in a huge airplane was an exciting experience for an Indian girl who knew civilization only as it touched the edge of the Amazonian jungle.

But it was not until after the plane had landed in Miami, Florida, that Rachel realized how much explaining she would have to do to her Auca charge.

"Dayuma looked all around at that great airport in Miami and saw crowds of people waiting for airplanes, and coming and going, a cross section of humanity," recalls Rachel. "She looked for about ten minutes, then turned to me and said, 'Do all these people love God?'

"That made me stop and think. I wondered why the question until I realized that I had told her that in our country we had

God's Word and we wanted her people to know it. That is why we had gone to her land."

But it was hard for Rachel to explain why people who had had God's Word for a long time did not love Him.

In Hollywood, however, Dayuma saw a number of people who did love God. One of them was a jungle Indian from the Shapra tribe of Peru who had been flown up as a surprise for the program. He was Tariri, the converted head-hunter who had heard the gospel from Wycliffe translators Loretta Anderson and Doris Cox. When Rachel was working in Peru she had served one year as Loretta's partner while Doris Cox was on furlough. That was before Tariri had accepted Christ. He was the progressive chief of the tribe who protected the foreign girls and called them sisters.

After his conversion, when Tariri heard that Rachel had gone to Ecuador to take the gospel to a tribe of spear killers, he wanted to go and help her. He probably thought of the first two girls who had gone to his isolated tribe and of how some of the Shapras almost killed them.

"Let me go with Rachel," Tariri said to Loretta in the Shapra language. "Let me go to those people and say to them, 'This is my sister. She has come to give you God's Word. Don't spear her. Build a house for her and listen to her. This is my sister.' "

"But," Loretta told him, "that tribe is far away, Tariri, you couldn't go."

"Couldn't I go in one of your airplanes?"

Two girls had gone over five hundred miles in a plane to bring him God's Word.

"But that would cost too much," explained Loretta. "It would cost lots of leaves."

"Well, if I couldn't go just let me talk to them on one of your radios." Tariri knew about the miraculous connection from the Shapra tribal system to the jungle base. "Just let me talk to them," Tariri continued. "I would say, 'This is my sister. She has come to you to bring you God's Word. Don't spear her.' "

"Tariri, they don't have any radios there. And if they did have you couldn't speak to them because they have other mouths. They wouldn't understand you."

Tariri's face fell when he realized that there was no way for

211

him to communicate with the Auca people. After a moment of reflection he thought of another solution.

"Then I'll just talk to God about it. *Surely* that will be enough."

And a year later in Hollywood Tariri met a member of the spear-killing Auca tribe. But he and Dayuma couldn't communicate, except in smiles of mutual understanding, or through the Wycliffe translators who served as interpreters.

Tariri had learned to "talk to God" because the translators to his tribe had put substantial portions of Scripture into his language and had taught him many lessons from it. Dayuma had not progressed as far. She knew God had pardoned her sins through the sacrifice of Christ, but she had not learned to pray to Him. It was while Rachel and Dayuma were in Wheaton, Illinois, following the television program, that Dayuma learned about talking to God. After explaining how to pray Rachel had given her what she thought was an acceptable sample prayer, in Auca.

"But we don't talk like that in our language," Dayuma protested. Rachel, thinking that she had made some grammatical errors, invited Dayuma to correct her. "But we don't talk to God in our language," explained Dayuma.

Rachel then told her that God, her heavenly Father, could understand Auca as He did other languages. She encouraged Dayuma to talk to Him.

"Then came the day," says Rachel, "out there in Wheaton when she prayed what may have been the first prayer ever prayed in the Auca language. My heart rejoiced! Since that day she has gone on praying, not stilted prayers but prayers from her heart to her heavenly Father.

"Though at first Dayuma had no interest in returning to Auca territory, she began to see her responsibility to her people, but had no idea where her family lived—or if they lived. We prayed together about it. The movies brought back from 'Palm Beach,' showing her aunt, Mintaka, gave her the first hope that some of her family had survived the spearing."

Dayuma was still in the United States when her relatives Mintaka and Maengamo came out of the jungle and took refuge with Quichua Indians living on the Oglán River at the edge of Auca territory. Mrs. Elisabeth Elliot, widow of one of the five men who passed "through gates of splendor" in an effort to give the Aucas the message of Christ, began an intensive study of the Auca language with Mintaka and Maengamo. Soon recorded tapes were sent to Dayuma in the United States. It was through an exchange of tapes that Dayuma discovered the two women were her aunts who had recently come from her own family group in the jungle.

"I am Dayuma, and Tyaento was my father," explained Dayuma on an answering tape. At that time she was living at the Wycliffe Home in Sulphur Springs, Arkansas. Dayuma tried also to describe her present location. "Now I am living here with another who is like a relative. Here, far away, big-water-other-side I live. Later, returning, I will come."

Dayuma had wondered for many years about her mother, and her favorite brother, and her other relatives in the fierce jungle. "Does my mother live?" she asked the tape anxiously. "Did they spear her? I don't know."

Back came the recorded tapes from Ecuador with up-to-date information. By this time her family had been considerably thinned out by enemy spears. Her favorite brother to whose house she had hoped to go to tell her people God's Word had been spear-killed long ago, along with several uncles and other members of her family. But her mother was still living!

News of the death of her brother was a heavy blow for Dayuma. "I loved him very much," she said. "He always brought me meat. We worked and played together in the forest."

"Days later the smoldering fires of resentment burned," wrote Rachel of those trying days through which Dayuma was passing. She had been plunged back into the hates and fears of her tribe.

One day when anger and resentment reached a high pitch Rachel reminded Dayuma that God's Word says not to let the sun go down upon your wrath—"and it was just about to go down!" Finally, at the close of the day, "she decided on God's way, as she often does these days, and said, 'Not being mad, I will sleep.' "

"I used to say that I was worn out from not understanding the language," Rachel wrote, "but frankly, it wears me out more to understand it. The picture of the Aucas is one of gross darkness."

In her despondency and resentment Dayuma had said that she wouldn't go back to the killers of the jungle. She had wanted to go and give her people God's Word, but now she was bitter. "I will not return," she had said.

This was serious. It seemed that Dayuma, the one member of the tribe who knew God's Word, was surely the chosen vessel to take the light of the gospel into the Bibleless jungle. What if she wouldn't go?

Rachel thought, and prayed. Then one day she said quietly:

"Dayuma, what if the Lord Jesus had said, 'I won't go to those horrible people down there on earth. They are too wicked and sinful. I will stay here in heaven with my holy Father. I will not go down to earth, to that place where people do only evil things.' What would have become of us if the Lord Jesus had said that?"

Dayuma made no comment. Several days passed. Then one day she said to Rachel:

"When are we going back to my land? I want to tell my people about God."

By February, 1958, Dayuma's desire to return to her people was growing. A visitor at the Wycliffe Home in Arkansas was impressed by a long prayer in Auca when Dayuma had been asked to say grace at a simple repast of toast and tea. Rachel then explained to the puzzled visitor that it was more than asking blessing for the food. Dayuma was taking every opportunity to pray by name for her kin in the jungle, beseeching the living God that they should soon hear of Him.

Within a few months Rachel and Dayuma were winging their way back to the edge of the Auca jungle where Wycliffe's new Dawson Trotman Memorial Base, Limoncocha, was waiting to welcome them. Dayuma's joy was complete when she saw face to face the aunts with whom she had been communicating on recorded tapes.

"The God our grandfather used to tell us about—I know Him now!" was one of Dayuma's first greetings. For hours she told them about what she had learned of Him since leaving the jungle years ago.

By the quiet shores of Limoncocha Dayuma "taught them in the Auca language the stories of the living God which I had been able to teach her in those months apart at Sulphur Springs last winter," wrote Rachel.

By early September Dayuma and her two aunts were making

plans to return to the jungle home. Dayuma's mother had commissioned her aunts to bring her home if they found her. Most of the Aucas believed her killed by the foreigners, but her mother had not lost hope. Should Rachel and Betty Elliot accompany the women into the jungle?

"They themselves ruled out the possibility of either of us going in at this time," wrote Rachel on September 2. "Dayuma, after a series of deep emotional reactions, felt strongly that she should accompany her aunts. She has a deep desire to teach her people God's Word, to see her family again, and to try to bring harmony within the tribe and with the outside world.

"With God's blessing all three may soon be back again in what is left of the village where Nate started making gift drops . . .

"Before they left, both Mintaka and Maengamo had begun to pray to God in heaven, as Dayuma had taught them. Shall we not take this as a cloud the size of a man's hand and trust for the showers to come?"

In the days that followed the Missionary Aviation Fellowship plane unsuccessfully searched for signs of the three women who had gone into the tribe. By September 25 the worst was feared. But on that day Dayuma, leading a party of Auca women and children, came out of the jungle at Arajuno singing "Jesus loves me!" Commenting on the reason for their return, Dayuma said:

"The planes didn't see us and I thought you would think we were dead. Besides, I didn't have any soap to wash my clothes!"

Dayuma along with Mintaka and Maengamo brought an invitation from her people for Rachel and Betty to go back with her. They agreed to do so, and early in October entered Auca territory, on foot, accompanied by Dayuma and a small band of Aucas.

On October 27 Rachel wrote to friends at home:

"It is my joy to greet you from this pretty little jungle clearing dotted with Auca thatched huts beside the Tiwaeno River, a spot the Lord led Dayuma to when she returned home after twelve years. We have been here almost three weeks now and rejoice at the apparent friendliness of all Dayuma's related family group.

" 'Not understanding we killed your men,' they say, and some add, 'Now we will hear about God.' Every Sunday Dayuma gathers the whole group together under one of the thatched roofs (most of them in their birthday clothes!), instructs them not to laugh,

215

and teaches them little by little about God, the Creator, and His Son, Jesus."

As if they had heard the words Tariri wanted to speak to them, the Aucas have built a house for those who entered the tribe with the Word of God. And the Aucas are hearing that Word, in their own language.

On entering the tribe Rachel wrote to her parents on October 9:

"It surely was a sweet picture to me to round the bend in the river, and see the buff roofs of the little thatched houses, and the lovely bronze bodies of the Aucas gleaming in the sun. To be able to communicate was wonderful.

"Kimo proudly showed me the house well under construction and said, 'All alone I built it.' Dayuma's mother and the rest had gone back to 'Terminal City' * for the necessary food, and this morning Kimo set off for the day over rough trail to tell the others that Dayuma is back, with the foreigners.

"It seems the most natural thing in the world to me to be here, a thing I have felt the Lord was leading me to over five years ago."

---

* The Auca settlement where gift-drops were made by the five missionaries killed on "Palm Beach." For the full story of this contact with the tribe, see *Through Gates of Splendor* by Elisabeth Elliot (New York: Harper & Brothers, 1957).

26. Home Base on the Equator

Less than an hour by air from the Auca clearing is Rachel
Saint's other home in Ecuador, the Dawson Trotman Memorial
Base. Overlooking Lake Limoncocha, the placid body of water
shaped like an arrowhead, are a number of rustic buildings beside
a neat airstrip cut from the thick growth. Like Yarinacocha, the
Ecuador base is located strategically to serve translators in their
tribal locations. Donald and Helen Johnson who pioneered in the
construction of the base have made it a haven for translators needing a break from tribal work, for Ecuadorian government officials,
and for other visitors. It is far enough out, one hour by air from
Shell Mera, to be close to the tribes to be reached, convenient for
Indians to be brought in for school, and for informant and translation work.

Limoncocha is the home base of the JAARS operation in Ecuador. From here planes take off to other isolated areas to provide
transportation to patients needing medical help. One such passenger was the bishop of the Salesian Order, a kindly old gentleman
whose eighty years made difficult a trek over the trail.

The lake is long enough for the Catalina from Peru to land, and
the airstrip is being enlarged to accommodate the Ecuadorian
government's aircraft.

At the invitation of the Ministry of Education relayed through
the embassy in Washington, the first group of translators headed

217

by Robert G. Schneider had flown from Peru in 1953 and set up headquarters in Quito, Ecuador.

Prior to Wycliffe's entrance into Ecuador other missions had already made appreciable progress among several Indian tribes. The Missionary Aviation Fellowship operating out of Shell Mera has served missionaries in the Oriente for more than a decade.

Twenty-five minutes by air from Limoncocha live Orville and Mary Johnson in a Secoyah Indian village.

"We had lived in the tribe almost two months before getting an insight into their beliefs," said Johnson. "This came when I unknowingly violated one of their beliefs. We were constructing the airstrip and one evening after work one of the Indians came and said he wanted me to kill a jaguar. I went with him about a mile downstream. We could hear it roaring over on the bank in the woods. It was a large one and the Indian was afraid to go up on the bank. So he started calling it. About twenty minutes later the jaguar came out on the bank and I shot it. The first shot killed it, but the Indian wanted me to shoot it again.

"I found out later the jaguar is supposed to have two beings, that of the jaguar itself and the other that of a person. According to them, I had killed a person. Not knowing their beliefs any better, I wanted the hide and tried to get the Indian to help get the jaguar into the canoe. He wouldn't help. When we got back to the house, the whole tribe had gathered to see the jaguar, but not one of them would help get it out. Next morning a woman with a newborn baby came to see Mary and said, 'Everyone says my baby will die because your husband touched the jaguar.' Even though the baby didn't die, they hold to their beliefs. They explained that if I had been an Indian, the baby would have died!"

The head of the Secoyah religious system is the witch doctor who through a drink, *yahe,* related to marihuana, sees visions. When hunting is poor the witch doctor calls the people together to drink *yahe* and thus bring the game closer. In the case of sickness *yahe* wins the favor and support of very strong demons living in the heavens. The same root occurs in words for diseases and that for witch doctor. In one illness that nearly caused the death of the chief, the Secoyahs said the demons were actually eating him.

"When the Indians drink *yahe,* they see things that would scare the authors of horror stories," according to the Johnsons. "One of the worst is a gigantic snake with a forked tail, large enough to swallow a person, which lives in the rivers where there are whirlpools. They tell of how it will come up and tip a canoe over, and the riders are never seen again. Another common idea is that when a witch doctor has a child by his wife, at the same time a jaguar gives birth to an offspring which is considered to be the child of the witch doctor."

The Johnsons look forward to the day when the Secoyahs will be set free from the power of the witch doctor and *yahe,* and will come to exchange the reign of fear for the reign of love and freedom in Christ.

Through the translated Word of God primitive Ecuadorian tribes such as the Aucas and the Secoyahs are at last hearing of a Savior powerful to free them from Satan's clutch.

27. Hitch Your Airplane to a Treetop

"On a recent flight to the Chacobo Indians of Bolivia," wrote Pilot Baughman, "we found that the water of the Beni River had risen to treetop level. Normally, the village is about a forty-minute walk from the river. On this flight I merely tied the airplane to a treetop near the village and waited for the Indians to come with a canoe.

"They soon arrived, and a quick survey revealed that these particular Indians do not specialize in making canoes. They choose a tree with a thick bark which they split, then slip it off. Sticks hold the bark open, making it look something like a canoe. The open ends are then packed with dirt to prevent the water from coming in.

"Well, we made it to shore after having rammed several trees and nearly dislodging the dirt. I might add that it was comforting to think back on the day I learned to swim. The trip back was uneventful. So ended another routine flight."

But life in the jungle is in no sense "routine" for Wycliffe's Bolivian Branch members. Airmen, radio men, translators, and teachers all share in the daily thrill of life composed predominantly of the unexpected.

Life for the jungle inhabitants of Bolivia has not been the same since the advent of the translators. The people of the town of Ivón on the banks of the Beni River well remember one afternoon in June, 1955. In the words of Leon and Betty Schanely, members of the Bolivian advance, the amazed spectators "raced to the river bank to watch the sad fate of the big airplane as it glided down close to the muddy water. But it did not sink as they expected. Instead, its motors roared, bringing it close to the shore where they stood. In wonder they watched as the four men of the crew climbed out, followed by fifteen adults, ten children, and three tons of cargo.

"They have been very friendly, providing housing, helping us move our supplies, bringing us food, doing our laundry, and many other kind and helpful acts. Ivón is about fifteen miles upriver from Riberalta, the central town for this district and our mail town. We were to live in Ivón until the jungle could be cleared and some houses built on the shore of a lake three miles from here."

Within record time, dense jungle growth was chopped down on beautiful Lake Tumi Chucha, "Palm Island," and a temporary house of palm-thatch roof and palm-leaf walls was ready for occupation. Soon a colorful caravan of oxcarts, piled high with foreign belongings and children of all shapes and sizes, was weaving its way over the dry road a short three miles through palmy jungle to the new base. By August the group of pioneers were set up for work in the jungle, happy to have beaten the rains. The oxcart road would soon be knee-deep with mud, making the moving of men and material more difficult.

While one team of workers was busy constructing temporary shelters on the lake shore another team scanned the jungle by plane and foot, surveying the Indian tribes to be occupied. After the Chacobo tribe had been located, Gilbert and Marian Prost packed their duffels in preparation for living with the tribe and learning the language. Two other tribes had been contacted, and possibilities of translator teams for them were being discussed at night under the palm roof.

Efficiently marshaling the forces of his team was energetic Harold Key, a former United States Army major, who had had eight years of varied experience in Mexico, principally in a tribe of Aztec Indians. He and his wife Mary had translated a substantial amount of Scripture for the tribe, in addition to making numerous dictionaries, primers, and textbooks.

Since August, 1954, when President Paz Estenssoro and Cameron Townsend had signed a contract calling for the rapid occupation of Bolivia's needy tribes, plans for working in the country had developed quickly. Who should lead the work there? Harold Key was in Mexico City when his name was suggested. It was a big order—and he wanted to stay with the Aztecs—but he was willing to go to Bolivia.

Before hearing of the proposed uprooting Mary had written Harold that she had had some serious dealings with the Lord of late. "In fact," she wrote, "I'd even be willing to pack up and move if that were the Lord's will." Her attitude was a perfect preparation for the news Harold brought back to the Aztec village where Mary was waiting with the three little Keys.

The date for departure from Mexico toward Bolivia was set—December 10, 1954. The Keys had paid two years' rent in advance for their house in the Aztec village. "We'd better check on the rent," said Harold, as he rummaged among the stacks of stored papers to find the receipt for the rent last paid. There it was, signed by his Indian landlord. The rent was paid to December 10, 1954! Harold treasures the paper as concrete confirmation of the Lords' perfect timing for them, and for Wycliffe in Bolivia.

Every step forward in Bolivia has been marked by blessing, although sometimes accompanied by deep trial and searching of heart by those seeking neglected elusive Indians in the wild back country where until now only rubber hunters and a few white men have ventured. When the twin-engine Catalina belonging to the Peruvian Branch carried the first contingent of Bolivian workers over the border to Riberalta, on the Beni River, it was truly a venture of faith. Donald and Mabel Van Wynen, who were also among the first settlers in the work there, wrote:

"This coming Monday, the 6th of June, we hope to land at Riberalta, Bolivia, which is in the northeast corner of Bolivia, near the junction of Peru, Brazil, and Bolivia. We have no permanent mailing address there as yet, but all of our mail will be forwarded from Peru."

When the pilgrims set foot on foreign soil they found that the Lord had gone before them. Key wrote:

"Some of you prayed for good government relations and the Lord has answered. A Bolivian cabinet officer welcomed our group into the country, giving us official introduction to municipal and department heads and providing us with every courtesy. On several occasions it was publicly mentioned that our job was to study the Indian languages and to translate the Word of God for them. The jungle area military commander put a river launch at our disposal and provided soldiers to help start clearing a limited jungle area as a beginning for a jungle base."

When construction on the base began the same providential care was evident.

"We needed some seasoned lumber for house-building," Key wrote. "In the nearby town there are four sawmills, and a year ago someone ordered quite a bit of lumber for flooring and had never picked up his order. The saw mill was glad to sell this to us. Other lumber is available as the need arises and as funds are available. Such are samples of the hourly care of our Father in response to your praying, as we make plans to deliver His Word into the languages of these jungle-dwelling peoples."

By August, 1955, Gilbert and Marian Prost were settled among the Chacobos where they were writing down words spoken by amused Indians. Friendly contacts with this tribe had been miraculously ordered of the Lord, for previous experiences with civilization had been tragically cruel. One white man had only recently asserted his authority by deliberately drowning a Chacobo before the eyes of his fellow tribesmen. They fled to find refuge in the jungle. But God prepared their hearts to trust and to welcome the Prosts into their midst.

From its inception the work in Bolivia has been necessarily dependent upon aircraft. Deep in the Amazon basin, isolated geographically from the rest of Bolivia which perches loftily on the great plateau averaging twelve thousand feet in elevation, the Indians of the jungle form a separate ethnic entity. Although constituting only one fourth of Bolivia's population, they are scattered through jungle lowlands representing seventy per cent of Bolivia's terrain. Several evangelical missions are working in jungle areas, but until recently few missionaries have devoted their efforts to the task of learning the dialects and translating the Scriptures. Spanish has proved to be an inadequate medium for reaching these primitive tribes, who still speak their own languages.

To meet the demands of the rugged terrain three planes have been provided for use in Bolivia. In June, 1956, in a unique

223

ceremony at the University of Oklahoma a Helio Courier, ideally suited for Bolivian needs, was given by friends interested in furthering the Indian work in that South American republic.

On the Oklahoma campus where the summer sun beat down in all its fury the United States Navy band played vigorously to welcome Bolivia's distinguished Ambassador Victor Andrade to the outdoor platform. A nineteen-gun salute honored the official representative of the government that was to receive the high-performance plane now gleaming in the sun a few feet from the speakers' platform. After an address by Dr. George Cross, president of the university, the plane was christened with a cruse of crude oil "Friendship of Oklahoma" and soon was on its way to serve linguist-translators in the palmy wilds of Bolivia. Most of the Wycliffe members located by that time either at the base or at tribal stations on the Beni River had studied linguistics at the University of Oklahoma, and were doubly grateful for this gift.

Parts and supplies for the planes in service had to be shipped from Glendale, California, where trained JAARS personnel answered requests from the field. Once, after long waiting, a shipment of much-needed materials from California finally arrived at the river town of Riberalta. Arrangements were made to transport it on a launch up to the base. But days later the shipment still had not reached its destination, so a reconnaissance flight was made in the Aeronca plane looking for signs of a sunken boat. Sure enough, just seven minutes by air the searching party spotted what looked like some crates stacked up on a sandbar. They reported:

"We landed and found that they had salvaged every bit of our shipment and dragged it up to dry ground. Everything was good and wet and pretty well covered with rust, but there was very little loss. We spent several days tearing down and cleaning out sand from a couple of tribal generators and motors, and sorting out nuts, bolts, washers, etc., but we do rejoice that those things are here and not down at the bottom of the Beni River."

Early in 1955 the Van Wynens had located an amiable group of nomadic Tacana Indians on the Beni River, and made contacts and preparation for translation work among them. As they were making plans to move in, however, their three-year-old daughter Ruthie was taken ill. In spite of the care of her mother who was a trained nurse, she became steadily worse. In August she was taken to a Catholic hospital in Riberalta, but still she did not respond to treatment. "Finally, it was decided to fly her to La Paz, the capital of the country, where X-ray was available. Four hours after arriving, she passed away. The doctor there diagnosed her ailment as an intestinal obstruction, the same that she had been miraculously delivered from over two years before in Mexico.

"Through it all we've found God's promises sure and steadfast. God did some marvelous things for us which were strong reminders of His presence with us. We had never been to La Paz before and as we approached the city we asked the pilot to radio ahead for a cab to be ready to take us to the hospital. Instead, we found a United States Army captain ready to take us in his personal station wagon.

"We also had the services of a Bolivian man from the captain's office who knew the town well and also spoke English. Thus all arrangements for the funeral were made, smoothed out before us by the Lord's hand.

"We thought we would be quite alone in this large city, but remembered that two group members had just left Lima to join our work here in Bolivia. We remembered the name of the hotel where they were expected to stay, and that night we located them. They were with us all the time in La Paz, and one of them sang at the funeral."

Through their tears the Van Wynens rejoiced that "a big victory had been won while we were gone," for the Chacobo tribe had actually been entered, and language work begun. Perry Priest and Gil Prost, surveying the tribe preparatory to the Prosts' work there, had already made an initial contact, as reported by Perry:

"When the Indians saw Gil and me, they ran into the jungle fearfully to hide. But can you blame them? In a previous contact with a 'civilized' man, the man had openly murdered one of the Indians. After the murder, they had gone farther into the thick jungle, and we had located them from the air, gone upriver by canoe, and inland by foot. And now they were running away. But our God was with us, and as we spoke the few Chacobo words we knew—'friend,' 'hello,' etc.—they began to come toward us,

225

afraid but friendly. They allowed us to stay in the village, so we spent all last week with them hunting, fishing, and learning a few words of their language.

"May I tell you a bit about these primitive Chacobo Indians? They wear bark cloth for clothes, red feathers through their noses, animal teeth through their ears, and hunt and fish with bow and arrow. While we were there they killed wild pig, monkey, and other animals. They killed enough fish in just a few minutes to last all day. I went fishing with the old chief, and he'd shoot into the water where I couldn't see a thing and pull out a beautiful fish."

The first months of living among the Chacobos were devoted to the tedious job of learning some of the language and committing it to paper. The Prosts observed the customs of the Indians and one experience especially spurred them on in their desire to learn the language to communicate the gospel adequately:

"One dark night we accompanied our Indians down the twisted jungle path by the light of brightly burning torches to witness a strange tribal custom. When we arrived at our destination there was stretched before us a huge animal called an *anta*. It resembles a pig about five feet long and three feet high. One of the men had just killed it. As we witnessed the butchering, we were taken by surprise when two of the Indians began to wash their bodies with the blood of it and stood before us, crimson and shining. As the rite was being performed, we whispered to one of the nearby Indian women, 'Why are they doing this?' We understood her reply to be that both of these Indians were sick and that by washing in this blood they would be healed. We tried to explain to them that this would not make them well, and that we had medicines for their sickness, but they did not seem to understand us."

By March, 1958, the Prosts had made good progress. They brought their informant to the base on "Palm Island," a rich experience for both the Chacobo and the Americans at the base, as reported by Director Key:

"The Prosts brought one of their Indians to the base so they would have some time to concentrate on the language and get help on the linguistic problems. This visitor is a fine gentleman. He

226

moves with quiet dignity and poise. He wears bright red feathers in his nose and animal teeth through his ear lobes. And with these he wears a warm smile—and a few more clothes than in his jungle home. Our children, although not being able to speak his language, take him gifts of sugar cane, and he graciously presents gifts of fish he has shot in the lake with his bow and arrow."

By December, 1958, the Prosts reported a welcome question from one Chacobo: "Why should a Man come to die on a cross?" The Indian had heard the gospel through a chorus Gil had written in the Chacobo language. He understood the words but could not fathom their meaning. But the man showed great interest in the song, and was quick to learn it. He asked Gil to tell him more about "this Jesus." Gil could not have dreamed of a better Christmas gift; this interest in the gospel had been his heart's prayer.

In their study of the Chacobo language the Prosts had been helped considerably by a Wycliffe linguist from Peru. Olive Shell had analyzed a related language, the Cashibo dialect, belonging to the Pano language family. Of Olive's visit the Keys wrote:

"Up to this time Gil and Marian Prost had worked entirely with a monolingual approach, which means that every word they were able to get was with sign language or acting out some scene and guessing at the meanings of their growing vocabulary. This technique is possible, but is slow and tedious and costs many months of laborious effort. Now Olive had come to help them and to give them a push equivalent to many weeks or months of difficult guesswork in getting meanings and understanding the system of this aboriginal grammar."

Thus do Wycliffe's linguistic consultants in various countries as well as at the Summer Institute of Linguistics at the University of Oklahoma speed their younger colleagues on their way by sharing results of their investigation.

In other parts of the Bolivian jungle, tribes were being occupied and Indians were hearing the story of Christ. At the 1958 conference of Wycliffe members at the Bolivian base thrilling reports were given of progress in almost a dozen tribes where language work had actually begun, or where friendly contacts had been made.

Perry and Anne Priest were able by May, 1958, to explain

227

the rudiments of the gospel to their Siriono Indians who listened in wide-eyed wonder.

"No mosquitoes in heaven?" they asked as Anne Priest explained the way to heaven, and cleansing through the blood of Christ. "Is there no mud there?" continued the Indians, pursuing the subject with interest. "No, no mud," the answer came. "Beautiful!" exclaimed the Sirionos, who work and hunt through the rainy season in deep mud, so that their feet crack open and cause much suffering.

"We took a trip upriver and spent the night with some of the Indians," wrote Perry Priest. "For supper they gave us yucca and turtle liver. There must have been about thirty-five of us, plus chickens and dogs, who slept under that one thatched roof, our only privacy being our mosquito net. We had a little service with them out in the moonlight, sitting on logs and baskets of corn."

On Bolivia's high, cold, and barren plateau where Aymara Indians and llamas roam, the Summer Institute of Linguistics also has workers who are co-operating with the government and with missions that for years have been faithfully laboring with the largest tribe in the country. Although the Aymara Indians have the whole New Testament translated into their language, few can read it. Translators Alan and Iris Wares, aided by other Wycliffe workers, have prepared primers and are collaborating with the Christian Literacy Mission in its gigantic task of teaching thousands of wandering Aymaras to read and understand the Word.

Mary Grantham related some of the contortions involved in learning the Aymara language:

"I've run into a weird phonetic combination. Most of the people like my backed 'k' just fine. It's the back of the tongue kicking the roof of the mouth at the place where you gargle. The schoolteacher's helper was here the other day, and he didn't like my 'k.' I would start making a 'k' further front in my mouth and back it up. Then when I got to the strangling point he would shout, 'There! That's it!' "

A Canadian schoolteacher, Marion Heaslip, has been spending some time at the base helping the missionaries' children learn to read and write English, as well as imparting some fundamental knowledge of the history and geography of the "foreign" lands in which they were born. Three of her charges are the Key children. Of them Harold wrote:

"Mary Helen, our gentle, ladylike little daughter, collects fungus plants from the jungle. Hayden studies snakes and alligators and wants to be a Cub Scout. Tommy sneaks up on insects and collects them in bottles, boxes, and his pockets, and calls them 'my friends.'

"The other night we heard a firm discussion going on in the corner where our small sons sleep. Tommy wanted to bring a 'friend' to bed with him and Hayden refused to sleep with it even if it was just a small frog carefully wrapped so it wouldn't get 'squashed.'

"The children are collecting more items for a museum, such as claws of anteaters and porcupine, alligator teeth and giant land snail shells. Incidentally, they are learning to read, too."

Marion, according to the parents of the children whom she teaches, is a true "lover-of-children." And she loves her job in the jungle. She delights in the place of service God has given her as a link in a long chain that is drawing Indians to Jesus Christ.

One Christmas she wrote from "Palm Island" where she was giving her pupils a notion of the holiday season in other lands:

"We have just finished reading a book at school called *Treasures of the Snow*. It is a delightful book about Switzerland and the 'treasures' were the hearts of children who were changed by the gospel. Since reading it, I have been thinking about the 'Treasures of the Jungle.'

"Not all treasures appear to be so on the surface. We found one recently while on a hike down a trail looking for pottery clay. It was not something you could put your finger on and say, 'This is it!' It was rather a feeling of deep gratitude and quiet peace. The Lord was good. We had found Him so. It made me appreciate more this beautiful land in which we live. We did see things of real value that day.

"There were the tall straight rubber trees with the tin cups to catch the dripping milk, and the giant kapok trees that give us the soft silky cotton used to stuff pillows. There were the palm trees which provide roofs for our houses and the big Brazil nut

229

trees we all appreciate so much. Out of reach were dozens of beautifully colored butterflies and down low were the monkey vines that the children love to swing on.

"Then in my mind's eye I could see treasure of eternal value. Brown-skinned dark-eyed treasures with only bark cloth for covering and feathers for decoration. Hidden away in swampy jungles, they wait for peace which does not come. The message of salvation will go winging around the world this Christmas time, but for these there is no word of hope, for there is no Word."

28. ". . . Tongues, They Shall Cease"

Since 1900, an estimated seventy Indian tribes of Brazil have become extinct.

Seventy small nations have perished without hearing one phrase of Scripture in their own tongues.

When Wycliffe leaders heard this news they were alarmed. They were reminded of the divine word in Proverbs, "If thou forbear to deliver them that are drawn unto death, and those that are ready to be slain; if thou sayest, Behold, we knew it not"— but now they knew it. What of the other tribes similarly "ready to be slain"? How many remained without a witness from the Word to be preached to *every creature?*

According to figures released in 1950 by the government of Brazil, one hundred and eighty-six tribes still roamed the vast Amazon jungle. The government was concerned for the welfare of these uncivilized Indians within its borders. Anthropologically and linguistically, the disappearance of seventy tribes was a loss, but spiritually, it was a tragedy. Those who had been burdened for the tribes of all Amazonia prayed that this tragedy not be allowed to continue.

Wycliffe was not the first organization to be concerned for the evangelization of South America. More than a century earlier, the first missionaries had laid down their lives for the sake of the gospel. It was in September, 1851, that the British Captain Allen

231

Gardiner and his valiant companions starved to death in Spanish Harbor, Tierra del Fuego, while waiting for promised food and other supplies.

Such a tragedy naturally awakened the church both in England and in the United States, and from that time on efforts were increased to evangelize the continent. Into this great morass went many brave warriors of the cross. They fought courageously, but the history of missions reveals that lasting results have been limited.

As early as 1872 the South American Missionary Society occupied Santarem, and in 1880 a launch was obtained for an effort among the Ipuriná Indians of the Purús River in western Brazil. After the drowning of a worker in the first instance, and the expenditure of ten thousand pounds in ten years in the second, both these undertakings were abandoned.

In the middle twenties the South American Indian Mission made a number of exploratory trips into the interior of Brazil, with a view to starting work in that section of the Amazon basin. On two of these trips one member of the party was L. L. Legters, field secretary of the Pioneer Mission Agency, and later a cofounder of the Wycliffe Bible Translators. One notable attempt to reach the tribes within the basin itself was that of Mr. and Mrs. Arthur Tylee among the Nambiquara Indians. The work of the Tylees was terminated abruptly after six years of labor by the massacre of Arthur Tylee, nurse Mildred Kratz, and other coworkers.

When Dale and Harriet Kietzman led Wycliffe's advance into Brazil in 1956 they wrote at the outset:

"We are not alone in the work among Indian tribes. Other missions have been on the field for a number of years and are going ahead with plans for expansion into new tribes. The Unevangelized Fields Mission, with Neill Hawkins as field superintendent for Indian work, has been granted permission to enter a large number of tribes in northeastern Brazil, in the territory of Rio Branco. New Tribes Mission has occupied seven tribes scattered throughout Brazil. The South American Indian Mission has a number of mission stations in central Mato Grosso, an area with many tribes."

And still there was room. "With one hundred and eighty-six

living tribes," Kietzman wrote, "Brazil represents a tremendous challenge. A great many workers will be needed before the last of these tribes can be occupied. We trust that the Lord will lay the burden of this country on many of the students who may be planning soon to attend the Summer Institute of Linguistics."

By January, 1959, translators had settled in twelve of the one hundred and eighty-six remaining tribes. In a few cases beginnings of translation had been made. Several of the first tribes occupied had already been contacted by other missions who invited Wycliffe to co-operate in Scripture translation. In cases where Christian informants were available, the work of translation was immediately advanced. Meanwhile, surveys into the unexplored tribes continue, and contacts with shy or hostile Indians are attempted.

In urging future workers to consider the needs of the tribes of Brazil, Kietzman wrote:

"The point we would like to emphasize about these tribes is that they are uniformly small. The largest tribe in Brazil is said to number about fifteen thousand Indians. Some of the smaller tribes have just twenty or thirty members left. The average tribe will not be much greater than one thousand persons. We do not know just how small the smallest tribe may be with which we will work, but we are sure that as we survey some of these extremely small tribes, there will be many of them to whom we will want to give the gospel message.

"One of the redeeming features of this situation is that the languages are often quite closely related to others within the family. There are, however, a great many linguistic families represented here, of completely varying structures. Within the same language family we believe that it may be possible for our people, once they have learned one language and translated into it, to shift to another of the same family with little difficulty, giving added value to their investment in language learning."

Dr. Sarah Gudschinsky, who had had extensive experience in making linguistic comparisons of Mazatec and related dialects in Mexico, arrived in Brazil in June, 1958, to make surveys and comparisons of the great mosaic of dialects as yet unstudied. Results of this investigation, undertaken at the request of the government of Brazil, will guide translators in the order of

233

selecting locations among the dialects urgently needing Bible translation.

The first workers to settle in a Brazilian tribe were nurse Lynn Borman and Loraine Bridgeman, allocated among the Kaiua-Guaraní Indians of the state of Mato Grosso near the borders of Paraguay and Bolivia. After six months of study in a center near the government Indian post of Dourados, these two translators did some extensive research on other dialects of Guaraní, a large language family extending throughout several southern states of Brazil.

Early in 1958 Loraine Bridgeman, accompanied by Ursula Wiesemann, a Wycliffe translator from Germany, undertook an initial survey of the area. Traveling more than thirty-five hundred miles by foot, horse, cart, canoe, second-class bus, tobacco and lumber trucks, train and plane, the surveyors made some fascinating discoveries. In addition to turning up a fair-sized stack of data about Guaraní dialects, they also had the unexpected opportunity of making a word list of the Xetá language spoken by a stone-age tribe similar to the Aucas of Ecuador and until 1955 living undiscovered in the forests of Paraná.

Another find was a contingent of Polish immigrants who "are marrying the Guaraní Indians—and learning to speak Guaraní!"

Muriel Perkins and Muriel Ekdahl, another pair of translators, settled on a government Indian post at Cachoerinha, a village of more than eight hundred Terena Indians. Although previous work has been undertaken in the dialect, including some translation by Margaret Harden of another mission, the New Testament has not been completed. In all there are an estimated five thousand Terena Indians, living in eleven villages. A number of Christians are presenting a solid witness for the Lord among their people, but are hindered in their full understanding of the Portuguese Bible. Some of them, especially one faithful informant working with the two Wycliffe translators, are eagerly anticipating the day when God will clearly speak to them in Terena.

Because of the vastness of the tribal area, Wycliffe faces unique problems in Brazil. Covering forty-seven per cent of the area of all South America, Brazil is large enough to hold the United States apart from Alaska! But the varied terrain and the difficult modes of travel—there are no superhighways linking the states, nor even adequate waterways—greatly increase the complexities of settling in scattered nomadic tribes. In order better to approach the problem, Wycliffe in Brazil has fanned out to establish centers of operation closer to the tribes to be occupied. The main base of operation is in Rio de Janeiro, but strategic inland locations are being selected to provide a link between coastal communication and the tangled interior. A center has already been established in Belém, in the far north of Brazil at the mouth of the gigantic Amazon River.

To help Dale Kietzman in the heavy task of allocating the new workers entering Brazil at a heartening rate, and to assist in cooperation with government projects, James and Joyce Wilson landed in Rio de Janeiro early in 1958. Within a few months Wilson had traveled the length of the country, searching out Indian posts and villages for translators.

Miriam Stout, working with Ursula Wiesemann, wrote of some of the early experiences with the Kaingangs. These Indians had a reputation of unfriendliness, an attitude the translators attributed to shyness "easily overcome after a greeting in their own language." Speaking their own dialect afforded immediate opportunity for communication. Miriam stated:

"You may have heard of the 'country hicks' that can never learn. Some of the Indians were doubting that we would ever learn their language because we're from the *city!* Our informant told the skeptics that of *course* we'll learn—he's teaching us!"

Some at least must have been convinced, for Miriam was invited to make a "speech" of "the few appropriate phrases I had learned in Kaingang for an Indian couple who came to the government post to be officially married." One of the forty Indians present at the ceremony enthusiastically translated the "speech" into Portuguese for the government family in charge of the post.

Trials such as malaria and undiagnosed fevers always plaguing the Wycliffe workers of Brazil are a small price to pay, they feel, for the joy which shall be theirs within a few years when the Word of God will speak in nearly two hundred tribal tongues. "O death, where is thy sting?" is the message, in Indian accents, which will echo soon throughout the jungle, a welcome sound to the many tribes waiting to hear it.

Wycliffe's advance in Brazil is expected to continue even more rapidly as prepared reinforcements press the occupation of tribes as yet unexplored.

One impelling word comes from a Wycliffe leader calling to remembrance the tragic death of Captain Gardiner. While starving to death, alone after his companions had died, that faithful missionary wrote the story in his journal before he went before his Lord to give account.

"But will Christians have to wait for further tragedies," asks the leader, "before they rouse themselves to the needs of Amazonia? Here, whole Indian nations are lost and dying, never having heard the Word. It is *now* within our means to take it to them—if we will."

29. "God Speaks Navajo" *

"Yes . . . yes, this is Mr. Blount . . . What was that, please?
. . . Who is speaking, please? . . ."

Suddenly Turner Blount had an idea. Perhaps the uncertain
voice on the other end of the line was that of a Navajo Indian
having trouble communicating in English. He switched into
Navajo. From there on the conversation flowed.

But why would a Navajo Indian be calling Turner Blount in
Los Gatos, California, more than a thousand miles from the
reservation where Blount learned to speak Navajo? Finally, after
the happy Navajo greetings had been exchanged, the purpose of
the call began to emerge. Did Mr. Blount know anything about
"a good book in the Navajo language"? The inquirer had heard of
such a volume, and someone had referred him to Mr. Blount for
more information.

Before the conversation ended Turner Blount assured his new
Indian friend that a Navajo New Testament would soon be on its
way to him.

"Word is certainly getting around!" Blount said to his wife
Helen as he hung up the phone. The demand for the good book in
Navajo has exceeded the most optimistic hopes of its translators,
and has silenced the critics of such a project. Some who had
heard of the Wycliffe undertaking back in the middle forties felt
it was foolish. Even spoken Navajo will shortly disappear, they

* Title of a film portraying WBT work among the Navajos, produced
by Frederick A. Roberts.

237

argued, so why bother laboring over a translation of the Bible in that language? All of the Navajos will soon be speaking English. Who would read a translation in Navajo?

Within five months after its publication in 1956 by the American Bible Society the first edition of two thousand five hundred Navajo New Testaments was sold out, and a second printing was in process. Within a year the second printing was exhausted, and in 1958 a third was selling well with no signs of waning interest on the part of the Navajo public.

The Blounts and three other members of the Navajo translation team, working under the Wycliffe Bible Translators, labored for more than ten years to produce the New Testament in its present form and to teach many Navajos to read it. In their extensive project they were assisted by Navajo Indians and missionaries working under a number of various agencies on the reservation.

Veteran of the Navajo translation team is a gentle gray-haired lady nearing seventy years of age. But to see Faye Edgerton walking briskly to a hogan to visit her Indian friends, or driving across the reservation in her Volkswagen, one would never guess she had passed the age of retirement. "Her repeated winters" with the Navajos—to use their own expression—have produced an understanding love for them. And Faye Edgerton will very likely repeat many more winters among the Navajos and Apaches, with whom she is also working with her partner, Faith Hill.

But Faye Edgerton did not begin her missionary career in the Arizona desert. As a young woman she spent several years in Korea, only to have her mission work there prematurely terminated by an illness preventing her return to the Orient. It was in 1924 that she went to live on the Navajo reservation.

During her period of service in Korea she had been impressed with one great fact: the faith of the Korean Christians was strong and contagious because they had the Bible *in their own language.* Hence Christianity was no longer a foreign religion; it was distinctively Korean. The missionary transplanted from Korea to the Navajo reservation could not quench a burning conviction that the Navajos, too, needed the Bible in their mother tongue.

But not many missionaries on the reservation in the twenties shared her conviction. Navajo was very difficult for English speak-

Cameron and Elaine Townsend with their four children: Billy, Elainadel, Joy, and Grace. (p. 188)

Wycliffe translation and education continues among American Indians. Here, Turner Blount teaches Navajo to read in a hogan on Arizona reservation. (pp. 237 ff.)

Frederick A. Roberts

President Magsaysay, inspired by Townsend's biography of Mexico's Cárdenas to invite SIL workers to the Philippines, greets the first translators in 1953. (p. 279)

Translators concentrate on initial language study at the University of the Philippines.

Tribal groups along Luzon's east coast live mainly by fishing. Constant net-mending is required to maintain their meager livelihood.

On Philippine beach, Tom Lyman reads Scripture he has
translated for Cotabato Manobos.

Bontoc tribesmen of the Philippines squat to read
"pre-primer" of their language.

Though wary of foreigners, nomadic Philippine Negritos
like this fisherman have responded to the gospel presented in
their own tongue.

Wycliffe work is growing in remote areas of New Guinea.
At the Aiyura base in the highland area, Gadsup tribesmen
assist in the translation of their language (left) and the
building of a "prefabricated" bamboo house (right). (p. 304)

Neighboring chieftains visit Aiyura
to request translators for their people.

A Wycliffe jeep, laden with
supplies for Aiyura, needs extra
manpower to ford the swift
Uni River between Lae
and Kainantu, New Guinea.

New Guinea's Tairoras arm themselves
against the "Poison Man"
who strikes by night. (p. 303)

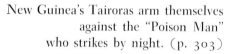

Laurie Nicholson relaxes with Forei friends at tribal
house-warming for her translator parents. (p. 305)

ers to learn, and there were few written helps, for there was no written tradition. Faye Edgerton could study only on rainy days when other mission activities were curtailed. But she was always listening, learning, and trying to master the intricate language which intrigued her. She developed a trial-and-error technique for approximating the explosive, disjointed syllables of a language utterly different from English or Korean. In 1941, while still searching for an efficient way to write and to speak Navajo, she met the Blounts. Fortunately, their studies that year at the Summer Institute of Linguistics had attuned their ears and trained their tongues to cope with the Navajo "noises." It was a happy meeting, for the trio found they had a common purpose—the mastery of the Navajo language for translation of the New Testament. They began working together on phonetics. Occasionally Turner Blount would suggest a "glottal stop" or a "voiceless l" that Faye Edgerton might be missing. With characteristic frankness she told him he was "hearing things." After all, she had been studying the language a good deal longer than he!

"Well," said the easygoing linguist from California, "if you don't believe me, why don't you go over and take the course at the Summer Institute of Linguistics?"

So she did, in the summer of 1942. "And then," says Turner Blount with a hearty laugh, "Faye began to 'hear things'!" And she really began to speak Navajo!

To her delight Faye also discovered that Drs. Edward Sapir and Harry Hoijer, eminent American linguists, had already made a scientific analysis of Navajo. "We simply studied their work and learned to speak the language," she says modestly. However, anyone who has attempted to speak Navajo realizes it is quite a feat.

In 1944 the translation trio joined the Wycliffe Bible Translators and began a concentrated effort to complete the translation of the New Testament. Several attempts had previously been made by other missionaries, but only a part of the Testament had been completed. Of others who had worked on Bible translation Faye says:

"Navajos have had small portions of the Bible for some years. Translation work was begun about fifty-five years ago by Christian Reformed and Presbyterian missionaries. Roman Catholics had begun work among them some years before this, but nothing was published by them until 1938 when the Scripture readings for Sundays and Holy Days appeared in book form. The first portion of the New Testament was published by the American Bible Society in 1910. This was followed in 1917 by a few other portions of the Old and New Testaments, printed in one volume. After the printing of Acts a few years later, nothing more appeared, and it seemed that very little was being done to complete the New Testament. One missionary of the Christian Reformed mission was working at it very slowly, because of his full schedule of other work."

In 1946 Faith Hill joined the Wycliffe team, followed in 1950 by Anita Wencker. The five worked steadily until in 1954 the manuscript of the New Testament was completed and submitted to the American Bible Society for printing. With Faye Edgerton carrying the main burden of actual translation, other members of the team devoted themselves to literacy work and testing trial versions with their readers. Only a translation in genuine idiomatic Navajo would communicate the Scriptures to Indian hearts and minds—and not be just "the white man's book of heaven" in white man's Navajo! And the team wanted a translation that would be *read* by the Indians.

For their literacy work and as a written medium for their translation, they adopted the alphabet used by Robert Young and his associates of the United States Indian Service. These, in turn, had also benefited from the studies of Sapir and Hoijer. The alphabet used in the readers and newspapers prepared by the United States government personnel was effective as a tool for literacy. The New Testament printed in 1956 by the American Bible Society made use of the same alphabet.

Translation accuracy constantly depended upon the collaboration and judgment of competent Navajos. Blind Geronimo Martin was a strong right arm through the long tedious years of work. Although he was deprived of physical sight, his keen mind and spiritual insight were invaluable to the translators in preparing the basic drafts of the New Testament.

Another Navajo friend was Roger Deal. He was always eager and enthusiastic. "It's just like God speaking to me!" he exclaimed after looking at a manuscript copy of the Navajo New Testament. Of Roger's preparation for helping in the translation Faye says:

"The son of a medicine man, he was denied the privilege of going to school and spent his youth herding his father's sheep. During World War II he contracted tuberculosis while working in the shipyards in San Francisco. Then, in a government sanatorium, he and a fellow patient taught themselves to read their own language. Released from the sanatorium he later became for a while one of our translation helpers. In the sanatorium he had begun to believe in 'the missionaries' God' whom he knew only through what others had told him. At the translation desk he began not only to hear but to read for himself and to know in truth not just 'the missionaries' God' but the great Holy One who gave His Son for the Navajos as well as for the white man. To know this great Holy One became the passion of his life, and he spent most of his free time poring over the manuscripts, correcting the translators' errors in writing the difficult language of his people, and in absorbing that life-giving Word."

English is still a foreign language to most of "the people," as the Navajos call themselves. Even those who speak and understand English better than the average often do not get the implications. Around the translation table as the precise significance of expressions was ferreted out, the English-speaking Navajo helpers would exclaim from time to time, "I didn't know it meant *that!*"

And no wonder, for the grammatical categories of the Navajo language do not coincide with the thought patterns familiar to the native speaker of English. The points at which the two language structures differ are potential trouble spots in actual communication and also made a good vernacular translation of the New Testament difficult.

In illustrating the many ways in which a simple English verb such as "give" may be translated, Faye says:

"You don't just say, 'Give it to me,' in the same way for any kind of object, but you say it with twelve different stems or roots for the verb form, according to what kind of things you are asking for, whether it is a round, bulky object; a long, slender rigid object like a stick; a paper or blanket-like object; a live object, animal or human; a liquid in an open vessel; a flexible object like a rope or stocking; plural separable objects; something carried on the back; larger plural objects, etc. This grouping of objects is

249

carried through every verb that has to do with handling them in any way."

Another characteristic is the picturesque way of computing time by the passing of nights; for example, "Three nights passed over him in that place." Years are counted by winters. In order to say that his boy is ten years old a Navajo father would say, literally, "His repeated winters ten." If a baby is almost three months old a Navajo mother says, "It will have monthed three times with him."

Navajo equivalents for ideas expressed in the Bible may lead to very thought-provoking results. For example, a Navajo term for "cares" or "anxieties" is "that which sticks into," a close parallel to the English slang for something that "gets under the skin." Thus First Peter 5:7 reads literally, in the Navajo translation, "Those things which stick into you, all of them, turn over to him one by one; for he, being much interested in you, cares for you." Adaptations of the translation to tribal culture throw new light on familiar Bible expressions. "Take my yoke upon you . . . for my yoke is easy and my burden is light" comes out in Navajo, "Be harnessed together with me in the double harness. . . . For working with me in double harness is easy and the work is light."

The Navajo New Testament is clear proof that "God speaks Navajo" as well as English. The growing number of Navajos desiring to know what He says has amazed some who predicted the rapid disappearance of the language. In spite of the great changes of the last decade, "the people" and their language are still vigorous. Population is increasing at the rate of one thousand a year, and today the tribe is eighty thousand strong. Industry and education have produced changes, too. Of this shifting scene Faye says:

"During the last decade, especially the last five years, great changes have taken place on the Navajo reservation. Gas and oil wells, and uranium mines have increased the tribal treasury to such an extent that the Navajos themselves have undertaken numerous projects, such as building roads, providing schools, financing young people in special training, providing medical care, etc. Most of the children are in school. . . .

"But the need for the Bible in Navajo still remains, particularly for those of teen-age and up, who missed the chance to go to school and learn English. Many of those who speak English cannot grasp spiritual truth except in their own tongue. And this will be true of many of those who are going to school now, for many will not go very far in school."

The sales of the Navajo New Testament are eloquent witness to the truth of Faye Edgerton's statement concerning the need for the Scriptures. Many missions on the reservation are encouraging the reading and use of the Navajo New Testament, and many church services use it. As one Navajo pastor said, "It is so *plain* in Navajo!"

One revealing report came recently from the reservation:

"At our mission every new believer is expected to make an honest effort to learn to read the Navajo New Testament. One of our older Christians who could not read the Bible in English said, 'I thought I was a pretty good Christian, but since I have learned to read God's Word in my own language I find that I am not such a good Christian after all. I've found out many things I did not know about the Christian life.'"

With the Navajo New Testament in use, Faye Edgerton and Faith Hill have moved on and are making good progress in a translation of the New Testament in Apache, a related language. During their first winter in the new field they prepared a draft of the Gospel of Mark. With the help of an Apache Christian a few hymns were also translated, thus whetting the appetite of the people for the Word in their own language.

Missionaries who have been evangelizing the tribe in English are now beginning to learn to read Apache. The reading classes with the Wycliffe team bring a new spark of life into the work.

The first Scripture portions, the Gospel of John and the Epistles of James and First John, have been printed and selections from them recorded to be played on hand-operated machines. The American Bible Society is making three hundred sets of Scripture material and records available to the Apaches at a nominal sum. In October, 1958, Faye and Faith had the joy of taking a sample set to each of the twenty mission stations on the San Carlos and White Mountain Reservations.

Although Townsend had realized many years before that some tribes of the United States would benefit from translations of the

251

New Testament in their languages, no specific surveys were made until 1944. At that time he and Turner Blount, assisted by personnel of the Summer Institute of Linguistics and other American Indian investigators, began a detailed study of the need. They found that in Oklahoma alone there were representatives of twenty-six tribes. Not all of these warranted Bible translations, however, for in some cases there were only a few speakers of the language, or some Bible translation had been done by earlier missionaries.

As a result of careful surveys Wycliffe, by 1958, had allocated workers in a number of languages and dialects in the United States and Canada. The principal locations of workers were among the Navajo and Apache, Comanche, Keres and Tewa Pueblo, Hopi, Papago, Seminole, Paiute, and dialects of Athapaskan and Eskimo in the Northwest Territories and Alaska.

Because of the live interest of American linguists in the Athapaskan dialects stretching from the interior of Alaska to the southwestern United States where live the Navajos and Apaches, an Athapaskan Workshop was conducted during the summer of 1958 at the University of Oklahoma. Professors Harry Hoijer of the University of California at Los Angeles and Kenneth Pike of the Summer Institute of Linguistics directed the workshop financed by the Wenner-Gren Foundation. In addition to personnel of the Summer Institute of Linguistics working in Athapaskan dialects, other related language groups were represented by workers of the Northern Canadian Evangelical Mission who contributed data from a Chipewyan dialect, and by Mr. and Mrs. Philip Howard, Jr., missionaries working with the Slave tribe. Results of the research are being prepared for publication.

Many English speakers acquainted with the work of Bible translation in the United States and Canada are surprised that a need for the Word of God in the vernacular still exists in certain tribal groups. Some are astonished that the number of North American Indians vigorously living and speaking their own tongues is far more than a few individual tribesmen scattered over the continent. According to a report of the United States Congress dated December 12, 1952, there are an estimated 368,401 "living persons on tribal rolls in the United States." If the number of living persons in the Canadian tribes were added, the total would approximate five hundred thousand. The report warns that "a distinction must be made between historical Indian tribes and the tribal entities of today with which the Bureau of Indian Affairs administratively deals. . . . Altogether there are two hundred and seventy-nine such entities throughout the country." There is no indication, however, of the extent to which the Indian languages are used.

The report further reveals that there are "over three hundred separate and distinct areas of land in the country which are occupied by Indian groups and maintained in Federal trusteeship for their use and support." These areas range in size from a few acres to the Navajo reservation covering an expanse of fifteen million acres in Arizona, New Mexico, and Utah.

Observation and investigation of these tribal entities dramatically reveal the persistent use of the Indian languages in some areas. Although standing as ethnic islands in a sea of English speech and culture, they often retain many cultural traits distinctive of their individual groups. One Indian authority, Harry Tschopik, Jr., cites an eloquent example:

"The Iroquois retain their curing societies and other religious beliefs; many make their living, however, as steel construction workers, tossing white hot rivets high above metropolitan New York as they converse in their native language."

North American Indians today do not use bows and arrows or hunt buffalo, as legend and even modern movies would imply. Many of them drive late model cars, and some of them are successful miners of uranium in the Southwest. But their cultures and languages are still as varied as their geographical locations and their occupations in the modern United States.

Wycliffe's work among the North American tribes is based upon the need of Bible translation. Because in some cases English is replacing the tribal language at a greater rate than in others, not all tribal groups will require a full translation of the New Testament. In the Navajo, however, it has proved to be a help and blessing to numerous native speakers.

With the Navajo translation completed, Turner Blount is now serving as director of the North American Branch and assistant in the Alaska advance. Anita Wencker has moved to Arizona to help in Hopi literacy work. Her partner is Iva Chizek whose nursing among the Zapotecs in Mexico was terminated by a health condition no longer permitting her to live there. They have joined forces with translators Jonathan and Molly Ekstrom who had been welcomed to the tribe by Hopi Christians. Otto Lomavitu, who had served as an informant for an earlier translator, is helping to complete the Hopi New Testament. As he tells his own story:

"Forty-four years ago, while attending Chilocco Indian Agricultural School in Oklahoma, I accepted the Lord Jesus as my personal Savior and was baptized in a lagoon on the school campus on April 5, 1914.

"Two months later I returned home to my mother in Kiqotsmovi (Lower Oraibi) from whom I had been estranged by my grandparents through accusations of witchcraft. The Lord not only turned my heart to Himself but He also put light and love into my heart and caused me to fly into the open arms of my long suffering loving mother. (Praise the Lord! Mother accepted the Lord in her old age and passed away peacefully to be with the Lord. Marvelous grace!)

"My grandparents and all my relatives were worshipers of idols. There were two fearful-looking tallish gods in our ancestral home kept in the innermost recess of our three-storied house, and I was taught to worship and feed the gods on ceremonial days which came often. On such days, when the ceremonial food was placed on the floor for our meal, I would take a pinch of each food and carry the food to our gods as offering. As I approached the gods through devious narrow passageways in the terrible silence of the smelly rooms, I would seek to stifle any fear which came up my spine. Facing the two hideous creatures with bulging eyes and long beaks, I would offer prayer for health, rain, and prosperity; then placing the food before the gods I would walk away with great emotion calling into play all reserves of my manhood bravery. However, before I was halfway through the rooms . . . I would 'feel the spirits clawing at my back' which made my steps become faster.

"On that happy day in 1914 light came and darkness fled away as my eyes became fastened on the glorious person of Jesus Christ, blessed be His holy Name.

"In late fall of that year Rev. John R. Duerksen and his family came . . . and I joined them. Mr. Duerksen mastered our language perfectly and we began to translate the Scriptures into our language; also some gospel songs and a book of catechism. . . . In 1929 the Four Gospels were printed by the American Bible Society. . . .

"Now after almost thirty years have elapsed, it is necessary to revise the Gospels, and to prepare the rest of the New Testament for printing. To this end a young brother in the Lord, Mr. Jonathan Ekstrom and his wife, came to the field and together we are now engaged in that blessed work."

With such help Jonathan Ekstrom completed a draft of the entire New Testament in only two years.

For the Comanches among whom L. L. Legters earlier spent twenty years, it would seem that the time for translation has gone by. After working among them for several years Elliott and Viola Canonge feel their work drawing to a close. Cultural transition in the tribe has brought about such a change that now most Comanches, excluding those sixty and over, are either bilingual or speak only English. The Canonges have translated the Gospel of Mark into Comanche. But they are persuaded that they should go instead to other Indians still using their tribal tongue.

In the course of his work among the Comanches, Canonge collected the texts of many tribal stories. Some of these he edited for a compilation of *Comanche Texts,* the first in a Linguistic Series of such texts from various tribes being published by the University of Oklahoma.

Another interesting tribe are the Seminoles. When early in the nineteenth century Indian tribes were relocated in the Indian Territory, the Seminoles refused to move. For seven years they fought the United States Army for the privilege of remaining in the Florida Everglades. During those years of bitter struggle four thousand of the tribe were captured and taken west. But a remnant of the tribe withdrew into the cypress swamps where their descendants live today, an independent people whose tribe is the only one in the United States that has never signed a formal treaty of peace with the government.

Early in 1955 David and Virginia West undertook to live among the Seminoles and learn their language. They wrote of the beginning of their venture:

255

"Since we arrived on January 10, the Lord has been most gracious to us, giving us a friendly reception at each of the three Indian reservations. The government agent favors a written language for the Seminoles. Permission has been given for us to live on Big Cypress Reservation, about fifty miles northwest of Miami. An Indian shelter will be our new home. It has framework of cypress poles and a thatched roof of cabbage palm leaves."

A year later they reported progress:

"Albert Billie was eating lunch with us. He had come to ask for a ride to town and accepted the invitation to our table. As we ate, a neighbor's dog barked just outside our house. 'Mahs-tick-shah (stop that!),' I said. 'Can you talk?' asked Albert with about as much surprise as a Seminole ever registers. This little incident serves to remind us of many things that God has accomplished during our first year here.

"At last we are *beginning* to talk in the language of these Big Cypress Seminoles. But it is easier to put words and sentences on 3 x 5 slips in the file than to be able to use them at the proper times and places. Seminole words are the only ones that really 'talk' to these people. Gradually, the reserve of the people toward us has been broken, and many of them are genuine friends to us. Several adults and a number of children have come to visit lately. The number should increase when we can really talk."

There is a Baptist church on the reservation with a Seminole pastor, Henry Cypress. Hymns are sung in Creek which is used by another part of the tribe and is related to Mikasuki, the language of the Big Cypress Seminoles. The pastor reads from an English Bible, but English is a foreign language to him too, and the rest of the service is in Mikasuki. The necessity of translation for the tribe has been questioned, but the Wests are convinced:

"You may ask us: Since there is an Indian church with an Indian pastor at Big Cypress, why are *you* there? We reply: Because Mikasuki Seminoles need an understanding of God's Word that they cannot get through English. Henry Cypress and others have expressed a desire for the Bible in their own language. Anthropologists realize there is a problem. One wrote recently: 'The Seminole seems to accept Christianity not as a religion but as an aspect of all religions. . . . he retains his own convictions because he cannot conceive that everything that he and his ancestors have believed

256

and practiced all their lives is false. To simplify matters he naïvely blends the two.' "

After four years of living in Big Cypress the Wests can say:

"We are preparing for the planting of spiritual seed in Seminole hearts by language study and cultivating the friendship of the people. For the most part we are still busy developing a new form of the seed—the Word of God in Seminole—which can best grow in Seminole hearts. We are encouraged by the words of Amy Carmichael: "The Seed is not your poor little word. The Seed is the Word of God.' The process seems long but we are confident of the harvest."

30. Operation Deep Freeze

The weather is news in Arctic Training Camp. In the fall of 1958 George Fletcher, director of the camp and pilot for Wycliffe's Alaska program, wrote a greeting to the Jungle Training Camp in Mexico from the first session of the camp in Nenana, not far from the Arctic Circle:

"Greetings from Alaskan sourdoughs who inhabit a land where one of the biggest problems is getting too warm. Now, don't laugh. Extra warmth leads to freezing. The other afternoon as the sun was setting behind Mt. McKinley at two o'clock, I slipped into my down parka and pants and canvas mukluks and headed down the Lake Menchumina trail. The temperature was −5, but it wasn't long until I was warm, extra warm. So I threw back my hood, opened my parka and continued padding my way through frost-covered trees toward the blazing sky. I finally decided that if I was to get home before dark (between three-thirty and four) I had better turn around. It wasn't much cooler going in the other direction so I became warmer and warmer until my undershirt was beginning to get wet. I kept up a good pace for if I had stopped for a few minutes, my clothes would have begun to freeze from the inside out. 'Clothes control' is, therefore, very important here. One must be warmish-cool, no more.

"We haven't had any long stretches of cold weather yet. It did stay around −25 to −30 for three days once, but that isn't a long stretch. Our record low so far has been −41. When the

258

winds start blowing it gets warmer; when it stops, the mercury nose dives. However, −30 is a lot more enjoyable than ten above with wind.

"The other afternoon four of us made overnight camp in slightly more than a foot of snow. We had an enjoyable time making camp and eating supper, though it is a bit cumbersome to make and eat supper with mittens on. Down sleeping bags are cozy but the trick is getting out of your clothes into the bag, a very cold bag to begin with. Another trick is getting out of the bag and into your clothes in the morning in zero weather."

Arctic Training Camp at Nenana, fifty-five miles southwest of Fairbanks, is one of the coldest spots in Alaska, the temperature sometimes dropping to seventy below. The "overnights" George wrote of are spent in makeshift shelters in the icy wilderness on the outskirts of the town. There is a landing field one mile from Nenana, and it is also accessible by car from Fairbanks in winter when the river is frozen deep enough for cars to drive across. The campers occupy seven insulated cabins flanking a main street. Each cabin, as one camper described it, "is about fifteen by fifteen feet with a central coal-burning stove. Somewhere you will find a fire extinguisher, a water bin, a curtained-off 'bathroom,' and a kitchen area and wooden beds or bunkbeds."

The population of Nenana is approximately two hundred and fifty of whom a little over half are natives, mostly Athapaskan Indians but also a few Eskimos. Arctic Missions, Inc., have had missionaries there for several years ministering chiefly to the white people. The campers have enjoyed the fellowship at the chapel, where occasionally they teach Sunday school or preach. Visits have also been made among the Indians of the area and some study begun on their languages.

The orientation program is not all centered on cold-weather survival, important as that might prove in the event of a plane crash or being lost or "weathered in" on the trail. Long periods of isolation from civilization and from fellow workers coupled with the confinement of the long winter nights may create emotional problems popularly known as "cabin fever." Workers must be prepared for these times and be ready to keep wholesomely occupied. What a chance for uninterrupted language study!

Besides the Eskimos and Indians of Canada and Alaska hundreds of other indigenous groups live in the Arctic area. Of these the larger language stocks have been studied, and relationships determined. Some of the dialects have been given alphabets, and literacy projects launched. But an unknown number of these Arctic tribes still await linguistic discovery—and Bible translation.

This Arctic phase of Wycliffe's work stems from Cameron Townsend's burden for the aboriginal tribes in the area. The way was paved by four years of prayerful investigation and careful preparation.

In October, 1954, Wycliffe's deputy general director Richard S. Pittman and his wife took opportunity to stop in Alaska while en route to the Far East. Dr. Pittman sent a careful report to the board of directors concerning his investigation and his conviction that certain of Alaska's tribes needed Bible translation.

Later, in the spring of 1956 and again in 1958, Turner Blount made extensive surveys of particular Bible translation needs in Alaska's northwest, coastal, and central regions. On the second of these trips other Wycliffe members of the survey team were George Fletcher; David Shinen, assigned to the St. Lawrence Island Eskimos; Herbert Zimmerman, assigned to the Yukon Delta Eskimo dialect; and Earl Adams, director of Wycliffe members in training and since 1948 Jungle Training Camp director in Mexico.

Some Bible translation has already been done by other missionaries in Alaska, including the Moravian Mission translation of the New Testament for the Kuskokwim Eskimos. Blount found, however, that there is still a need in the following languages: the Siberian dialect spoken by natives on St. Lawrence Island; the Kuchin (and several other Athapaskan dialects) of the Alaskan interior; the Thlingit dialect of southeastern Alaska; the Barrow Eskimo dialect of the far north.

The Rev. Walter Soboleff, Thlingit Indian pastor of the Memorial Presbyterian Church in Juneau, has invited Wycliffe to do Bible translation. Soboleff, who has had both college and seminary training, preaches in his church in Juneau in the English language, but carries on a radio ministry in his native Thlingit. He states that it will be another seventy years before his people will think in English as well as in Thlingit. Both he and other native

Christian leaders on the islands of the nearby Alexander Archipelago heartily approve Wycliffe's proposed translation program and are convinced that a Thlingit translation will be widely used.

In September, 1958, a Canadian couple, Victor and Anita Monus, began their work with the large Slave tribe at Fort Laird in the Northwest Territories of Canada. For two months during the fall freeze-up they were absolutely cut off from the outside world. Mail comes to them only three times a year. Ski planes drop by now and then in the winter and boats come up river in the summer. But they have a comfortable log cabin with Slave Indians nearby and have already set their teeth into the difficult Athapaskan language of their area.

On the north shore of Great Slave Lake in Yellowknife live the Dogribs, an Athapaskan tribe of Northwest Territories. With a population of four thousand, Yellowknife is the largest town in the Territories. It is a thousand miles north of Edmonton from which a gravel road runs to the south shore of the lake. Less than ten per cent of the residents are Indians: Chipewyans, Slaves, Crees, and Dogribs. However, the Dogribs are nomadic fishermen, so that living among them in their own settlements where they are largely monolingual presents problems not the least of which is housing. Their country is a barren one and building materials have to be brought in by dogsled or by plane.

Although they seem outwardly friendly, an underlying antagonism toward outsiders makes it difficult to win their confidence. In November, 1956, a Canadian couple, William and June Davidson, and their two children went to live among the Dogribs at Yellowknife. That the Davidsons want to learn their language pleases them, especially since Mrs. Davidson is the first white woman they have seen who has tried to learn to talk with them. They are growing less suspicious and more co-operative, but language learning has been very slow.

However, Davidson sees some progress in being accepted by the tribe. Recently, in helping some of the Dogrib people he was stranded away from home with the river freezing up and planes grounded. It was a serious situation but God graciously spared his life. The people appreciate his willingness to sacrifice for them.

It is a far cry from the steaming equatorial jungle to the streets of Yellowknife where the children walk along eating ice cream cones at thirty below, but the need for Bible translation is the same in all latitudes.

Wycliffe's Operation Deep Freeze aims to make Alaska a Bible-reading area in as many languages as necessary. Also from Alaska will radiate the light of the gospel to other Bibleless northern neighbors whose life like their winter is one long night.

31. Wycliffe Lives Again

Bracing himself on a motorcycle and driving into the bitter cold wind and rain, John Bendor-Samuel journeyed from London to northern England and Wales. During that winter of 1953 he traveled throughout Britain bent on a historic mission. He was fanning into flame a spark that had been lit in England five centuries before him by John Wycliffe.

Both John Bendor-Samuel and his predecessor were Oxford men. Wycliffe's "poor priests" devoted to the Word of God went about the north of England preaching from hand-copied manuscripts. The forthright directness of their everyday language pricked the hearts of the listeners.

Impelled by the same love for the Scriptures as Wycliffe, John Bendor-Samuel was making a tour of the British Isles presenting the cause of Bible translation in the mother tongue. Instead of hand-written parchments the twentieth-century "poor priest" had modern equipment wedged beside him on his little vehicle. In one parcel was a moving picture projector, a screen, and a film entitled "O For a Thousand Tongues." Through these means and his own strong conviction he would lay the cause of Bibleless tribes before his countrymen.

John Bendor-Samuel was training for missionary education when he heard of the Wycliffe Bible Translators. He had finished at Oxford and was studying at London University preparatory to a career of missionary teaching.

263

In 1953 John attended the first Summer Institute of Linguistics to be conducted in England and known there as the Wycliffe Language Course. During that summer John sensed a burden for publicizing the need for translators. The course over, John set aside his own plans in order to tour England and proclaim the message that had now captivated him.

Several years of planning, praying, and corresponding with mission leaders in England had preceded the initial session of the Wycliffe Language Course. Among the first to be interested in the possibility of such a course in England were Norman Grubb, director of the World-wide Evangelization Crusade, the Rev. Ernest Kevan, principal of the London Bible College, Fred Mitchell, then Home Director of the China Inland Mission, and Ashley Baker and A. H. Long of the Scripture Gift Mission. Missionary linguistics would complement the courses already offered in theology and medicine for full-orbed missionary training. In 1951 when Kenneth Pike was returning from a linguistic assignment in Europe he visited friends in London. A training school for the following summer was discussed, a sponsoring committee set up, and Mr. Jack Kemp of the Scripture Gift Mission was loaned to help with the secretarial duties.

About to sail for England in 1953 to inaugurate the course, the Pikes and George Cowan received word that only four persons had enrolled. Was it worth three round-trip transatlantic fares? In reply Pike stated that the Wycliffe organization had never hesitated at beginning small and trusting the Lord for growth in the future.

After the arrival of the party in England more students enrolled, bringing the total up to fifteen. The session was held in the old London Bible College building located in central London across from Regent's Park. With competing noises on all sides, central London was not an ideal spot for phonetics classes.

The American staff members had prayed from the beginning that God would send English students of high scholastic caliber who could later assume the responsibility for the training of candidates in their country. John Bendor-Samuel was an encouraging answer to their prayers. Pamela Moxham, a graduate of the University of London, was another. Harry Rosbottom of the University of Manchester also did outstanding work.

264

From its inception the Wycliffe Language Course enjoyed cordial academic relations with institutions interested in language research, such as the School of Oriental and African Studies, and University College where for many years the eminent British linguist Daniel Jones was the head of the department of phonetics. Dr. Jones visited the first Wycliffe course and was pleased with the quality of work done. With only six weeks of study and practice several of the students passed the phonetics proficiency examination usually given by Dr. Jones after six months of study.

"Everyone spoke English, but what a dialectical potpourri it was!" commented one observer during the first summer. And no wonder, for in that small gathering were representatives of New Zealand, Scotland, Ireland, Wales, England, Canada, Italy, the United States, and Mexico. Nina Peasland, born in England but taken to Mexico by her parents as a small child, returned to her homeland to serve as the first Wycliffe office secretary there.

Mr. and Mrs. Stewart Dinnen, directing the Worldwide Evangelization Crusade Training College in Glasgow, and who had attended the course at the University of Oklahoma in 1952, were loaned by their mission for teaching duty the first and several succeeding summers. Later Dr. William Lees, who had left British colonial medical service for missionary work with the Borneo Evangelical Mission, together with his wife Shirley, were gladly loaned for teaching duty "out of appreciation for the help that Wycliffe linguistic training had been to the entire program of the Mission."

The new brand of linguistics was not the only innovation that summer. American volleyball had been imported along with the books on how to learn unwritten languages. Passengers atop the London double decker buses looked over the high wall and gaped in astonishment at the strange antics of players as they bobbed up and down whacking a big ball over a net. Passers-by strained to see what in the world was going on! To the American players, volleyball was an old Wycliffe tradition. After a grueling hour of voiced implosives or glottalized stops, a turn on the court worked wonders. "We shake the linguistics down with volleyball," says George Cowan, "so we can pour more in!"

For the second session of the Wycliffe Language Course in 1954 a new site far from the jangle of London traffic was

265

providentially supplied when the old building of the London Bible College was abandoned.

A British army doctor from East London had returned with his wife to general practice in London. Longing for a home in the country away from the downtown din, the Beattys found their dream house in the "green belt," an area around London preserved as natural countryside. It was an old manor house of 1500 vintage, in disrepair and unwanted, probably because it was considered haunted. Next to the old mansion was a listening post used in the war and equipped with a number of buildings. The Beattys invited Christian young people to weekend meetings in their country home, and Mrs. Beatty could visualize the listening post as an ideal set-up for a camp. So she began to pray that the property would become theirs. Plans to convert the post into a county school suddenly changed, and shortly thereafter it was purchased by the Beattys. Later as they talked with John Bendor-Samuel they learned of the need for a location for the Wycliffe Language Course and were overjoyed to grant use of the grounds for such a purpose.

The camp site in the "green belt" is a holiday setting for the students. It was originally equipped for seventy persons, but each year as the course grew tents were added. By 1958 there were one hundred and fifty students and staff members, half of them living in tents, enjoying country life while working intensively on the language course.

"Now the students can try their phonetics out on the cows instead of making queer noises on the streets of London and having bobbies looking at them as though they were mad!" says George Cowan. One drawback is that the frequent summer rains make living in tents far from ideal. "But this is good pioneer training," Cowan philosophizes.

Since 1953 British staff members emerging from the course have shared responsibility for training new recruits. In 1958 John Bendor-Samuel, who in 1955 had married Pamela Moxham, became associate director of the course. He had by that time completed his work for a Ph.D. at the University of London, his dissertation being based on a grammatical description of the Jebero language of Peru where the Bendor-Samuels spent a year.

When an acute need arose for a Wycliffe representative in England to continue the vigorous efforts of John Bendor-Samuel,

266

George Cowan thought of John's father-in-law, A. R. Moxham, who from the beginning had shown keen interest in the program.

Cowan called upon Moxham, who remained silent during the "sales" talk. After Cowan had given several strong reasons for Moxham's assuming the responsibility, the latter said, "Well, isn't this wonderful! My wife and I have been praying about this very thing."

They had told the Lord that if there were anything they could do for Wycliffe they would be most willing—but the request for their services would have to come first. They confided in no one but their daughter Pamela, who was sworn to secrecy. Moxham is now Wycliffe's honorary secretary, while Mrs. Moxham helps by preparing Wycliffe literature for England. With the impetus which they and like-minded Wycliffe friends have given the movement in their land, thirty British translators, from many denominations and with a variety of training, academic and otherwise, are now serving in Wycliffe's various fields.

One of the thirty was Desmond Derbyshire, a qualified accountant sent by his firm to British Guiana. While visiting missionary friends among the Waiwai Indians of the Guiana Brazilian frontier, he was impressed with the need of such tribes. Following the unpleasant experience of being lost in the jungle, he felt that God was clearly calling him to leave his profession to reach another such tribe. Returning to England, he and his wife Grace, a trained nurse, enrolled in the Wycliffe Language Course as the first step in preparing themselves.

Another was John Callow, a mathematician from Cambridge who appeared at the course after having been challenged by a Wycliffe film, "Each in His Own Tongue." In making a case for academic missionary training Pike had looked out from the screen straight into Callow's eyes with the pointed question, "Have *you* ever considered a mental retooling in linguistics?" John Callow began to consider it, and soon left mathematics for Bible translation. Kathleen Callow, a philosophy major and honor student from the University of Glasgow, also joined her husband in linguistic studies. In 1958 the Callows sailed for Brazil for language research under the School of Oriental and African Studies in preparation for future Wycliffe service.

Informants at the Wycliffe Language Course, corresponding

to the American Indian language helpers at the University of Oklahoma in the United States, are overseas students. One was from Assam studying in Glasgow. His native tongue was Hmar, spoken by a hill tribe of Assam, and he furnished the Wycliffe students with live phonetic data. He had translated the New Testament for his own tribe at the request of the Hmar Christians who educated him for that purpose. His studies in Glasgow were preparatory to translating the Old Testament into Hmar.

Another informant was a Zulu music inspector doing research in London. One summer the Wycliffe students analyzed his speech which included fifteen varieties of clicks the novices strove to imitate.

At the end of the course Cowan told the Zulu informant a story of a Zulu chief who expressed great pity for the British in his country who could not enjoy the beauties of the Zulu Bible. Expecting that the educated Zulu music inspector would smile at the naïveté of the chief obviously unaware of the existence of the English Bible, Cowan was surprised by the quick reply, "Yes, that's right. The Bible is *far* better in Zulu than in English." With deep feeling the Zulu inspector quoted the Twenty-third Psalm in his own language. "Oh, it is much better in Zulu!" he said.

The Zulu inspector was delighted that British young people were devoting themselves to the unfinished task of Bible translation. In 1958, in addition to Wycliffe members, students representing twenty-eight different mission boards took the Language Course preparatory to missionary work in various countries of the world.

32. A Call from "Down Under"

When Wycliffe went "back to England" in 1953, training centers for Bible translators had already been opened in two other places in the British Commonwealth. In 1944 a school had been inaugurated in Canada, and in 1950, one in Australia.

With characteristic foresight Townsend had suggested to his younger colleagues that a training center, in addition to the one in Canada, should be undertaken somewhere in the Commonwealth. Australia might be a likely area, inasmuch as England was still recovering from the war. Townsend continued to pray and look for an opening.

About that time an Australian missionary to Brazil, back in his homeland, read an article in the *Moody Monthly* about the work of the Wycliffe Bible Translators. Having seen the dire need of tribespeople in Brazil, and surrounded by it in Australia and New Guinea, Robert Story began to ponder what he had read.

Subsequently Story, having lost track of the article but remembering the Moody connection, wrote a letter to "Wycliffe School of Languages, Moody Bible Institute, Chicago." Finally it reached Pike's desk. In essence it read, "Are you thinking about opening up work in Australia? If so, we would like to know about it. If not, would you send us your syllabus?"

The reserved answer went back to Australia, "We have been praying about it."

269

The "syllabus" sent was an imposing set of technical books on phonetics, phonemics, morphology, and principles of Bible translation, enough to frighten all but the most determined.

Soon Pike received a letter from Australia, saying:

"After looking at your materials, we feel it would probably be better if one of you would come over and show us how to use them."

The work of Wycliffe was unknown in Australia, and the concepts of descriptive linguistics new. But Robert Story and other Australian missionaries sought help, and Wycliffe seemed a logical source.

"They really didn't know us," Pike says. "They didn't know what we were—but they were very courageous. When we arrived, they sighed with relief when they found that we were in truth Christian brethren!"

The immediate steps leading to the formation of the Wycliffe School of Linguistics, as it is known in Australia, were clearly ordered of God. Great obstacles were removed in response to earnest prayer on the eve of the venture. By correspondence it had been arranged that Kenneth and Evelyn Pike would conduct the first session of the school, to be held in Melbourne in the early spring of 1950, under the direction of the Interdenominational Missionary Fellowship of the State of Victoria.

The first mountains were financial ones. Pike recalls vividly the suspense of those days:

"The Australians didn't have the money to meet their share of the quota, so they had a prayer meeting. It was the day before I was to take a plane from California to Australia, and they were having a prayer meeting to decide whether they should call it off.

"They prayed, got up from their knees, and said, 'We'll go ahead.' Then a man handed them a check for two hundred pounds with the words, 'I was told to give you this *if* you decided to go ahead with the program.'

"I went to Australia by plane, and three weeks later my wife Evelyn followed me with Stephen, who was not yet a year old. We had bought our tickets through a travel agency so that there would be no hitch in plans. We had spent our last dime getting ready to go.

"When Evelyn arrived at the airport with the baby the officials said that there would be a ten per cent charge on him which the travel agency hadn't told us about. And Evelyn didn't have the seventy dollars.

"But it just so happened that that morning before leaving her parents' home in California for the plane she had received a check for seventy dollars made out to me. She tried to give it to her folks—it really belonged to them, she said—but they wouldn't hear of it. So she had said okay, and stuck it in her purse. Finally the officials let her sign my name to the check, get on the plane with Stephen, and come over to Australia to meet me."

Another concern was for God-given personnel. Again Pike recalls how the Lord provided:

"We started the work in Australia with two prayers. One of them was that the Lord would give us some 'bull-dogs.' By 'bull-dogs' we meant people who were basically of the character that would continue on with the work, and not get frightened out. We have never opened any work in Wycliffe without problems. We didn't want people starting a work unless they had strong stomachs. We said, 'Unless there are those who will *hold on* when everything seems to be in turmoil, we might as well not start.' We prayed for strong men who would *hold on* when the going got rough.

"Then in addition, we said, 'We need some *young* men who can learn to teach. We can't send people over from Mexico every year to teach.'

"As to the answer to the first prayer, I found when I got there that the men of the committee who had invited us over were made up of the directors of the Sudan Interior Mission, Australian Branch; Unevangelized Fields Mission, Australian Branch; Africa Inland Mission, Australian Branch; and every other member of the committee, with one or two exceptions, was the director of a mission, because the committee inviting us over was an executive committee made up of directors of these member missions. God gave them to us, and they have stuck by us since 1949, and they have never wavered. God answered that *serious* prayer.

"As to the second prayer, it didn't look as if God was answering at first. The well-trained teachers whom the committee had invited to come and learn the new methods of linguistics couldn't come, for one reason or another. Finally in desperation the com-

271

mittee began looking for 'young sprouts.' Among them was a schoolteacher whose parents had been missionaries to the Australian aborigines. There was another schoolteacher by the name of Joan Rule. She had taken a government scholarship for five years, and had had to teach five years to meet the obligation. But she wanted to serve the Lord in missions. The day that her contract was finished and she had met her obligations she resigned from schoolteaching. Her mother objected at first, for she hadn't wanted her to be a missionary.

"Just at that point her mother attended an evangelistic meeting at which she surrendered her daughter to the Lord. The day after Joan resigned from her job, without anything in sight, she received a letter from our committee asking if she would help teach phonetics. She had been teaching phonetics to three hundred students for the government in a training school for teachers. This was the hand of God.

"Another of the teachers who came was Wilf Douglas who had been out in western Australia. He had been working for eleven years in a tribe where missionaries had served for fifty years in English but where no missionary had learned the tribal language. This young fellow was discouraged by the situation in the tribe. He heard of our course, and his own fellow missionaries paid his way to take the work, so that he could go back and help.

"At the end of the course, during the week of language demonstration which we put on for visitors, we tried to get as much of one language from a bilingual informant as we could and attempted to translate with his help a verse of Scripture, just for fun. The students worked with him, and translated and wrote a verse on the board to show the visitors the kind of thing that we tried to do. In that meeting there was another aborigine from that same tribe. She took out her notebook, and started copying that verse to use it in teaching. It was more Scripture than she had ever had in her language. She needed it, and to our astonishment she thought it was good enough to use."

Wilf Douglas wrote back to his wife and said, "Bess, I have learned more of this language in one week than I learned in eleven years!" Later he became the head of the phonetics department in the Wycliffe School of Linguistics.

272

Another student, hand-picked, was all ready when Pike found him:

"I had gone to the University of Sydney, in accordance with our custom of contacting university people. I spoke with the head of the department of anthropology, and with a well-known Australian linguist who assisted him. When I told them of our plans to establish a linguistic training school one of them said, 'I don't want to discourage you, but you must realize in the evangelical group you cannot expect to find students who can handle this academic work.'

"Later I went to a mission meeting where I spoke and someone made an appointment to see me. He said to me, 'I have a boy who ought to know about this.' So he arranged for me to meet his son Harland Kerr who was working on his Ph.D. in agriculture at the University of Sydney. Harland had considered leaving his research to enter the ministry. When he heard of our work he said, 'This is what God had been holding me for.'

"I took him back to the office of the head of the department of anthropology the next day and I said, 'Professor, you told me yesterday that if I found a boy who could handle the work you would help us train him in linguistics. How about this fellow?'

"The professor looked at Harland and asked him his name. He could tell immediately that he wasn't from the bush. He found that he was an honor student getting his Ph.D.

"And from the professor's own university God called out a student for the work! Harland Kerr finished his degree, studied anthropology. He is now thinking of getting another degree, in linguistics, and is the director of our school in Australia.

"This is the way God answered those two prayers. He gave us the 'bull-dogs,' and He gave us the trained men to do the work!"

From that vigorous start in Melbourne, Australia, with a strong committee of mission leaders and businessmen determined not to turn back, and with thirty-nine students from eight denominations and sixteen mission boards, the Wycliffe School of Linguistics began with mature personnel. Singularly prepared tutors assisted immediately in the teaching, and undertook the responsibility for the organization of future work.

At the second session in 1951 Richard Pittman, then director

273

of the Mexican Branch of Wycliffe, was dean of the school. The prospective fields of service of this second group of students were about as varied as the boards with which they were associated. New Guinea and India led the list, with others looking to fields in Africa, Borneo, New Hebrides, Java, Pakistan, and with the Australian aborigines. Increasingly through the years mission candidates who receive training at the school have gone to many tribes under numerous mission boards.

Many of the students at the 1951 session were to become choice colleagues for the vast Pacific area where Dick Pittman would one day be directing Operation Oceania.

33. "M–A–G–S–A–Y–S–A–Y"

Firmly balancing their delicate electronic recording machines on their laps like babies needing protection, a group of technicians in a dugout canoe were making their precarious way around a swift bend in the river. They ducked from time to time to avoid a lash across the face from the overhanging trees growing luxuriantly on the banks of the narrow waterways in the rural Philippines. The travelers were a team from Gospel Recordings, Inc., led by their director, Joy Ridderhof, who in 1949 captured on electronic tape many unwritten languages of the Philippines.

Overwhelmed by the great need of the tribespeople of the islands, Miss Ridderhof had urged Cameron Townsend seriously to consider undertaking a program of Bible translation for the many tribes where she was able to make records, and for many more where the gospel was unavailable in any form. She and her team of technicians had made gospel records for several tribes in Mexico where Wycliffe translators had found them to be a valuable supplement to their written materials. She knew that both records and translations were necessary for a lasting Christian witness for the Philippine tribes.

Therefore, in 1951 Dick Pittman, en route to the United States from his teaching assignment in Australia, visited the Philippines at the request of the board of directors of the Wycliffe Bible Translators to investigate the need Miss Ridderhof had reported. As he entered Manila he found many of the thoroughfares blocked, or

275

barricaded by sandbags. Machine guns were everywhere with soldiers prone beside them "sighting guns which were aimed at me!" said Pittman. "What have I done?" he thought. He soon learned that Manila was under threat of attack and every precaution was being taken to defend the city. The situation was tense in April, 1951, when Pittman made his exploratory trip.

That spring, however, at a very crucial point a young Filipino by the name of Ramon Magsaysay was appointed secretary of defense. "He took over the situation with amazing ability," said Pittman, and disaster was averted. Although he called upon a number of officials during the linguistic survey, Pittman failed to meet Secretary Magsaysay. After completing a six-week survey in the Philippines, Pittman reported to the board:

"I was able to record word lists in thirty-four different languages and dialects, and to double-check lists in four of the languages. My basic list consisted of approximately two hundred different words and seventy-five grammatical constructions, giving a brief, but fairly useful sample for comparative purposes.

"In reply to the question of whether or not additional translation is needed in the Philippines, the situation is roughly as follows. Whole Bibles are now available in eight different Philippine languages, besides English and Spanish. The American Bible Society estimates that eighty per cent of the people can understand one of these languages.

"Of the 100–200 different languages and dialects spoken on the islands, some are no doubt mutually intelligible, but many are so different as to resemble one another no more than, for example, French and German. Many of these are spoken by rather small groups of people (one thousand to ten thousand) among whom little or no missionary work is being done. Many persons, considering the size of these groups and the prospects of their learning a trade language, doubt the advisability of undertaking any extensive translation projects for them. My own conviction is that extensive translation should be undertaken as soon as possible for all which are not mutually intelligible with a language already having the Scriptures.

"A base in the Philippines would also serve in the near future, I trust, as a staging area for sending translators into Formosa, Borneo, and other Pacific islands which still need translations."

276

After prayerfully considering the report the board asked Dick and Kay Pittman to lead the Wycliffe advance in the Philippines.

This request weighed heavily on Dick Pittman. He had been working contentedly in the Aztec tribe in Mexico where Townsend had pioneered, and hoped to complete the translation of the New Testament. "We had been very happy in Mexico," Dick said, "and I did not fancy pulling up stakes and going over to the Philippines." Furthermore, he recalled gloomily some of the warnings about the rigors of the Orient.

Thus Pittman's final expression of willingness to undertake the new work was based purely on the evident need of the step to be taken, "not supported at all by feelings—rather, contradicted by them."

The following winter he completed his work for a Ph.D. at the University of Pennsylvania. His dissertation was an Aztec grammar published as a special supplement of the technical journal *Language.* But because of the assignment ahead of him, it was "an unpleasant winter."

Early in 1952 Townsend's book *Lázaro Cárdenas, Mexican Democrat* appeared. "It described a man who was of a kindred spirit with Magsaysay," said Pittman who was following with interest the activities of the energetic secretary of defense in the Philippines. At his earliest opportunity he sent a copy of the book to Secretary Magsaysay with a letter congratulating him on the way he was restoring peace and order to the country.

Later in the spring someone in the Philippines attempted to communicate by phone with Pittman in Philadelphia. On the third try a connection was made, but the message was not clear. Pittman could not understand who was calling, nor what was being said. He caught the words "book" and "thank you," and something about "important for my people." He was left to guess the rest.

"Even after the call had been completed and I had hung up," Pittman said, "I still did not know to whom I had been talking. I called the Philadelphia operator and said, 'Could you please tell me who it was on the other end of the line?' 'Sorry,' she said, 'I'll give you the San Francisco operator.' When the San Francisco operator came on she said, 'It was a Mr. M-A-G-S-A-Y-S-A-Y.'

"Ramon Magsaysay! The 'man of the hour' in the Philippines!

277

"I wrote Magsaysay a letter thanking him personally for his phone call, expressing my appreciation for the work he was doing in the Philippines, and telling him more about our work."

The plans for advance into the Pacific area matured rapidly during the summer and fall of 1952. The University of North Dakota had invited the Summer Institute of Linguistics to establish a branch on the campus at Grand Forks. In view of the need for special preparation for the Pacific area it was decided that in addition to the basic linguistic courses offered first-year students attending the session in North Dakota, an advanced course would feature an intensive study of one of the Philippine languages, as well as orientation to the Pacific area, culture of the people, and other information pertinent to successful work in the new field.

Howard and Barbara McKaughan, who had been working in the Chatino tribe of Mexico, were asked to assist the Pittmans. Accordingly Howard McKaughan pursued his graduate study at Cornell, and assisted by Jannette Forster, produced a textbook entitled *Ilocano: An Intensive Language Course*. This served as the basis for the specialized course at the University of North Dakota where more than twenty linguist-missionaries were groomed for the advance in the Pacific.

But the official invitation for Wycliffe to work in the Philippines had not been received. Some skeptics predicted the project would miscarry, basing their assumptions on flimsy data that the government would not welcome an extensive work in the lesser-known languages of the islands. Would passage and support be forthcoming for the optimistic band of workers who had volunteered to go?

The Pittman circle of intercessors in Illinois, in New Jersey, and in Pennsylvania were alerted. New friends in North Dakota agreed to pray faithfully for the work that loomed frighteningly large to Pittman.

In October, 1952, Howard McKaughan, appointed to assist in the advance, preceded the Pittmans to Manila. By the time they arrived all was in readiness in official circles for rapid completion of plans initiated only a few months before.

"The friendship which began with that telephone call widened and deepened," said Pittman, and Magsaysay became the instrument in the hand of God to place sixty-four translators and other

278

technical workers in twenty-six aboriginal tribes of the Philippines in a miraculously short time.

But Dick Pittman was not prepared for the welcome awaiting him. From the inception of the advance his spirit was overclouded. "I didn't even have enough joy about the occasion to put on a fresh shirt," he said of the arrival in Manila.

Secretary Magsaysay had cordially sent his personal aide to greet the Pittmans. That very day Secretary Magsaysay had been proposed as a coalition candidate for president of the Philippines. Later Magsaysay told Pittman he had fully intended to meet the ship himself, but because of the announcement in the papers had thought it wiser not to.

The day after his arrival Pittman was plunged into a round of interviews with government officials as arranged by McKaughan. The following days were also filled with interviews with the secretary of education, the director of the National Museum, the presidents of universities and schools, the director of the Institute of National Language, and other leading men of the country.

And finally Pittman saw Secretary Magsaysay. During the conversation an aide said to him, "You are talking with the next president of the Philippines."

"I gulped," said Pittman, "for it was an awkward situation. As a foreigner it was not appropriate that I express an opinion. Besides, Magsaysay was only a few years older than I, and I wondered if he were really old enough to be the president of the Philippines!"

Within a few weeks a contract was signed by the Philippine government and the Summer Institute of Linguistics.

Alice Lindquist, one of the new recruits who had been preparing to go to the Philippines, wrote:

"A shout of victory went through the group. Beginning in Manila, it crossed the ocean to be taken up by teams in the United States and Canada preparing to proceed to the Philippines. Elijah's God still lived! This was clearly the Lord's doing, and it was marvelous in their eyes!"

And twenty-two translators in the first group in the Philippines soon arrived with all the equipment needed for settling in to study aboriginal languages and translate the Scriptures.

From their first tenuous contact Magsaysay and Pittman were

279

drawn together on many occasions. Their relationship was strikingly similar to the Cárdenas-Townsend friendship Pittman had observed in Mexico. Even before Magsaysay was elected president Pittman had several interviews with him. Each time some word from the Scriptures was given the high official. From the beginning of their friendship God had impressed Pittman with his responsibility to speak faithfully for Him to the one who had been used to bring the Word to neglected tribespeople of the Philippines.

After Magsaysay's tragically sudden death in a plane crash in 1957, Pittman recounted numerous occasions when the open-hearted official had welcomed a personal word from the Scriptures.

While Magsaysay was still secretary of defense he had become ill and Pittman visited him in the hospital, but not without misgivings. He had "almost no money—certainly not enough to buy a bouquet appropriate for the secretary of defense." But he gave him a bunch of flowers with a card on which he had written some Bible verses for the sick friend. He was warmly welcomed by Magsaysay.

In order to transact business with Magsaysay, Pittman often called upon him early in the morning in his home. It was through such visits that the men became well acquainted. One morning Magsaysay invited him to breakfast. "I was struck by the simplicity of his meal," Pittman recalled, "which consisted entirely of a plate of rice and one small smoked fish."

Magsaysay's heart and home were always open to the missionary linguists whom he had invited to help his people. "From the beginning of our work in his country," Pittman reported, "he always gave us free access to his presence. He personally signed the papers for the majority of our members to do their work in the Philippines."

When Magsaysay was elected president, Pittman took the opportunity to give the new chief executive a special message from God's Word.

"I had just gone through a terrible experience of spiritual defeat and warning," said Pittman. "The Lord had reminded me that I must not allow such a thing to happen again. In the early morning following the experience, I felt compelled to present a Bible to the new president. I was under such conviction that I felt

I did not have time to wait for the store to open to buy a new one, and I found one in the house which was in good condition.

"I typed off the passage from Deuteronomy 17, verses 14 through 20, which gives instructions for the kings of Israel when they came to the throne. They were 'to keep all the words of this law and these statutes to do them.' They were not to turn aside from the commandment of the Lord, to the right hand or to the left.

"After having congratulated Magsaysay on his election, I told him that I wanted to present him with a copy of the Bible. I said to him, 'You might be interested in the commandment to the kings of Israel on the occasion of their coming into their official responsibilities.'

"He was standing in a room with a large number of well-wishers, and in a loud, clear voice, he read the entire passage I had typed, and he thanked us for it. We reminded him that the ancient rulers were to have a copy of the Scriptures before them, and to read them all the days of their life.

"Some time later I noticed in *Time* magazine on the first page, at the time President Eisenhower was preparing for his trip to Geneva, this little sentence: '. . . President Eisenhower was preparing his Geneva talks in the second floor study of the White House in which Abraham Lincoln used to read the Bible every morning before breakfast.' I took my red pencil and underlined those words. I knew that President Magsaysay was a great admirer of Lincoln, and the next time I saw him I presented him with the page, and said to him, 'Mr. President, we would like some day to be able to write in your biography that you read the Bible every morning before breakfast.' "

On another occasion Pittman presented Magsaysay with two verses written out from Matthew 20, with the further word that this was the motto of Cameron Townsend: "And whosoever will be chief among you, let him be your servant: Even as the Son of man came not to be ministered unto, but to minister, and to give his life a ransom for many." Magsaysay read the passage aloud in the hearing of his aides. "But his voice faltered," said Pittman, "when he read the words, 'Even as the Son of man came not to be ministered unto.' 'That shows me what kind of a man I ought to be,' he said."

281

After Pittman had left the Philippines for the United States in November, 1956, he received a letter from Magsaysay written December 15:

"I regretted to learn from your letter that you left the Philippines with your family last November 30. It will please you to know, however, that I have the Seventh Semi-Annual Report and other publications which you presented in my absence to Executive Secretary de Leon before your departure. From the contents I can see that the Summer Institute of Linguistics is realizing its objectives, and I therefore wish you continued success in your work.

"From the information you gave it also appears that Key West yams of high quality have been planted in Bukidnon. I hope that yields will be better and better for yams are indeed suited for production in many of our rural farms. Although you will be away until November of 1957, I hope that we shall have the opportunity to see each other even before that time."

President Magsaysay later received a sample crate of the luxurious Key West yams grown at the base on the Island of Mindanao. The president had encouraged the introduction of new types of plants and animals that would basically improve the economy of the Philippines. And the field headquarters at Nasuli on the Island of Mindanao was becoming a showcase where new products were springing from the rich soil under the skilled care of a specialist called of God for that purpose.

Benjamin Needham had successfully grown oranges and avocados in southern California, and after retiring made a trip around the world with his wife. While in Mexico he became acquainted with the projects of Wycliffe, so that in his travels he was also led to visit the work of the translators in the Philippines. He was impressed with the need—and the rich potentiality—of agriculture as an adjunct to Wycliffe's program of Scripture translation and literacy in the area.

Accordingly in 1956 Mr. and Mrs. Needham went to help develop the base at Nasuli. The property had been leased in 1954 by Howard McKaughan and Richard Elkins, who immediately saw in it the possibilities for a base. One of the attractive features of the property was a big unused spring at the source of a river. The inhabitants of the area believed that anyone who dived into

282

the spring was never seen again. Tall grass and trees covered the fertile plain.

Within two years after the Needhams' arrival the beautiful virgin area was blossoming. Today the pure spring is capped, and water pumped daily up the bank to the personnel houses. The base serves as headquarters, translation center, and vacation spot for Wycliffe workers. There are neat cottages with woven bamboo walls; a rustic, shingle-walled administration building with airy office rooms; a nursery for children; a laundry-shower building; and a kitchen-dining-meeting hall with attractive basket-weave walls.

A pond has been stocked with fish, and a small herd of Brahma cattle feed on the fat of the land. Fine strains of pineapples, bananas, and many other fruits and vegetables have been introduced.

And the huge growing pile of rocks beyond the housing area indicates progress on a hydroelectric power project. A dam has been built and the spring channeled to provide electricity for the base.

Surrounded by a colorful, fragrant profusion of fruit trees, translators at the base are well fed as they turn out primers and Bible translations in many languages. Nasuli is a busy Babel as national helpers from tribes scattered all through the islands from Luzon to Mindanao come to assist in the language work.

Accompanying the happy chatter in many tongues, and the pleasant bird songs in the luxuriant trees, is the industrious clicking of a Davidson offset press heard at almost any hour of the day or night. Howard McKaughan and Elmer Wolfenden, who first operated the press when it arrived in Manila in 1954, also trained other Wycliffe personnel in its use. When the Nasuli headquarters required a full-scale publications department, the press was moved to the new location where there is room for expansion. Readers for children in the public schools, and gospel portions in a score of languages are issued steadily. The Philippine government has welcomed the bilingual materials that are being used successfully in several public school systems, in adult education, and in individual instruction in the faraway places where the translators work.

Ben and Hilda Needham are active not only at the base but at every opportunity go out to the more primitive areas for a first-hand view of the translation work and tribal needs. This trekking often involves travel on dangerous rafts over swift rapids, encounters with many animals and insects, and a very unpredictable diet. "They are a tremendous boost to our morale," says Pittman.

Concerned about their indefatigable efforts Pittman said to Needham one day:

"I'm curious about this, Ben. Don't you and Hilda feel that you are shortening your lives, or kind of wearing out too soon by all this gallivanting around? Don't you think it would be better to husband your strength and not kill yourselves off so fast?"

With a radiant smile and an amused twinkle in his eye Ben Needham replied:

"That's kind of a joke, Dick, because I'm in better health than I have been for a long time. It's really a joy to be working here. It has just the opposite effect to wearing us out. The thing is that we feel we're accomplishing something, and the Lord has blessed the effort. When you're doing what the Lord wants you to do your whole attitude and mental condition—and even physical condition—are good. We're having the time of our lives!"

34. Philippine Gems

Crawling cautiously up the jagged cliff overlooking the sea, Simon Gato poised on a sharp peak and eyed the water swirling below. Then he pointed and plunged, skillfully avoiding an encounter with the rocks around him. He swam rapidly out to the ship making ready to sail for Manila.

Simon had determined to leave and never return to his home on Batan Island just off the northern tip of Luzon. Typhoons frequently swept the island lying unsheltered in a vast expanse of ocean between the Republic of Free China and the rest of the Philippines, so that ship schedules were not dependable. Simon knew that he must make this sailing.

The enterprising tribesman living on a lonely island separated from the main stream of life in the Philippines had heard of Manila as a young boy. He knew that there he could learn the way of the world and its books. Thirsting for knowledge, he first left his rocky home in 1937 and made his way to the milling metropolis. Through a providential ordering of circumstances he heard the gospel and accepted Christ as his Savior. With the help and encouragement of missionaries of the Association of Baptists for World Evangelism he dedicated his life to serving the Lord, and entered a Bible school.

Vacationing back home, he told his family of his plans. Infuriated, they forbade his return to the Bible school, under threat of death. It was then that he determined to leave for good on the next ship.

But after graduating from the training school he felt impelled to give God's message to his people. They spoke the Ivatan language; only a favored few who had ventured out beyond the rockbound village knew one of the major trade languages of the Philippines. They must hear what God had to say, and in their own tongue. Returning again to his home he was persecuted by his friends and disowned by his parents. A compassionate old aunt was the only one to offer him food and lodging. As he went about proclaiming the gospel his people mocked him and called him a devil.

Simon, like the weather-beaten crags of his island home, withstood the storms that constantly lashed him. Despite much persecution his testimony resulted in a growing group of more than two hundred believers. But Simon knew more than ever that his people needed the written Word of God. He and his followers prayed fervently to God for someone who could help them translate it.

In 1951 when Dick Pittman made his first exploratory trip to the Philippines, he met Simon who begged him to "send someone to help us." After returning to the United States Pittman presented the need of the tribes of the Philippines to the recruits gathered at the University of North Dakota. Morris Cottle offered to go to the Ivatan people. Eventually he and his wife Shirley found their way to the rocky village of Mahatao on Batan Island. They lived in a strong stone house, built to withstand the typhoons.

All around them were Ivatan speakers tilling tiny patches of potatoes on the rugged hills or fishing in small boats along the craggy coast. To learn the language they would often accompany the peasants to their fields to plant or harvest. Simon Gato faithfully helped with the translation of hymns and Bible stories as soon as the Cottles were able to start communicating the gospel message. With Simon's help they prepared primers for teaching the Ivatan people to read their language which for the first time was appearing in written form.

From the group of Batan Islands lying north of the big Island of Luzon, to the tip of Mindanao, the southernmost island of the great archipelago, live scores of ethnic groups each with its characteristic speech and customs. The people of the Philippines are in general of the Malayo-Polynesian family, and are divided into three main racial types: Pygmy, Indonesian, and Malay. The Pygmies represent remnants of aboriginal races, of which one is the true Negrito. The Indonesians settled principally on the two large islands of Mindanao and Luzon. Some of the more progressive tribes of this racial stock are the Igorots and allied tribes of northern Luzon. The Malayans make up the major portion of the people of the Philippines. From this group come most of the agricultural and industrial laborers, business and professional men, educators, social and political leaders.

For years missionaries have carried on extensive work in the Philippines. In recent times the Overseas Missionary Fellowship of the China Inland Mission as well as the New Tribes Mission have concentrated on some of the tribal dialects not previously studied.

Since the independence of the Philippines in 1946 the republic, comprised of seven thousand islands stretching from China on the north to Indonesia on the south, has made great progress industrially and socially. At the present rate of exploitation of large mineral deposits, the republic is a promising mining area. It is the second largest coconut-producing country in the world, and the abaca plant supplies the world-famous Manila hemp. Rice is the largest cultivated crop, with sugar cane a runner-up. Tropical fruits—papayas, bananas, pineapples—abound.

Manila is a noisy modern metropolis from which exports are made to markets around the world. In this cosmopolitan capital scores of languages are heard on the streets. Although since the period of American government of the Philippines, English has been the medium of instruction in the schools of the main centers, Tagalog is now the national language and is taught from the third grade. Spanish is also used extensively in trade communication. Ilocano, Visayan, and other languages of the Philippines serve in some areas for trade and education. One of the most widely-used tribal languages is that of the Moslem Maranao living in Lanao province on the Island of Mindanao. It was among the

Maranaos, numbering approximately two hundred and fifty thousand, that the famous literacy expert Dr. Frank Laubach initiated his first literacy campaign. His followers sponsored a translation of the Gospel of Mark that has been printed. To date this is the only portion of Scripture available to the Maranao people.

Every government courtesy possible has been extended to the translator-linguists, beginning with the provision of living quarters in the University of the Philippines, away from the noise and heat of downtown Manila. The guest house on the beautiful campus was a delightful place for the newcomers to be introduced to the culture of the country. In addition, rent-free headquarters downtown have been provided in the buildings of the Department of Education. This is a convenient center for directors Pittman and McKaughan who are in constant touch with government and educational leaders.

But most of the Wycliffe personnel working in the Philippines are scattered throughout the islands, living in lonely mountain villages or in primitive nomadic settlements where they can learn the aboriginal languages.

A number of workers are located on the northern Island of Luzon, best known for Manila, Corregidor, and Bataan. Luzon is famous also for its varied tribal groups. The Igorot tribes carve fantastic rice terraces from the steep mountain sides, and the Negritos timidly shrink from civilization in forest areas of the island. Scattered throughout Luzon and even over onto the long sliver of the Island of Palawan on the west live the elusive Pygmy Negritos. Centuries ago they probably occupied large tracts of land in the Philippines, but other more powerful tribes came in, and gradually the Negritos retreated into the protecting pockets of the mountain forests. Wary of newcomers, they rarely venture into the towns and barrios. The common problem in all areas where Negritos live is to maintain a daily and personal contact with them in spite of their nomadic characteristics.

The Agtas of Central Cagayan, Luzon, were the first Negrito group to be reached by Wycliffe. William and Lynette Oates, members of the initial party of translators from Australia, made contact with these scattered folks and began a study of their language. Others have joined in the work among the Agtas.

Another pair of Australian workers, Rosemary Rodda and Jenny

McKay, went to live among the Batak Negritos of the Island of Palawan. A cluster of palm-leaf shelters by a stream is the preferred group-living pattern of the Bataks. Translators live quietly beside them, observing their way of life and learning to speak their language. They watch the Batak as he prepares to plant his rice fields, clearing off tall trees and thick underbrush by slashing and burning them. The seed is then dropped into holes in the ground made by a stick. At harvest time the long hunger season is ended and rice is plentiful—for a few weeks.

Also interesting to watch is the *babalian,* or doctor of the tribe, who sings for the sick. The men follow his lead in low voices, then the women join in on a high nasal pitch. The performance is aimed at appeasing the spirit responsible for the sickness. It may be the spirit of a man, or perhaps the evil spirit of the *biangunan.* This bearlike animal is said to have such piercing eyes as to cause a chicken to fall from its perch. The *biangunan* will also eat a man should he foolishly wander into the forest alone. Or perhaps the spirit seen as a big fire flying through the air has caused the sickness. Whichever spirit it is, the singing is meant to appease it.

Down south on the big Island of Mindanao live many tribes whose languages until recently had no alphabets. Now translators are living in a number of these.

Richard and Betty Elkins who went to the Manobos of Central Mindanao in 1953 did not find an ideal location in which to work. Their house was a ramshackle shelter a distance from the center of the village. Dick Pittman who helped in the allocation found one redeeming feature about it. "The posts are solid!" was his cheerful comment. The hut was taken as the only housing possibility in this spot in the rain forest where the Manobos lived.

The chief of the area promised to supply someone to help the Elkinses with the language. Soon Lumundaw was assigned to teach them Manobo. He not only gave them words but assisted Dick in making the shelter more livable.

At first Dick and Betty's morale was a bit low. The days were hot and dismal, and the droning of a melancholy guitar did not help. But one day Dick heard someone singing a tune in startling contrast to the usual pathetic strains. "Jesus is Tenderly Calling Me Home"—yes, it was unmistakable, but he could hardly believe

289

his ears. He followed the song, and came upon Lumundaw busily sawing a log to repair their house.

"I always sing it when I'm lonely," he answered Dick's query with a smile. To his amazement Dick discovered that the Manobo carpenter had once found his way out of the rain forest to a group of believers from whom he heard of the Lord and learned to sing several hymns. Dick told Lumundaw of his desire to translate the Word of God for him and his people.

"This is the hand of God," Lumundaw said. "For a long time I have prayed that my people might have the Word of God in my language!"

The gloom lifted. The complaining guitar suddenly struck a major key as the Elkinses worked with a new joy and incentive.

As they learned to speak the language and began writing it down they encouraged their Manobo people to tell them stories and legends. One of the tales concerned the beginning of alphabets. The first two people on earth gave each of their sons the gift of writing. The ancestors of the Spanish and the Tagalogs took the gift, treasured it, and used it well. Likewise the forefathers of the Americans, the Visayans, and the Moslem peoples. Unfortunately the great-great-great grandfather of the Manobos was hungry and ate his alphabet right on the spot. That is why other peoples have prospered, the legend goes, and the Manobos alone have remained poor, content to be wanderers of the forest.

Today, with the help of Dick and Betty Elkins, the gift of writing is slowly being returned to the descendants of the first legendary Manobos. As they receive reading materials and translations of the Scriptures, the Manobos are seeing their language written for the first time.

While on a recent survey of the interior area of the Bukidnon Manobo people, Dick Elkins carried with him a completed translation of the Gospel of Mark in Manobo. He asked one man if he had ever heard of Jesus Christ.

"Yes, I've heard the name, but I don't know who He is," was the answer. Dick read a passage about the power of Christ over demons, over creation, and over life and death itself. Then he closed the book and looked up. A crowd had gathered. An old man who had been listening took the book, held it upside down, and stroked it lovingly. He wanted to hear more. For two days

Dick continually told the story of Christ's love. It was the subject of conversation on everyone's lips. The people did not tire of asking how their sins might be forgiven.

As Dick Elkins and his companions boarded the bamboo rafts to travel downriver, the old chief of the newly-contacted Manobos said:

"Come back soon. I want my people to have the Book of God."

Great responsiveness to the gospel has encouraged translators in various parts of Mindanao. In the southern province of Cotabato, Harland and Marie Kerr from Australia worked on another dialect of the Manobo language. After completing the translation of the creation account, Harland one day read it to Ugow, one of his helpers. He listened in rapt attention, but because he was partially deaf Harland was not sure the message had reached him. And Ugow gave no real indication of having understood.

After supper the next evening there was a commotion at the doorway. Someone pushed Ugow forward, saying, "Go on, you ask." With a bit of prodding Ugow finally said to Harland, "They would like to hear the story." Overjoyed, Harland began to read. Interest was intense, and others also joined the group as word spread that "the story" was being told.

Then Harland spoke of the Lord Jesus. As he recounted His death there were exclamations of sympathy and awe and disapproval of those responsible for His sufferings.

In the days that followed, many came to hear the news. These in turn would bring others. Leaders from the neighboring areas continued to hear the message of God. Their curiosity gave way to the belief that they were listening to God's Word, and a number expressed a sincere desire to know more that they might follow the Lord Jesus with understanding.

One of the major deterrents to reaching the tribes in the Philippines meriting translators has been the lack of adequate transportation. Travel from island to island is dangerous and unpredictable, with much time also lost in waiting for a launch or other conveyance. On the islands the mode of travel is often by small canoes, through churning rapids.

Lester and Madeline Troyer, translating for the Gaddang tribe of Northern Luzon, depend on canoes to take them the last two days up the Siffu River to their home. Because food is scarce, Lester is forced to travel six days each month for supplies. On one trip when the water was treacherous his canoe was caught in a swift current and overturned. He barely escaped with his life.

In 1958 a Helio Courier plane given by the City of Seattle, Washington, for use in the Philippines arrived there with Larry Montgomery, chief of Wycliffe's JAARS operations. The maiden voyage of the high performance plane was made to the Troyers' location. The trip requiring three days' land and water travel was made in just four minutes in the plane! The Troyers were especially pleased for the surprise flight because their food supply was low, and they had not ventured out because of a dangerously high river. Pilot Montgomery, following the custom of such flights in Amazonia, had thoughtfully taken in a shipment of assorted foods.

Montgomery hopes that JAARS will soon be able to provide safe and quick transportation for all Wycliffe personnel in the Philippines. "Challenges like this have always thrilled me," he says, "when I realize what a wonderful tool the airplane is. I am thinking also of Elmer and Beverly Wolfenden who have to use guides through headhunter territory to reach their tribe. Commercial pilots flying chartered planes hate to go over this country, and some even refuse to go."

One of the members of the Philippine Branch of Wycliffe found that dangers exist even out of the tribe, in modern surroundings. Myra Lou Barnard, a nurse from Oklahoma, was among the first translators in the Philippines. She and her partner Jannette Forster had lived for two years among the Mandayan people. On August 8, 1955, they were in Malaybalay, Bukidnon, near the Wycliffe base of Nasuli, visiting friends of another mission. When it was discovered that the kerosene refrigerator was on fire Myra Lou tried to smother the flames with potholders. Suddenly she was showered with flames as the refrigerator exploded. She received the full impact, although four others were caught in the fire. In the nightmare that followed, Myra Lou fell down in the unbearable heat.

Several hours later when Dr. Lincoln Nelson of the Association of Baptists for World Evangelism had finished dressing her burns, Myra Lou was a solid bandage. The instant medical attention had saved her life, but the fight was not over. Nearly eighty per cent of her body was covered with second- and third-degree burns. Next day plasma was flown from Manila, and as soon as she could be moved a Philippine Air Force ambulance plane took her to the American Hospital in Manila. There her temperature reached 106 degrees, and doctors marveled that she was still alive.

The fight for life continued through days and weeks and months of excruciating pain. Each week Myra Lou was taken to surgery for débridement and change of dressings, but the pain was so intense she could not be moved without anesthesia. In order to prevent contractures of her knees an autograft was done. Following that both her legs were put in casts. Myra Lou cried out in spasms of pain. Her companions watched her suffer through long months when their only recourse was prayer. At one point when her agony seemed beyond endurance Vivian Forsberg and other co-workers called upon the Lord in desperation. Rest was granted and Myra Lou slept. When she awakened she said that she dreamed her legs had been put in new casts which "just fit." For almost twelve hours there were no spasms, and they never again reached the same intensity.

Blood transfusions were her steady diet for months. Filipino, Negro, and Scandinavian blood; Baptist, Presbyterian, Catholic blood; Army, Navy, and Marine blood—fifty-nine transfusions in lots of 300 to 600 cc. dripped slowly into her veins. The bond of love sealed by these donors was wonderfully encouraging—a blood pact indeed!

Large areas of Myra Lou's body were patched with skin grafts from cadavers and live donors. Through the meticulous care of the doctors in attendance spots of skin started growing where there had been only an expanse of raw redness. Dr. James Laico, foremost plastic surgeon in the Philippines, sometimes worked seven hours at a stretch patiently stitching the patches of skin onto Myra Lou's burned body.

Came the day—exactly one year after the explosion—when Myra Lou stood on her own feet. Stiff as a board, the first bungling attempt got her up to a thirty-degree angle. In the excitement no one noticed the bleeding below her knees. As soon as her legs had been lowered more than her body, capillaries in raw areas not accustomed to the additional pressure spurted blood. But finally Myra Lou stood briefly.

293

Days later she began taking a few faltering steps. It was a day of great victory when she took sixteen steps without assistance. A little boy had prayed, "Dear Lord, help Myra Lou to stand on her feet so she can get out and see the world again"—and his prayer was being answered.

In October, 1956, a United States Air Force ambulance was backed up to the hospital and Myra Lou wheeled into it. Soon a Super-Constellation United States Navy plane was on its way bearing her to an Oklahoma City hospital. By the end of 1958, with fresh new skin Myra Lou was able to return to the Philippines and to the Mandayan tribe still waiting for the translation of God's Word. Before hearing of her preparation to return Dr. Laico had written:

"I have been praying for her rapid recovery. I hope she comes back to the Philippines. We would call this a second life. There is a saying in the Philippines, 'You stand where you have fallen.' "

Dick Pittman believes that united prayer brought Myra Lou back to life, and that it is also the strong bond drawing the Wycliffe family in the Philippines into close fellowship with their Lord. He is convinced that united prayer accounts for much of the very evident blessing which has marked the advance into more than two dozen tribes where translation of the Scriptures is in progress.

Recent surveys reported by Howard McKaughan indicate that at least twenty-six more tribes in the Philippines need translators. Future exploratory trips may uncover other tribal groups, perhaps smaller, needing separate translations, or adaptations of materials in use in a neighboring dialect.

Pittman has been challenged concerning the wisdom of sending talented young translators to small tribes of the Philippines and other Pacific areas. His answer is in the form of a parable:

"Here, Your Majesty, is the royal crown," said the officer as he bowed low and presented the jeweler's masterpiece. The diadem was encrusted with jewels: a 48 karat Japanese ruby, a 39 karat English sapphire, a great Persian amethyst. The King's face lit up with pleasure as he looked at it, then darkened with a frown.

"Where are the Agta diamond, the Ivatan pearl, and the Batak opal?" he demanded.

The jeweler wrung his hands nervously. "We thought perhaps Your

Majesty would not care for those particular stones," he stammered. "They are very small. They would hardly show beside the large gems."

"Go," the King commanded, "and do not let me see that crown again until every stone is in its place!"

35. The Second Thousand

Wycliffe translators worked steadily toward the goal of the Scriptures in one thousand languages known to be without them. But until 1955 one thousand was only a minimal estimate. There were areas of the world as yet unexplored, and linguistically unsurveyed. One of the largest of these enigmatic locations was the Pacific with hundreds of islands, large and small, awaiting investigation. It seemed to be anybody's guess how many separate indigenous groups speaking distinctive languages were living in that part of the world.

In 1951 when Dick Pittman returned to the United States from Australia via the Philippines, he envisioned a Philippine base of operations as a potential "staging area" for sending translators into Formosa, Borneo, and other Pacific islands. He hoped that Australia would train and send linguistic missionaries to New Guinea and Indonesia which were Australia's immediate responsibility.

In 1955 Australian Robert J. Story, the Unevangelized Fields Mission executive who had appealed to Wycliffe for help in training Australian personnel, again challenged his American colleagues with a task demanding help. He flew from Australia to Arkansas where Wycliffe was holding its biennial conference. With him he carried a briefcase fat with documents that soon proved to be "dynamite."

Story had come to issue a Macedonian call to his American brothers. Millions of souls in the immediate vicinity of Australia representing no less than *thirteen hundred different vernaculars* were his burden. Most of these, said Story, were without any part of the Word of God. Would Wycliffe in the United States send translators to help in the overwhelming task—before it was too late? The example of countries now closed to missionaries was fresh in Story's memory as he urged action.

For the first few hours of the conference while Story read page after page of evidence, including the names of tribes and the numbers of souls involved, Wycliffe members in attendance were almost too stunned to react. They had not expected their job, already looming large, to double overnight. There were at least two thousand tongues to go.

Recovering from the impact of this revelation, delegates in the 1955 conference solemnly voted to do all in their power to "lengthen their cords" and send personnel to the Pacific as soon as possible. And the responsibility for implementing another advance in co-operation with Australian comrades fell squarely on Pittman's shoulders. Specifying the needs of the Pacific area under attention, Story conveyed the burden of Australia in the following words:

"Australia has a special responsibility toward the islands immediately to her north and northwest. The war emphasized the needs of the islands of New Guinea. American and Australian soldiers mingled together in the fetid, steaming jungles of New Guinea and Borneo. Indeed, right through the island world they met and together repelled the enemy who had planned to strike with lightning rapidity down southeast through the Pacific world in order to invade Australia before the Allies could marshal their forces. Through the contacts begotten of war experiences, we of Australia learned to love the island people, particularly those of New Guinea.

"This led to the discovery that we were in the middle of the most complex linguistic medley in the world. Surveys of more recent days indicate that in New Guinea, in the Australian section alone, the million natives speak no less than five hundred different vernaculars. Some of these are related, but for practical

297

purposes, for preaching and teaching and giving them the Word of God in their own mother tongue, only separate translations will really do the job.

"In the Dutch section, which is the western half of the island, there are known to be seventy-nine different vernaculars. But most of this Dutch territory remains unexplored! The strong opinion has been expressed by missionaries and others who know this island that the complete exploration of the Australian New Guinea territory may add another two hundred to the present official list of five hundred and the eventual opening of all Dutch New Guinea may bring to light several hundreds therein. It is thus concluded by knowledgeable men that a reasonable expectation for this second largest island in the world will be a figure in the vicinity of one thousand vernaculars.

"Outside of New Guinea the linguistic situation is no less astonishing. Throughout the islands of Indonesia, the Dutch Bible Society says there are over two hundred languages. The native peoples of the Solomon Islands speak one hundred and three languages. In the New Hebrides and New Caledonia another one hundred and five languages have been listed. These areas alone, without bringing in the Philippines, Malaya and Indo-China, present a problem unequaled in any like territory of the missionary world today, if the inhabitants are to have the opportunity of reading the Scriptures in their own mother tongue.

"Undoubtedly, Wycliffe was brought into being for such a time as this. Australian Christians are most grateful for its coming into the Pacific and Australian spheres. We need the prayers of all Christian people that young folks from America, Canada, Australia, New Zealand, and England will respond to this tremendous challenge of the unreached and Bibleless tribes of this Southwest Pacific island world."

Beginning with Australian personnel and a few others trained in the Philippine field, Wycliffe entered the tribal work in New Guinea in 1956. Also in that year Dick Pittman made visits to Viet Nam and Indonesia where contacts with government leaders and missionary groups resulted in cordial relationships. The first Wycliffe workers entered Viet Nam in 1958.

Before leaving the Philippines for his trip to the two countries, Pittman was given several letters of introduction. One from

President Magsaysay was for the latter's personal friend President Diem of Viet Nam. Another was from Pittman's Indonesian dentist in Manila to his brother in Indonesia. Arriving in Indonesia at an unpropitious time, Pittman was unable to present the letter of introduction which the secretary of education in the Philippines had given him for the secretary of education in Indonesia. The cabinet was changing, and the secretary of education was going out of office. At the end of Pittman's visit in Indonesia he called upon the dentist's brother. During the conversation the brother told Pittman, "The new secretary of education is living in my house. I'll take you to meet him." The result was a cordial visit with the education official who had just taken office.

"Those things are not accidents," Pittman wrote his colleagues. "We believe that before long we will be expected to undertake linguistic studies and Bible translation in Indonesia."

In Viet Nam Pittman was cordially welcomed by members of the Christian and Missionary Alliance. Through their faithful work extending over a number of years the whole Bible had been translated into the Viet Namese language, as well as Scripture portions in a few of the tribal languages. Realizing the vital need for the vernacular New Testament as the basis for a solid indigenous church in each tribe, the missionaries urged Pittman to bring in translators as soon as possible to work in the twenty-five tribes still needing the Scriptures. They regretted that the door to China had closed before all of the tribes in that land received the Scriptures. "They remember with great sorrow," wrote Pittman, "the many Bibleless tribes of North Viet Nam which are now cut off, and are eager that all tribes of South Viet Nam get the Bible as soon as possible. Providentially, there are large refugee groups from some of the North Viet Nam tribes now in the south, so some of the northern tribes can still be given the Word through these refugees."

Presentation of documents and visits with officials of Viet Nam resulted in the invitation to undertake linguistic research and Bible translation. Before his interview with President Diem, Pittman talked at length with other officials and educators. One day he met a Viet Namese poet who chanted Viet Namese translations of Chinese poetry in the forms almost identical to those Pittman had heard in various areas of the Philippines. "When I

299

remarked on the resemblance," Pittman wrote, "he graciously admitted that there might be a little, but that I would be unqualified to judge since the nuances escape the foreigner's ear. This I cheerfully admitted! He gave me copies of three books of Chinese and Viet Namese poetry written by his father."

Pittman also conferred with Indonesian scholars who gave him much valuable information about the tribal languages, and the customs of the people who spoke them. The widespread practice of sacrificing buffalo concerned some of the educational leaders. Pittman explained that the translation of the Bible and the teaching of its principles would change that. One linguist expressed an opinion, differing from the generally accepted view, that many of the Viet Namese mountain languages are related to Malayo-Polynesian. Future research will help to establish relationships as translators settle among the mountain tribes.

One of the officials with whom Pittman talked was doubtful that the president of his country would favor Bible translation. "He recommended that we give up the thoughts of Bible translation altogether, confining our efforts to scientific and literary work," reported Pittman, who explained to the official that Bible translation was the principal motivation in undertaking work in Viet Nam. "We prefer to commend ourselves by an open statement of the truth," Pittman concluded.

But the president of the country was favorable to the complete program of the Summer Institute of Linguistics, including Bible translation. He was grateful for the prospect of help in reducing the mountain languages to writing, and for the literacy work the translators would undertake as they had in other countries.

Early in 1958 David and Dorothy Thomas, whose service in the Philippines equipped them to spearhead the Wycliffe move into Viet Nam, settled in Saigon for an intensive study of the Viet Namese language. Later they were joined by Milton and Muriel Barker. Because French is also used extensively in the country, a study of it will be necessary as a trade language medium in some parts of Viet Nam. By the end of the year Dick Pittman and a group of sixteen new recruits had joined the Thomases and Barkers.

After becoming conversant in Viet Namese and French, the translators will settle in tribes from the seventeenth parallel south.

300

In addition to languages belonging to the Malayo-Polynesian and Indonesian groups, they will make alphabets for other unwritten languages, including dialects of Cham, Thai, Moi, and Khmer. They will begin to identify the pieces of an intricate jigsaw comprising about as many remnants of races as are found in Europe. These linguistic leftovers are jumbled through Viet Nam over into Laos and Cambodia. In addition to inventing symbols for new sounds they will hear in the unrecorded languages, the translators will also be making maps as they explore interior mountain areas as yet sealed to the Western world.

But the reward of their labors will be the uncovering of small but precious jewels hidden in those hills, waiting to be set beside the Agta diamond and the Ivatan pearl in a royal crown.

36. New Guinea—and Beyond

The morning mist had just begun to lift in the eastern highlands of Australian New Guinea. It seemed too early for public proclamations in the Tairora village, but two white men were awakened by a sonorous voice coming from the center of the cluster of huts. They listened. Although they had not lived with the Tairora people long enough to be proficient in their language, they made out occasional words in the address which continued for a good while. From time to time they recognized their names. Had something gone wrong?

The *tultul,* or chief of the village, was away on government patrol duty, and the two translators from Australia, Desmond Oatridge and Alex Vincent, wondered if there had been an attack. Curious, they dressed quickly and went out to ask their "cook boy" Ori what it was all about. He told them that the *tultul* had sent a message back to the village. It went like this:

"You people must look after my two white men. Carry their water for them and bring plenty of good firewood and plenty of vegetables. Sit in their house at night and teach them language. If they don't know more of it when I come home, you will all be in trouble."

Des and Alex made good progress indeed! In fact, they were besieged with teachers. Ori helped not only in teaching them the language but also with other information essential to successful

302

living with the fearful Tairora people. One of their chief dreads is that of the "poison man." Ori would be taken with a sudden impulse to attack him. One night he gasped to Des, "Quick—give me your flashlight—poison man!" Ori then quickly grabbed his bow and a handful of arrows and plunged into the dark.

"The words 'poison man' filled me with an adventurous spirit," said Des, "as ever since the first night when we heard of him I had wanted to meet him. I grabbed my kerosene lamp and ran hard on Ori's heels to the back door. There five or six men armed like Ori were standing close to the door. When one man opened it the others filed out on the run and began searching the tall reeds just outside the house. I was last in line, but soon found myself hunting all around with the men. After a thorough search we abandoned the chase and returned to the house. I think it was a pig that one of them had seen.

"Another time it was the feet of my cat seen in the darkness that frightened the men. In fact, each time there is a 'poison man' scare it is traceable to something like that."

But to the Tairoras the "poison man" is very real. They live in constant fear of him. The Australian translators were not inclined to take the myth too seriously until an arrow meant for the "poison man" struck too close for comfort.

"Where is Alex?" a couple of Tairora men asked Des one day at dusk.

"He went for a walk along the road."

"But which way did he go?"

It was getting darker and a growing uneasiness prevailed as the men went from house to house inquiring about Alex. Then they took a lantern and went down the road with Des. Not finding him they concluded he had taken another road. When the searching party arrived back in the village, Alex was already home. The foreigners couldn't figure out what all the fuss was about.

A few days later a national policeman came through the village with a prisoner. The unfortunate captive had been on his way home at night when suddenly he saw the figure of the "poison man." Startled, he let fly an arrow—and killed his own young cousin.

"That's why we were worried about Alex the other night," the

303

men of the searching party told Des. "If you go around at night without a light or without singing, someone might get frightened and shoot you!"

Within two years after the first contingent of translators arrived in Australian New Guinea ten tribes were occupied. Most of these were in the eastern highlands of Australian New Guinea, with two in the southern highlands of Papua. A base of operations was located in the mountains at Aiyura, eighty-three air miles west of Lae, the Pacific port of the island. Five thousand feet up in the highlands, the base is situated in the center of a large area filled with a number of aboriginal tribes. These vary in size from a few hundred to larger tribal groups of twenty thousand or more. An exact census of the mountain tribal people has been impossible. Many of them are in territory uncontrolled by the Australian government.

Other pioneer missionaries working in New Guinea, particularly those of the Lutheran Mission, have prepared the way for translation work among the tribes. The aboriginal groups living near Aiyura have seen white men and have become conditioned to "book learning" which they associate with the outsiders. At the Wycliffe base tribespeople come to investigate the new way of living. The Gadsup people are the most numerous of the groups in the immediate area of the base.

When the first two houses at Aiyura had been finished, the *luluai,* or government-appointed chiefs, of the Gadsup tribe were invited to participate in the European meal in celebration of the event. After dinner the *luluai* asked Wycliffe men in charge if they had anything they wanted to say. Whereupon they were told of the missionaries' desire to learn the Gadsup language, make books, and teach the people to read them. The *luluai* were not impressed—until a reading program for the old men was outlined. Then the chiefs pricked up their ears and listened with interest. A spokesman delivered a speech in Gadsup which was translated into pidgin English for all to understand.

"I was a small boy when white men first came up to this area," the *luluai* said, "and I have heard the talk of many. But this is the first time I have heard wisdom like this."

Some younger people of the *luluai's* village who had gained a smattering of book learning had disregarded his authority. Now he was assured that the white men had something for the old men, too, and he was ready for it.

Under the capable direction of Dr. James Dean of Canada, and William Oates of Australia, the New Guinea Branch of Wycliffe has prospered and is expanding. Tribes are being occupied as rapidly as personnel is available.

The Forei tribe of pygmy-sized people numbering seven thousand stretches from an area near the base south almost to the Papuan border. Sturdy and independent, Forei visitors at the base are usually ornamented with feathers, tusks, and a good supply of flowers in their hair. Ray and Ruth Nicholson are studying the Forei language. This interest has endeared them to the tribespeople, and has made possible a ready access into their hearts and homes.

The Forei tribe has become well known even in foreign medical circles because of a rare endemic disease that also infects those marrying into the tribe. It is being studied by doctors and other scientists. Similar to multiple sclerosis, the malady is fatal once it attacks a victim. The Forei word for the sickness is "afraid," and is attributed to sorcery. Whenever anyone is stricken, the Forei people cook a rat in ceremonial fashion, and through divinations conclude what village is responsible for the curse. Through another process the responsibility is traced to an individual who must then pay the death penalty. Death is administered to the culprit by biting his windpipe or pommeling his kidneys until he expires.

Analysis of the Forei language requires great patience because of the fusion of words resulting from a very fast style of speech. One word may have several different forms, depending upon how fast it is spoken, and in what combination of surrounding words. Told that some of the changes may be caused by "linguistic mutation," Ray Nicholson prefers to call it "mutilation"—and he continues his battle for the mastery of the language. Adequate words for Bible translation already pose problems. The Nicholsons have found that the closest Forei word for "love" is one meaning "pleased too much." But they are hopeful that a fuller knowledge of the language will yield a more exact equivalent for Scriptural love.

In the central highlands of New Guinea, "about five valleys away" from the base at Aiyura, Kathleen Barker and Darlene Bee

305

are settled happily among the Usarufa tribe of six hundred people. Delighted that they would have the white women living in their village, the chiefs greeted them with a "sing-sing." Dressed gorgeously with plumes and flowery headdresses, and performing a dance with bows and arrows, the Usarufa tribe welcomed the translators in style and with a song about the white women composed in their honor. Kathy and Darlene are not only learning to speak Usarufa, but have discovered it is possible to cook vegetables in hollow bamboo over an open fire. They have found, too, that it is not necessary to import salt. The Usarufas manufacture their own by boiling a very savory bulblike part of a certain plant in a "pan" constructed from "the wonderful banana leaf."

Near the border dividing the territories of New Guinea and Papua, Ernest and Marjorie Richert have been welcomed among the Mid-Waria people. Through the help of Lutheran missionaries working in the area the Richerts were able to locate a place for their home and to obtain translation helpers almost immediately upon their arrival in 1957. Ready for the gospel in their own tongue, the tribespeople have already helped them translate the book of James, as well as verses and passages from other parts of the New Testament.

With the assistance of the Mid-Warias a translation house was built on the hill overlooking the Richerts' home. At the dedication of the building some of the tribesmen spoke: "On this very ground is where it happened," said one, pointing to the ground. "This is where we threw down our spears in a pile to be burned." Another said, "In those days I used to search my mind, wondering when the 'advice-sprout' would ever come to us in our language, and here we see it coming." The Mid-Warias are looking forward to further translation progress and the completion of the New Testament. Their appetite has been whetted by the sample mimeographed portions.

The Minaa people with whom Donald and Launa Davis are working believe that the human race originated in their Wantoat Valley in the highlands. According to them, the first two people were living in their valley a long time ago, when along came a huge monkey with cannibalistic intentions. After killing them he decided to cut them into small pieces. Then gathering local greens

306

which he chopped in with the people, he placed the mixture in several bamboo pots and put it on the fire to cook.

Suddenly a great wind caught the pots up and carried them away to all parts of the valley, dashing them to pieces. Bits of human beings were scattered throughout the area, each becoming a man or a woman. The white-skinned ones left through a gap in the mountains, promising to return some day with a knowledge of God.

An interesting sequel to the Wantoat tale is that the first missionaries to enter the region came through that particular pass, and were given a royal welcome.

In 1958 Earl and Betty Adams, who for years had directed the jungle training program in Mexico, were invited by the Australian Branch to help train personnel from Australia and New Zealand who were preparing to occupy tribes in New Guinea. The main base of the training program was located at Aiyura, where initial orientation was given. Then the trainees moved to advance base, located in a comparatively low section, only two thousand feet high, near the banks of the Markham River. The changing channels, and the sudden and heavy rainfall—sometimes an inch and a half in one night—challenge the ingenuity of campers who on overnight trips must pass through the treacherous river.

Jungle campers in New Guinea practice assimilating the languages of the tribes living around the base. In the high, cold vicinity of main base the tribespeople are very poor, and have little clothing. They cover themselves with pig grease and ashes to withstand the bitter cold. No one bathes because of the unwelcome temperature of the water. Once one of their number did so, and, it is told, died of pneumonia. Since then few will risk the dangers involved.

The highland people are friendly, and vociferous in their warm greetings. They also love to shake hands. "Their hands are caked with grease and grime, and every touch (of which there are thousands) leaves a smudge," wrote Betty Adams.

Their friendliness is manifested in requests for more white men to take the Book to more of their tribes. "The chiefs keep coming here asking the director if they can't have a couple come and learn *their* language and live among them" is the message

307

from the highlands of New Guinea. "How can we share this burden? If only we knew how to make this open door *real* to young folks at home! Wycliffe could use hundreds of recruits here. . . ."

East of New Guinea myriads of smaller islands lie clustered in the Pacific Ocean where island-dwelling tribes wait to hear God speak in their languages. To the west is Indonesia—"linguists' nightmare"! The age of language discovery and Bible translation has just begun in the Pacific island world—a world speaking more than half of the two thousand tongues to go!

Set in linotype Fairfield Medium
Format by Nancy Etheredge
Manufactured by The Riverside Press
Published by Harper & Brothers, New York